Advance Praise for
365 Ways to Raise Your Frequency

"*365 Ways to Raise Your Frequency* presents an eclectic and insightful perspective on the many ways we can connect to our core spiritual essence by raising our vibration emotionally, physically, mentally, and spiritually. Some primary keys to success are to practice, trust, and believe in your inner self!"
—Dawn James,
author of *Raise Your Vibration,
Transform Your Life*

"I am always on the lookout for other modalities that I can segue into my work with tarot. Melissa Alvarez has given me exactly what I need and 365 ways to do it. Deceptively simple, this book can help you on your own path."
—Stephanie Arwen Lynch,
professional Tarot consultant and reader

"A must-read for everyone who wants to move forward on the path of life. Melissa Alvarez has given us a daily road map for achieving happiness and success through simply shifting our vibrations. Not just another 'how-to' book, there are 365 engaging methods of doing so. Brilliant and highly recommended for all!"
—Dyan Garris,
author and New Age musician

365 WAYS

✳

to RAISE *Your*

✳

FREQUENCY

© Isabel Barney

ABOUT THE AUTHOR

Melissa Alvarez is an internationally known spiritual intuitive coach and an award-winning author of metaphysical nonfiction and paranormal romantic suspense, published under the alias Ariana Dupré. She has appeared on many radio programs as both guest and host, and has written numerous articles in her previous position as the original paranormal expert at Examiner.com and as the Guide to Romance Fiction at About.com. She is listed as a publishing expert at *Moonspinners Ask the Experts* (Writer's Digest Top 100 Website), a spirituality and publishing expert at BookPromotionNewsletter .com. Formerly the owner and publisher of the small press New Age Dimensions, Alvarez has been a freelance editor, graphic artist, and website designer. She conducts workshops teaching others to connect with their intuitive abilities and spirituality, and has done intuitive readings for over twenty years. Alvarez and her family share their home in South Florida with their many animals. She and her husband breed champion KFPS Friesian and ECHA Barock Pinto horses, as well as German Shepherd dogs. Melissa can also be found online at www.MelissaA.com or www.APsychicHaven.com.

Melissa Alvarez

365 WAYS

to RAISE *Your*

FREQUENCY

SIMPLE TOOLS TO INCREASE
YOUR SPIRITUAL ENERGY
FOR BALANCE, PURPOSE, AND JOY

Llewellyn Publications
Woodbury, Minnesota

FIRST EDITION
Eighth Printing, 2016

Book design by Bob Gaul
Cover design by Ellen Lawson
Cover art © flower: iStockphoto.com/14976504/_Vilor; texture: iStockphoto.com/323006/sx70; banner: iStockphoto.com/23349592/DavidGoh
Part page art © iStockphoto.com/Jelena Veskovic
Editing by Nicole Edman

Llewellyn Publications is a registered trademark of Llewellyn Worldwide Ltd.

Library of Congress Cataloging-in-Publication Data
Alvarez, Melissa.
 365 ways to raise your frequency : simple tools to increase your spiritual energy for balance, purpose, and joy / Melissa Alvarez. — 1st ed.
    p. cm.
 Includes bibliographical references
 ISBN 978-0-7387-2740-0
1. Spiritual life—Miscellanea. 2. Vibration—Miscellanea. I. Title.
 BF1999.A6353 2012
 204—dc23
                          2011031509

Llewellyn Publications, a Division of Llewellyn Worldwide Ltd.
2143 Wooddale Drive
Woodbury, MN 55125-2989
www.llewellyn.com
Printed in the United States of America

Contents

Introduction

What is frequency? It is the intensity of our spiritual energy within our bodies. It can be low, high, or just sort of in between. Each of us has our own unique frequency, which exists in direct relation to the culmination of all our life's experiences (past and present), outside influences, internal joy, and overall happiness. Where we choose to focus our attention and thoughts is what determines what level our energy is residing on at any given time.

The term *frequency* is relatively new in the metaphysical community. Previously this internal energy was called *personal vibration, vibrational level,* or *vibrational rate,* and many people still use these terms interchangeably, including me. It's only been in the last few years that we've taken the word *frequency* from the scientific community—where it is generally used in physics to mean "the number of regularly occurring events of any given kind in a unit of time, usually one second or the number of cycles or completed alternations per unit of time in a wave or oscillation"—and applied it to how we perceive changes in our personal vibrational rate. If you consider our internal energy in this way, as frequency, then the more regularly occurring positive events, the faster our energy will oscillate. The faster our energy moves, the higher its rate of frequency. So if we're trying to bring more positive factors into our lives, then we're increasing the number of regularly occurring positive events, thereby raising the energy within our body.

If you harbor negative feelings like fear, doubt, jealousy, envy, impatience, insecurity, imbalance, hatred, or judgment, you will live on the low end of the energy spectrum. This is because you're focusing on the negative in your life instead of the positive. Someone with an abundance of positive feelings like joy, happiness, elation, centeredness, love, peace, harmony, balance, kindness, compassion, and understanding will be at a higher frequency because they are focusing on the positives in their life. When you are able to look inside your own soul and see yourself for who and what you truly are—a spiritual being with lessons to learn in life—or when you look at the spiritual laws of the Universe and see the bigger picture, you are elevating your spiritual energy. You'll feel it; you'll know deep inside that you are different or have transformed your emotions because you attuned yourself with the principles of the Universe. Personal spiritual growth creates, nurtures, and elevates your frequency.

Have you heard the saying "What goes around comes around"? You can apply this same concept to frequency. What you send out to the Universe comes back to you, magnified and multiplied. If you're sending out feelings of love, you'll receive an abundance of love in return; if you're sending out feelings of hate, you'll get plenty of hate in return. Like attracts like. You can block what God and the Universe intend for you by living in negativity, but if you release those negative thoughts and feelings and live your life to the fullest, you may just surprise yourself.

Doing energy work specifically to raise your frequency doesn't mean you can never get angry or upset. Everyone has fears, worries, and doubts—it's part of human nature. There's nothing wrong with experiencing these normal emotions. We are on the earthly plane and must experience them to grow spiritually. It's when you allow these emotions to rule you that the problem begins. When you regularly act and react from a place of negativity, you're treading on thin ice. Emotions like anger and fear can get a foothold in your being and start you on a downward spiral toward unhappiness and discontent.

Intention is the biggest factor in controlling frequency. I'm going to say that again because it's very important: **Intention—your reasons for doing what you do, acting the way you act, and treating people the way you treat them—is the biggest and most powerful way to control and elevate your frequency.** Every intention carries a vibration with it, and that vibration can immensely affect your overall life.

How do you control your spiritual energy through intention? Through the emotion of love. That's simple enough to say but much harder to carry out. I've learned, through metaphysical experiences, that we carry our emotions with us when we pass over. If love is one of the emotions we carry with us, shouldn't it be the basis for all that we do while we're alive? Whether it's love for another or love for yourself and your own spiritual growth, it is still love. If everyone acted from a place of love, there wouldn't be any bigotry or hatred left. However, it's easy to get caught up in the moment, to let your ego and negative emotions take over. If you can learn to control your emotions while acting from a place of love, you will have taken a giant leap in maintaining and raising your frequency. It's a lifelong learning process. Remember that your emotions are going home with you to the Other Side. Consciously choose to base your actions and reactions to people and the situations in your life from a place of love instead of anger, jealousy, or bitterness.

Think about that saying again: "What goes around comes around." You can also say it in reverse: "What comes around goes around." Either way, it means the same thing. What you do, the way you react in situations, and the behaviors of the people you associate with (the company you keep) all come back to you, magnified and more intense than the energy you originally sent out.

Did you know your personal thoughts are a unique form of energy with specific frequencies? When you have a thought, you send it out into the Universe. It goes on its merry little way, collecting people and situations that equal its vibration, and then that thought comes home, bringing your original thought back to you along with all the friends it's picked up out in the world. Surprised? Consider this: If you're putting negative stuff out there, it's going to come back to you much worse than what you originally sent out. Instead, send out the most positive thoughts and energy you can and that's what will come back to you. The best way to do this is to think and act from a higher soul plane of existence and to associate yourself with people whose vibration is higher than your own. As you begin to learn from these people and your own vibration adjusts to a higher rate, you'll probably feel a little weird. That's normal. People often hang out with folks who are at the same vibrational level, since we are most comfortable around them. We feel weird around people with different frequencies. Adjust to this shift and test your limits.

The Core Four

There are four core areas that you will directly address as you do energy work to increase your personal vibration. Let's look into each of these areas in more depth.

Your Emotional Frequency

Your emotional balance (or lack thereof) has a big effect on your spiritual energy. If you tend to be led by your emotions, if they're out of control, unfocused, and go from one extreme to another, it will be harder to consistently bring your energy to higher levels and keep it there. Start by getting your emotions under control through breathing techniques or creative visualization so that you can look at life clearly and rationally. While you don't want to be a blubbering basket case, you also don't want to have your emotions under such tight control that you come across as an unfeeling jerk. Don't go to the extreme in either direction. The important aspect of emotional frequency is to find balance in the way you experience your emotions. Then you'll have a stable base from which you can work to increase your overall frequency. Without this base, the journey will be difficult. Find a way to relinquish emotional extremes to bring balance to your energy.

Your Mental Frequency

Understanding your mental capabilities is important in raising your personal vibration. If you find that it's difficult to make decisions, you're often mentally exhausted, or you feel like your brain went on vacation without you, it's time to let go of some of the stress in your life. When you can't think straight, it's difficult to focus on doing energy work. On the other hand, if you're too mentally focused, you may find yourself questioning every little thing that happens to you. Sometimes all you need is to accept what's happening. You don't have to analyze everything to death. Acceptance in and of itself raises your personal vibration. Sometimes, it is what it is. Faith and belief go a long way in energy work.

Your Physical Frequency

Your physical appearance affects your spiritual energy, especially if you're unhappy with the way you look. Do you need to work out more, lose weight, or take on an activity that will make you stronger? Are you noticing wrinkles that make you unhappy with your appearance? When it comes to your energy, you're working from the inside out. How you look isn't the issue here, but if you're unhappy about your appearance, that feeling can block you from realizing your fullest vibrational potential. If you're in excellent physical condition and have no hang-ups, then you shouldn't have any problems, but if you do have body image issues, what are you going to do about it? Since you've decided to do energy work to make changes on the inside, also make the decision to change what you're unhappy about regarding your outward appearance. Work on the two together; as you become more comfortable and accepting of your body, it will be easier to raise your vibration. Just remember that your body is a temporary home for your soul, not the soul itself. If for some reason you can't change your body, simply release any negative feelings about it and move forward. Get in your best physical shape today or accept yourself as you were created.

Your Spiritual Frequency

Spirituality is the area where you'll do the most work in order to increase your frequency. Connecting with your true spiritual self, beliefs, and ideals will enable you to reach higher levels of vibration. Spirituality does not necessarily have to include the way you feel about religion. While it can include your religious beliefs, you're going deeper than that. Examine your soul, your true self, your core spiritual being and light energy to find your pure essential being. Once you are able to look at yourself as more than just a human on Earth and can see yourself as a spiritual entity who is working to get closer to the source of all Creation (which I call God, but you may call by a different name), then you have taken great strides in increasing your frequency. It isn't about what church you go to, if you attend one at all; it's about your core beliefs, whether you are a good person with high moral values, and whether you have faith in your beliefs or are just putting on a show. If you don't have a belief system, now is the time to start doing research to find beliefs that feel right with your soul. What you believe may be totally different from what someone else believes, and that's fine—we all have our own truths and our own lessons to learn. Discovering your true spiritual self is imperative on the path to higher frequency.

My Case in Point

Sometimes it helps to know what other people have done in the past when you're trying to do spiritual or energy work. With that in mind, I'd like to give you a little bit about my background and share a time with you when I had to make a major decision, increase my frequency, and move forward on my spiritual path.

In 2001, I self-published my first book, *The Phoenix's Guide To Self Renewal*. The book was massive, over four hundred pages, and I was printing the book in my home. The book did very well—so well, in fact, that I couldn't keep up with the demand. Shortly after this, my family moved to Florida and I took the book out of print after burning out my printing equipment for the third time. I put my focus on writing a novel and picked the genre of paranormal romantic suspense, since I had a lot of knowledge in the area of psychic abilities and the paranormal. That book was *Night Visions*. The e-book market was just starting to come into its own, so I decided to change my company, New Age Dimensions, into a small press that published both e-books and print books using print-on-demand technology. When I expanded the company, I was working at About.com as their Guide to Romance Fiction. However, New Age Dimensions grew so fast that I had to leave About.com to run the company. I published *Night Visions* under the pen name of Ariana Dupré, keeping my identity a secret so it would either stand or its own or flop without my past or current jobs affecting the outcome. I'm happy to say the book went on to win numerous awards.

By 2006, New Age Dimensions had published over forty authors and nearly eighty titles. I did the majority of the work for the company, designed all the book covers and interior layouts, did marketing and promotion for the authors, and worked between seventy and eighty hours a week. I loved it, but I didn't have any time to write another novel. I could barely eke out short stories for anthologies.

I was also doing psychic readings at this time. I started doing readings online in 1994 and did them for free for the first two years because I wanted to make sure that I was accurate. At the suggestion of another psychic, I decided to add fees. That was a hard decision, but I couldn't keep up with the volume of free reading requests. Since this is a spiritual calling for me, I didn't feel that stopping this practice was an option. Sometimes I have to take breaks from readings through my website, but I'll always do readings in some way.

Then in 2006, Hurricane Wilma came through South Florida, and we were without power for two weeks. Due to personal situations resulting from the hurricane, I had a decision to make and it wasn't an easy one. I needed to close the company as a small press and revert back to a sole proprietorship for only my books. I was at a very upsetting crossroads, even though I knew what I had to do. My frequency was very low and though I discussed it with my family, I just couldn't move forward. I wrestled with this problem during the two-week power outage.

In order to bring balance back into my life, I implemented some of the techniques I've shared with you in this book to help center myself, elevate my frequency, and come to terms with closing the company. I would go to the beach and wash the negative energy away in the surf, walk around the lake and commune with nature, look for signs everywhere (especially in the clouds and the night sky), walk up and down the stairs dispelling negativity, and put my pride in my back pocket. Each one of these activities helped, but I was at a really low point emotionally, so it took numerous repetitions to get my frequency moving upward again. After two weeks of being cut off from the world and doing frequency exercises, I finally begin to sense my vibration elevating. I felt more centered and comfortable with what I had to do.

The exercises helped release the negativity of indecision. I saw numerous signs from the Universe containing the words *closed, shut,* or *ending.* When I closed the company, I feel I did it the right way, with respect to the authors and readers. The reactions to my decision ranged from sympathy to anger. I understood, having felt the same only days before, and I dealt with the negative reactions the same way I'd dealt with coming to the decision: I used exercises to balance my energy and raise my frequency, and I was fair and honest in my dealings with everyone, even when they didn't return the favor. Some of the situations got really ugly, but I stood up for myself—I couldn't do anything less and be true to my core spiritual essence. I cried many tears when I closed New Age Dimensions as a small press, but in the end I was filled with light and peace. I knew I'd done the right thing.

Closing that door, dealing with my frequency being at an all-time low, and being forced to look deep inside myself to elevate it again brought positive things into my life. Since then, I've sold several novels as Ariana Dupré, released several nonfiction books, and have been an online columnist for several large websites. Each of these things was a learning experience. My husband and I started breeding Friesian horses and German Shepherd dogs, which I love and would never have been able to do if the publishing company was still open. Yes, I've let some things go when they no longer served me, but I've remained true to myself. Now I focus on my family, my animals, my writing, my readings, and teaching others about their psychic abilities and spirituality. I've even invented a new technique of divination. I donate my time to workshops and worthy causes. So while life will always be filled with ups and downs, I know I can bring myself back to center and increase my frequency using the techniques in this book. I know that, in time, everything will work out exactly as it should be, and I will move forward on my spiritual path, no matter how difficult the decisions are along the way.

When life gets hard and you feel that you have nowhere to turn, I invite you to look inside yourself for the answers and to use these same techniques to help you regain your balance and increase your frequency. When everything is going well and you just want to increase your spirituality, use these techniques then, too. They'll only help you as you come to know the truly wonderful spiritual being that you are deep in your core.

How to Use This Book

The best way to get the most out of this book is to start at the beginning and work your way through each of the 365 ways, using one per day. Each of the techniques builds upon the previous ones, so I recommend that you don't skip around. If you do one a day, this book will last you for an entire year. It was my goal when I started this book to give you enough techniques to last a year, so that by the time the year ended, you'd have tried a wide variety of energy-raising exercises and would be successful in raising your frequency. The next year, feel free to start right back at the beginning.

Each day, apply the given technique to your life. Some days this involves hands-on work, while other days will simply ask you to read and consider a new idea. Some techniques you may accomplish right away; others you may have to do a couple of times throughout the day before you feel it's working for you. It may take several attempts to feel connected to what I'm asking you to do, but don't look upon this as homework. I want you to have fun as you learn to increase your frequency, as this will bring greater abundance, joy, and happiness into your life.

Some of you may feel you're too busy to do these exercises. I understand how busy life can be. While I was doing the second round of edits for this book, we had Thanksgiving, Christmas, and New Year's Eve, all of which are big events at my house. One of my kids got very sick with a nasty virus and almost ended up in the hospital, we endured two rounds of the flu, one of our Shepherds had puppies and couldn't deliver the last one so she ended up with an emergency C-section (can I just say right here that I have the best and most caring vet in the world at Chasewood Animal Hospital. Thank you, Dr. Maria!), and then mama bit one puppy's umbilical cord too short and she almost died. I nursed the puppy back to health and then—just when I thought it was going to be fine— mama lay on her and suffocated her between my hourly checks, devastating our kids and breaking my heart. Sometimes, despite our best efforts, the things we want in life aren't meant to be. With that knowledge comes acceptance, which raises frequency. But explaining death to a young child is challenging. To top it all off, I then came down with that nasty virus.

If I can teach you how to raise your frequency with all of this going on in my life, let me assure you that you'll be able to whittle out some time for energy work. It's difficult juggling a lot of responsibilities, but you can do it! You just have to steal a few moments here and there. When the kids are asleep, stay up later or get up earlier. Use creative visualization on your drive to or from work. (You can think and drive at the same time, just don't zone out or close your eyes.) Instead of cooking dinner one night, order in and use that extra time to do an exercise. If increasing your soul energy, growing spiritually, and progressing along your spiritual path are important enough to you and the time is right in your life, the moments and minutes will be available when you need them.

Overall, the easiest way to raise your frequency is to *practice*. Think positive thoughts daily during meditation or whenever you feel like it. If you can put positivity into all aspects of your life, you will be well on the way to a higher personal vibration. I also recommend keeping a journal to track your accomplishments and areas that need more focus. This book will give you motivation and support when life seems to be challenging you at every turn.

Following the Path

Sometimes, a frequency elevation can surprise you. This jump comes from someone pointing out something about you that you may not have realized. For example, I give psychic readings and have always been able to use many different abilities to tap into a client's situation. Most seers I know do the same, so it never occurred to me that it was unique. I was once told that I have a very high vibrational energy. I brushed it off, saying I was just like everyone else. Then I was told that other psychics may only receive information in one form—not everyone could see, hear, feel, smell, *and* know information like I do.

They didn't?

I was shocked. I didn't truly grasp the meaning of this until it was repeated. Then it hit me like a ton of bricks and I could feel my spiritual energy elevating from just that bit of knowledge. To date, that's been the only time I consciously felt such a dramatic increase in my frequency.

I didn't get all fluffed up about it and think "Whoopee me, I'm special." I did the exact opposite. I pondered what this meant on a Universal level. I started asking people how they experienced the metaphysical and how they did readings. I found out it was true: I did experience things differently than most psychic people. Granted, we're all individuals, so we'll all have slight differences in reception. I also discovered that most of my closest psychic friends experienced their impressions in the same way that I do. This is because we tend to attract others on our same vibrational rate. It was good to know that I wasn't the only one on this level of vibration, but this gave me a new sense of obligation to my work as a seer. After this realization—after actually feeling my frequency change with this knowledge—I knew I had more teaching to do.

In this book, I cover 365 ways to raise your frequency, but there are some basics you also need to know before you start. First, you have to *look deep inside yourself* and change the way you view life, how you act and react to situations and people, and acknowledge the core of your spiritual being on both a conscious and subconscious level. You have to *connect with your core spiritual self.* You need to *truly want this change.* Otherwise, it's like putting a tiny bandage over a huge wound—lip service won't do the trick. You must go deep, all the way down into your soul, and be willing to change your thought patterns and your way of believing to make positive changes. I know you can do it—I believe in you!

Start by using positive thoughts. Put daily affirmations around your house, stick notes on your mirror, in your car, on your desk, or scrolling across your computer screen. This may seem trivial, but it will be a gentle reminder to continue working on releasing negativity and holding onto positivity. You can also use creative visualization to raise your vibration. In a nutshell, creative visualization is holding a picture in your mind of what you want to happen in a particular situation, what you want out of life and how you see yourself in the future.

Once you've successfully raised your soul energy a bit, you'll find that people of the same vibrational rate will gravitate toward you. I suggest seeking out those who have a higher vibration than yourself as you start on this path. You can learn from them, which will also help raise your vibration. At the same time, you'll be leaving behind negative ways of thinking and negative people that may have previously influenced you. If you're having trouble increasing your energy, stop watching television and listening to the media for a while. Television and talk radio news is a wicked reality and we're usually shown only the negative in the world. It's a shame, since the media has such a huge influence on us—it should spread positivity instead of negativity and fear. As you work on yourself, release any medium that is providing you with negative influence. If you crave television sometimes, choose something with a positive message. The negative attitudes of other people can only affect you if you let them. Remember that your subconscious desires will manifest in your reality. Let those desires be positive.

Being Responsible for Your Own Path

One of my favorite sayings has always been, "You come into this world alone and you leave it alone, so you better take care of yourself." But, Melissa, you say, that isn't true at all! Well, actually, it is when you consider the concept from the spiritual plane. Your lone spirit enters your physical body before birth. Once you're born, you have a family to nurture and love you throughout life, but when you die, well, no one goes there with you. Yes, your spirit guides, family members, and master guides will be there to greet you when you pass over, but the actual birth and passing? That's all you, baby. It's one of the lessons you're here to learn. So, spiritually speaking, you come into and go out of this world alone.

The other part of this saying is also true: you better take care of yourself because no one else is going to take care of you. This also applies on a spiritual level. As children, most of us are cared for by adults. As adults, the responsibility shifts to you. But spiritually, you've always been responsible for your own path. That's why you're here. To learn life lessons so you can be closer to God (or whatever you call the higher power). If you don't take responsibility for your own path in life, who will?

Being responsible for your own path means to always do what feels right *for you*. You have different lessons to learn and a different path to follow than other people. My path is not the same as yours, and your path isn't the same as your neighbor's. It's up to each individual to discover on a soul level what their path is and to be responsible for following that path in the best way possible. How do you know? If you're unclear about your spiritual path in this lifetime, raising your frequency will give you a sense of purpose, and your path will be clearer.

Do your best and live your life in a way that feels right for you. We all make mistakes, we all change our minds, and what feels like the right path one minute might feel wrong the next. The main thing is to always do your best, treat people with kindness, stay positive in your outlook, and keep an open mind. I believe that one of the biggest problems in today's society is that people close their minds off to possibilities that they don't understand. They're quick to dismiss, but maybe they'd have a different belief if they'd taken a minute to listen and consider the idea.

As you travel down this road we call life, you're going to meet many people along the way whom you can help or hurt and who will help or hurt you in return. We have lessons to learn from one another, and by being responsible for yourself first—for your actions, attitudes, and beliefs—you can act in the way that will most benefit your own growth. When you do this, you are continually raising your frequency. When you learn your lessons, you don't have to repeat the past. This is a common theme in life, too. If you learn from your mistakes the first time, you won't repeat them later. Learn from life, be responsible for your own path, and watch your frequency rise higher and higher.

Self-Awareness

While discussing vibrational levels, we have to talk about your self-awareness. Have you ever met someone who blamed everyone else for the problems in their life? They just couldn't accept the fact that maybe *they* were the one screwing up? These people live in the negative. Everything is a dramatic problem, everyone's out to get them, life isn't fair, nothing good ever happens to them, etc., etc. Being around a person with this behavior is frustrating, which can make your energy plummet. You can try to get through to them, but eventually, you just have to realize that this is their path. If they want to live surrounded by negativity and despair, there isn't much you can do about it. Did you recognize yourself in the paragraph above? I hope not, but if you did, now is the time to pay attention to how you're living your life and start making changes.

Start by looking at the way you think. Are you a positive person or negative person? Is the glass half full or half empty? Do you look for the silver lining or do you wallow in the "what ifs?" What can you do to change the way you think? Can you let go of fears?

To become more self-aware, look at the way you act and react. Are you doing things out of spite? Are you into the "he said, she said" gossip grapevine? Are you going to hit someone because they looked at you wrong? Rip apart their feelings with cruel words if you don't like their looks? This behavior will only delay your progress along the spiritual path. Do you cheat, lie, or steal? I'm not saying you have to be a saint, but you can kick up your heels in ways that won't harm anyone physically or emotionally.

Take stock of yourself. Be aware of who you are, what you do, and why you do it. Can you be a better person? If you decide that you can, start to take steps now toward a deeper understanding of yourself. You'll find that you're raising your vibrational level and moving to new heights as a spiritual being.

Part One

*

Awareness

1. Tuning into Frequency

Do you know what your frequency is at this very minute? As you begin the journey through the 365 Ways, you'll need a starting point so you can measure your success. You can determine your current levels by looking at several different aspects of your energy. Are you outgoing, joyous, living life to the fullest? Are you in tune with your spiritual self, your psychic abilities, and your intuition? If you are, then you are living at increased levels. If you're constantly battling problems in your life, if you're often depressed, think that people look down on you, or feel life isn't fair, then you're living in the lower ranges. Before you start down this path, determine where you are right now so you have a point of reference from which to work. This is a great time to start a frequency journal to describe the techniques you do each day, to write down your emotional reactions, or to elaborate on how that technique worked for you. You may also want to draw a bar graph for each month—or any other type of scale that you prefer—so you can measure your daily results. Numbers, symbols, words—whatever describes your sense of frequency will work just fine. By recording your impression of your vibrational progress, you'll be able to compare "off" days and "breakthrough" days with previous ones. Many people start recording in the morning and continue throughout the day, while others write only in the clarity of morning or the reflectiveness of evening. Do whatever feels right and useful to you.

> *The measure of success is
> your truth at a soul level.*

2. Clarity of Purpose

Do you know why you want to raise your frequency? Is it because you want to become more in tune with your spiritual self, develop your psychic abilities, or be more joyful? Maybe you feel as if something is missing or just a little "off" in your life and it's keeping you from living to the fullest. Whatever the reason, you've made a decision to act, to take charge of your personal energy, and that's a big step forward. As you go forth with purpose, make sure to determine your goals and focus on the results you want to achieve. When you are clear in purpose with specific goals in mind, you'll find that it's much easier to meet those goals. Problems can arise when you're not definite in the reasons you've started on this path or the steps you need to take to achieve the desired results. If you're unsure of how to go about reaching a goal, then you may find that it's more difficult to achieve and maintain elevated vibration levels. Your frequency may increase, then fall down again, increase again, and then become even lower. Make sure that you're always achieving higher and higher frequency levels by being focused on your path with a clear goal in mind and are reacting in positive ways.

> *Be clear of mind—
> step forward and embrace
> the heights you can
> surely achieve.

3. Build Your Foundation

Now that you're aware of your unique spiritual energy vibration, you can build a solid foundation from which to raise it to higher levels. Your frequency has been with you since your birth, but now you know it can be increased through intention, thought processes, creative visualization, and other activities. Construct your foundation with strong and solid materials by believing in yourself and what you're doing. Don't let someone else's negative thoughts become a distraction that could weaken your foundation. Choose not to let negativity affect you, for in doing so, you're choosing to bring positivity to you. Keep a log of the positive actions you take today that will add to your foundation. Did you help a neighbor with some pesky yard work, or hold the door open for someone at the store? These may seem inconsequential but they are acts of kindness, which positively affect you. Keep track of them; these types of actions are the cornerstones of a foundation that will enable you to reach great heights of joyous energy. When building a foundation, you may encounter lessons that may need to be repeated before you feel your energy elevate. That's okay, because sometimes the repetition in and of itself is what ultimately brings enlightenment by making you look at the situation in a different way.

> *Build through acts of love
> and joy to stand up against
> the tests of negativity.*

4. Digital Catalysts

Have you ever noticed that you suddenly start seeing the same numbers pop up at random moments when you least expect them? These are usually repeating numbers, like 11:11 on the clock, 444 in a phone number, or 333 in a license tag. Maybe you saw 555 five different times in one day. These are digital catalysts and they are directly related to divine guidance. It is a sign that your spirit guides, angels, or someone else from the Other Side is attempting to communicate with you. These numbers all have specific meanings that you can find online or in books. (Doreen Virtue's book *Angel Numbers* is a great resource.) When you're searching for meanings online, be wary of negative definitions or people using scare tactics to frighten you into believing that these are signs of something bad. Digital catalysts are positive indicators from the Other Side, used to get your attention so a message can be delivered, to let you know you're not alone, that there's someone on the Other Side looking out for you in times of need, or to make you look deeper into the number's meaning for a specific message. These numbers are called digital catalysts because they spur you into taking notice, causing you to connect to the Other Side, become more enlightened, and increase your energy vibration.

> * *The numbers call*
> *to you; listen and receive*
> *their messages.*

5. FIND YOUR POINT
OF BALANCE

As you do energy work, you want to always be able to come back to center, the point of balance where you feel safe and secure within your core spiritual essence. In times of stress and anxiety, you will find that the more quickly you can get back to center, the easier it is to release any negative energy around you. The best way to do this is to give yourself a trigger.

First, find your center by sitting quietly and focusing on your inner self, your energy, and the exact moment when you feel a calm peacefulness settle over you. When you feel that, you've found your center point of balance. Now you're going to set your trigger. For this example, I will offer two possible triggers: the number seven (verbal) and a dove (visual). You could also use a motion or symbol, if you wish. When you are in the moment of your point of balance, feeling calm and peaceful, imagine that your trigger surrounds you in multitudes, whether it be a sight, sound, or movement. Give the trigger purpose. Now release the trigger sound or image, telling it that whenever you call on it, it will instantly bring you back to this place. Fully release your trigger and leave your point of balance. The next time you're upset, call on your trigger. For example, if you used one of the above examples, say the number seven aloud several times or picture a dove to activate this trigger.

There is calm within—
call it to you.

6. The Mind-Mouth Connection

You probably know people who speak before they think; they just open their mouth and shove their foot right down their throat. These people fill the space around them with negativity by making off-putting or callous remarks that offend another person without even realizing what they're doing. This is because they don't think before they open their mouths to speak—they have lost the mind-mouth connection.

When you're doing energy work, one of the first things you should focus on is making sure that you're thinking good positive thoughts about yourself and others; that you're mindful of other people's feelings and aren't too hard on yourself, either; and that you examine the consequences of your words *before* you say them. If you're always in hyperdrive, this may be more difficult to accomplish than it is for someone who goes about life in a slower pace—but it can still be done! If you're a master multitasker, your mind is on several things at once; when your mind is that busy, your mouth can have a field day. Always take a moment before you speak to focus on what you want to say or how you are going to respond so that you are making a mind-mouth connection and avoiding negative actions with your words. This will quite often avoid hurt feelings and embarrassment.

* Pause before speaking.
You may decide to keep your
thoughts to yourself.

7. Soul Song

Each of us has a soul song that is unique to our spiritual being. It's the core musical essence of us on a soul level. Have you ever caught yourself humming the same tune over and over again, but it's not a tune you know from a song on the radio or television? When you do this, you've tapped into your soul song. It's a clear expression of your essence coming out in song. Your soul song may or may not have words. When this song comes to you, it's as if you've known it forever (because you have)—it pours forth from you with little or no effort. Others around you may recognize your soul song because they recognize you as a spiritual being, yet they can't place the tune or they feel that they just somehow know the song. To tap into your soul song, start humming with the intention that you'll hit on your soul song eventually and that when you do, you'll recognize it. You may hum through a few tunes you already know but then suddenly, the song resonates deeper, you feel a sense of longing for "home," and you may even get teary-eyed without knowing why. That's when you'll know you've truly tapped into your soul song.

*Sing from your soul and
the Universe sings with you.*

8. Compassion Within

When you are compassionate, you are sympathetic to the suffering of another person and you desire to help that person in some way, even if it is just by being able to understand their suffering. When you are a compassionate person, you show kindness to others, are empathetic to their situation, and will often help those you feel compassion toward by taking action that will help them in some way. Let's say you're running to a department store to buy a few things. It's a cold day and you see a homeless woman sitting in a niche trying to get warm. You could forget about her, do your shopping, and go home—or you could pick up a thick blanket while you're shopping and give it to her. You wanted to alleviate this woman's suffering in the cold, so you did something about it by purchasing the blanket for her. Compassion is a wonderful ingredient in raising frequency.

Do you offer yourself that same kind of compassion? Most of us are harder on ourselves than we are on others. We'll beat ourselves up over stupid things that we do, where we'd offer another person understanding over that exact same action. Why do we do this to ourselves? Because we judge ourselves too harshly. To change this behavior and be more compassionate to yourself, try to look at yourself as a friend or loved one would see you.

*Spread compassion
throughout your world to
share light and love.*

9. CREATIVE VISUALIZATION GENERATES A NEW REALITY

Throughout this book I will use numerous examples of creative visualization exercises that can help you on your journey of enlightenment by showing you how you can see things in a different way. Creative visualization is envisioning what you want to happen in your life, and you can resolve problems or manifest things for yourself by imaging the situation and its end result in your mind's eye. You can use creative visualization with relaxation techniques to increase your energy and connect with your spirit guides or with your higher self. Creative visualization allows you to create a new reality in your mind's eye; by seeing it happen there, you can manifest it in your life. You give the new reality energy in your mind as you create it, and that energy follows the visualization into the Universe, where it gathers even more force. The visualization then brings what you desire back to you. It helps to keep you balanced and positive and allows you to release negativity or ties that are holding you back from happiness or successes in your life. This enables you to solve problems and think of things in new ways. When you do this, you are creating a new reality for yourself through creative visualization. If you can create it in your mind, you can create it in your life.

*What you visualize can
manifest in your life.
Think positive!*

10. Is Your Mind a Chatterbox?

Have you ever noticed that your mind can be the ultimate chatterbox? Your thoughts constantly run amuck, sorting possibilities, planning, organizing, and simply thinking about what you have to do, what you must do, what you should be doing, and what you want to do. If you're a busy person, you probably have several streams of thoughts going on at once. After a while this will really wear you out and send your energy spiraling downward. When your brain is in overdrive like this, you'll find it hard to focus on one task; instead, you'll be trying to do several things at once.

To raise your frequency, you need to calm down and quiet this constant stream of thought. If you're actively engaged in connecting with your mind's chattiness, then you can't rise above it to work on your personal energy vibration. If you become more conscious of this stream of thought and take vigorous measures to slow it down instead of actively participating in it, then you can begin to quiet the constant babble. Start by noticing what is happening around you. Consciously become more watchfully observant of the people, places, and things in your life. Notice your own actions and become aware of how your mind reacts in different situations. Once you've mastered this, you can take positive actions and make changes, which will result in a calm, quiet mind.

> * *When the chatter ends,*
> *enlightenment begins.*

11. Increase Your Awareness

Are you paying attention to both the big and small things that happen around you on a daily basis, or are you walking through life in a daze? It's easy to fall into the busy pace of daily life and miss the little things. If you make a conscious effort to become more aware of those little things, you'll make big strides in reaching your goals of a joyous and full life with high levels of vibration. Make a point of increasing awareness by noticing everyone and everything during your daily activities. Look past what you immediately see and pay attention to the details in the world. Start by really looking. Do you see that bee buzzing near that flower? Watch for a few moments. Really pay attention. What is that bee is doing? Does it land carefully on the petal or crash into it? Does it take long draughts of nectar or little sips? Do its wings stop moving when it's drinking or do they continue to rhythmically beat? Really notice its behavior and as you do, quiet your mind. Now, listen to any messages that may come to you from your inner self or your guides. You just may learn something about your own behavior, too. How are you similar to or different from the bee?

> *Don't let the little things
> in life pass you by simply
> because you didn't take the
> time to notice.

12. Feel the Energy Flow

We are all made up of energy, from our cells to our thoughts to our soul's life force. Intentionally directing your energy flow is a powerful tool that can be used to raise your energy at every level. Try this creative visualization exercise for a quick boost. Sit quietly, breathe deeply, and relax by releasing tension. Become consciously aware of the energy moving through you down to the subatomic levels within each cell of your body. Feel it swaddling and caressing your soul while flowing within you. Take a series of deep breaths. Expand your lungs to full capacity with each inhalation. With every exhalation, blow the air out until your lungs feel as if they're contracting and you can't release any more air. As you exhale, imagine that you're gathering all the negative energy built up within you, from the subatomic level upward, and watch in your mind's eye as it exits your body with your breath. Now visualize a wave of positive energy flowing from the Universe and into you as you inhale. Let this energy infiltrate each of your cells, filling them with calming, soothing warmth. Give this warmth intention. Just as heat raises the vibration of water, causing it to boil, envision this warmth giving a positive charge to your soul's energy, increasing the vibrations on a cellular level, thereby increasing your frequency.

> *Your breath is life—
> let it cleanse and energize
> your spirit.*

13. Find Your Mantra

A mantra is an uplifting phrase that, when said to yourself, gives you the feeling that you can do anything in the world and be successful at it. Many successful and highly motivated people use mantras daily to stay focused and moving forward toward their goals. If you don't have a personal mantra, choose one right now. Maybe your mantra is, "I will survive!" or "The world is my schoolhouse," or "I can be more than I am." When you think positively about yourself and life in general, you are raising your levels of joy and happiness. The more joyful you are, the easier life becomes and you'll feel happier overall. Big problems become smaller and little problems disappear. Success comes more easily for you. You'll see the situations in your life realistically without adding drama to the events or taking the things people say too personally. It's easy to fall into thinking that you aren't good enough, smart enough, or special enough to accomplish the goals that you set for yourself in this lifetime and to let the stress of everyday life get you down. Choose a mantra that connects to your unique energy and your unique goals. Say it out loud every day. Use it consistently and watch your frequency soar.

> *"I am a spiritual entity
> who succeeds in all I
> attempt. Even failures are
> successes in disguise."*

14. Answers to Every
Question Reside in You

Within you is the knowledge of all of time. It's just blocked from your memory because you're residing on the earthly plane. The good news is that with a little focused concentration, you can recall this information. While it's great to talk things out with friends or consult someone for their advice in situations, always remember that the ultimate answer resides within you. No one can tell you what to do. Others can give you their opinions, but only you can determine what's right or wrong for you based on your morals and ethical code of conduct. It's through your decisions that you will either learn your life lessons or set yourself up to repeat them. If you're unsure which path to take or which decision to make, sit down and focus on your life path. It is within this intricate plan that you set up for yourself prior to birth that you will find the answers you seek. Pay attention to your first impressions and believe in yourself as you discover the knowledge you need. Ask your guides to assist you and they will. Lie down or sit quietly and focus on your energy. Ask those on the Other Side to show you the information you need and then, when it comes to you, accept it as truth. Denying it—or doubting what you're seeing and the information you're given—will block your energy.

> *Look within yourself*
> *for spiritual solutions to*
> *everyday issues.*

15. Be Present in
the Moment

One of the easiest ways to raise your personal vibration is to be truly present in your life. As you grow older time may seem to move by faster. The way to slow this feeling down is to become more present in each and every moment of your life. When you're ignoring the special, precious moments you've been given, life will seem to fly right by you, until one day you'll wake up and realize that you're now an elderly person. You'll wonder how your life got to this point without you even realizing it. You don't want that to happen to you, do you?

I want you to stop reading and think about what's happening with you right now, at this very moment. Did you do it? I did. As I'm writing this there is an airplane soaring overhead, my air conditioner is humming, and my dog is snoring. There is a clock ticking and a slight breeze is blowing the leaves on the tree outside my window. Living in the moment means noticing what is around you, even the little things that you'd normally ignore, while staying centered and grounded. Kids are naturally great at living within the moment, since they don't usually have larger cares or worries. Young ones are also adept at recognizing the amazing and beautiful things all around us—flowers, a bird, a song. Thinking and noticing like a child does for a few minutes each day will raise your energy and keep you feeling young. This will help you enjoy every second of the time you've been given instead of living in the past "shoulda-woulda-couldas" or the future "what ifs."

> * View the world as a child
> does—full of awe, wonder,
> and appreciation.

16. Grade Yourself

Before you go to bed each day, review your accomplishments and the issues you encountered. Give yourself a grade on each of your successes, your reactions to any situations you had to deal with, and the positive ways you affected your energy today. Do you deserve an A for not blowing up at your boss when he blamed you for someone else's mistake? Or maybe that A is for being aware of the energies around you. Maybe you actually felt your spiritual frequency rising while working on your own enlightenment—then award yourself an A-plus and a gold star! When you were in elementary school, gold stars were a reward for accomplishment. You wanted those gold stars and to get them you had to learn. Why not use those as an adult, too? If a system has worked for you in the past, there's no reason it wouldn't work again. Include your daily grades in your notebook and when you deserve it, add a gold star (or a blue, red, or green one, if you prefer; little smiley stickers work as well). Not only does grading and giving yourself stars boost your confidence, it will raise your energy. It's important to reward yourself as you walk this path, for in doing so you'll experience more growth and understanding, not just when it comes to your energy, but in your entire spirituality.

*Shine like the gold
star you are!*

17. Awareness and Sensitivity

A good way to increase your frequency is to notice and be sensitive to it in other people as well as yourself. Consider the person who is always positive, looking for that silver lining when things are falling apart around them. Or think about the person who is always offering a hand, who teaches others by helping them understand themselves. They do this naturally—it isn't forced, it isn't an act, and they aren't doing it to receive something in return. People like this have high energy levels. They look like they're glowing, and they're so full of love, hope, and joy that it rubs right off on you. It is their true state of being and not something that they're forcing or that seems contrived. Once you're sensitive to how you feel at higher energy levels, you'll notice this air around yourself.

People who live in lower levels always see the negative instead of the positive. They try to make you as miserable as they are. They often start problems, yell, or scream. They have the worst "luck" in the world. If these people would simply pay attention to themselves, these negative qualities would fall away and leave them shining just as brightly as the eternal optimist described above because they, too, would have raised the level from which they're operating. Which kind of person are you?

*Release the dark to
live in the light.*

18. Learn Something New

When you take time to learn something new, you're allowing your soul to grow; you're stimulating your mind and expanding your person on many levels. Any new knowledge you can attain gives you a deeper understanding of yourself, of the world you live in, or of others. Choose something you feel drawn to and interested in, something enjoyable and stimulating. If you've always wanted to go snorkeling, take a trip to the ocean and don a mask and flippers. Or, if you can't take a trip right now, read about the different types of sea creatures you may encounter during a snorkeling adventure. It doesn't matter if you're actually in the water or not; it's the discovery of what's underneath that is important. If you've always wanted to learn how to play the guitar, then take lessons.

As you expand your knowledge base, you challenge yourself mentally and spiritually. The more you know, the greater your sense of accomplishment and inner joy, and the higher your energy will increase. Just don't become a know-it-all because the heaviness of that attitude will reverse what you're trying to accomplish. Strive for a vast variety of knowledge because it's something you desire for yourself, not something you want to show off to the world.

> *Challenge yourself to learn
> one new fact or attempt one
> new thing every day.

19. It Is Never Too Late— You're Never Too Old

Saying that you're too old or that it's too late for you to raise your frequency is nothing more than an excuse because you don't want to do the work necessary to bring about a change in your energy levels. Until you've breathed your last breath and passed back to the Other Side, it's never too late to learn something new on the earthly plane. That's true whether you're 1 or 130 years old. Maybe you're tired, or you just don't want to make the effort. If that's the case, then admit that to yourself. Get off the couch and make an effort. Or you may feel as if you don't deserve the great things that you'll receive on a soul level as you raise your spiritual energy. You do! As spiritual entities, we're always working to grow, but sometimes the heaviness of life can squash our best efforts. When you find that you're making excuses for yourself or are putting off a task, make a change, even if it's only a small one. Drop the excuses and do what you need to do to become a better person on a spiritual level because these actions will only help you as you progress along this path. It's positive, forward movement that brings about positive changes.

> *Be a seeker of spirituality.
> Don't hide behind excuses
> or laziness.

20. SPIRIT AWARENESS

Some entities aren't really on the human level of existence, such as spirits, ghosts, guardians, guides, angels, poltergeists, and fairies, to name a few. As you increase your soul's energy levels, you'll find that you're more aware of the spirit realm and the way you can connect to and interact with the entities in that dimension. The more you learn and understand about this realm, you may also begin to develop clairaudience, where you can hear what they're saying to you, or you may be able to see them manifest in front of you or in your mind's eye (clairvoyance). Some people are able to hear spirits, some can only see them while others can see, hear, and communicate directly with spirits. The higher your frequency, the more connected you'll be not only to your own abilities but to your ability to better understand those nonhuman entities you come in contact with. It can take some adjustment as you begin to experience the spirit realm, but in time, it will become second nature. You may begin by only being able to see spirits; after a few weeks of working to raise your spiritual energy, you may be able to directly communicate with them. When you reach that point, you can ask questions and receive answers that can lead to greater enlightenment.

> *Look to the Light and to
> the Shadows to step into
> other dimensions.

21. FREQUENCY SHOES

Because you are a human being living on the physical plane of existence, your spiritual energy is vulnerable to everything and everyone around you. The energy surrounding all of the situations that you encounter every day—both positive and negative—will have some kind of effect on you. It may be small or it could be huge, but you will feel a difference. Only you can decide how you will be internally affected by the external energy of the world. Your mood each day will affect how you deal with these situations, so it's very important for you to stay filled with positivity and harmonious emotions.

One way to ensure that your spiritual energy is positively affected is to wear "frequency shoes" every day. Before you put on your regular shoes each morning, imagine them filling with positive energy that is capable of blocking negativity and raising your own energy levels. Then, if you encounter stressful situations, angry people, or any other type of negativity, call on the positive energy of your frequency shoes. Imagine their energy saturating your feet, moving up your legs, filling every part of your body until you feel warm and radiant all over. Let these shoes help you walk away from negative situations and people while surrounding you with positive energy and light.

> *Energize and invigorate
> your soul from the tips of
> your toes to the top of
> your head.*

22. Save a Critter

They always sneak into your house at some point or another. Some can be an annoyance; others can give you a fright. A daddy longlegs, baby lizard, or harmless cricket isn't so bad. A snake, rat, or bird may be a bit more challenging. The next time you find one of these little critters in your home, save it instead of killing it. Catch the intruder and release it outside, even if you're deathly afraid of whatever it is. Use a broom to gather the spider, lizard, or other insect or animal between the bristles, then take it outside and release it away from your home. By taking positive action to save and release these animals, you're raising your personal vibration. It may be a pain trying to catch one of these critters (lizards are especially fast and I always have to catch them by hand), but once you've released them, you'll feel joy that you saved another living creature, even if you only saved it from yourself. A word of caution: leave the dangerous snakes, raccoons, and alligators (if you live in Florida like I do) to the experts. Once you've found where the animals gained entrance into your home, if the area is in need of repair, fix it so that you don't encounter the same situation again. You have higher intelligence; don't let fear dictate a path of death when it's not necessary.

** Saving lives results
in positive feelings and
encourages spiritual growth.*

23. Triggers

Noticing the things around you that act as a trigger or catalyst to an increased state of joy, happiness, and higher energy levels is an important step in your development. Start to really look for the things around you that cause your energy to soar. Is it the smell of fresh-brewed coffee? Does the sight and sound of a bird singing in a nearby tree, filling the air with song, cause you to feel joy? Does the feeling of a heartfelt hug from a family member give you a sense of love and belonging? Maybe your trigger is something as simple as sitting alone and enjoying the silence, connecting to your spiritual self, and communicating with your guides. Is it the smile on the face of an excited child? Or the happy antics of your dog when you get home from work? All of these examples are triggers because they catapult your energy to a higher plane filled with happiness, peace, and love. Once you've determined what your triggers are, you can purposefully use them as an instigator for future exercises. That's what taking this path is about: finding the triggers in life that cause your energy to move into higher rates of vibration when you connect with Universal Energy, which in turn brings you contentment and bliss.

*Become consciously
aware of things that inspire
love and joy.*

24. Connections
with Nature

Every individual person, rock, tree, animal, and grain of sand on the beach vibrates to its own rhythm. When you are open to experiencing higher vibrations, you will soon be able to identify the different frequencies of everything around you. While a rock may have a slower vibration than a butterfly or tree, all three still consist of energy that is free-flowing and vibrating at a given tempo for that entity.

Here is an exercise to feel the energy of everything around you. The next time you're outside, pick up a rock and hold it in your hand. Focus on connecting your energy to that of the rock. Feel its molecules vibrating. How does it compare or contrast with your internal motion? Notice the differences or similarities. Next, try this with a flower. Hold it in your hands. Feel the texture of the stalk, notice how its energy feels to you. Using creative visualization, look deeper into the stalk, move upward to the bloom and feel the energy, the life force, of the flower. Compare the energy on the inside of the flower to that on the outside. Make notes of what you feel from the stalk and the bloom. By connecting with them, do you feel your vibration rising? If you didn't, try again.

> *Be sensitive to your spirit,
> other's spirits, and the
> spirits of trees, rocks, and
> inanimate objects.

25. Signs around You

When you are troubled, you will often receive signs from the spiritual realms to let you know everything will be okay. For example, the tags on the car in front of you may be a digital catalyst if it contains three of the same number. Or you may look up in the sky and notice that the clouds are in the shape of a symbol that has a specific meaning to you or that reinforces something you felt. The clouds may spell out something that resonates with you. Perhaps while driving your regular route to work you notice a sign that you've never seen before and the message makes perfect sense regarding something you're going through. The sign could contain the word *angel, universe,* or *energy* or it could state something like *just wait* or *tomorrow.* Maybe you were doodling on a piece of paper and when you focused on it again you realized you'd drawn or written something that held a special message. Noticing these kinds of signs is an indication that you are raising your vibration by connecting with the Universal Energy and the spiritual realms. Your guides, angels, and departed loved ones often give signs to help you in life, but it's only when you've heightened your senses that you notice and pay attention to these comforting messages.

* Ask for a specific sign
that will let you know when
spirit is near.

26. Find Your Unique
Tonal Vibration/Pitch

We each have a unique tonal pitch that is connected to our soul energy. It's the sound our energy makes after it flows through our body and is expelled as sound. Your tonal pitch is distinctive to you; no two people will create exactly the same sound.

To discover your tonal pitch, use creative visualization to imagine your energy moving through you. When it's built up, release it as sound. Many people will say "ommm" when the sound is released, but you don't have to use this sound—it can be any sound, tone, or pitch that feels connected to your energy and that resonates with your soul. Try a variety of sounds, tones, and pitches including different words, a humming sound, or a grating sound. If the tonal pitch is lower or higher than you imaged it would be, that's fine. Don't try to change it. Accept it as it is and practice it over and over. Then, anytime you feel out of sorts with your energy, take a moment to repeat your unique spiritual tone to yourself to bring balance, stabilization, and ultimately an increase to your energy vibration.

The key element when using your unique tonal vibration is to let it naturally flow though you and be easily expressed as sound. Don't force it. Let it be an innate part of yourself, a sound that simply flows through your being, raising your vibration as it moves through you. If the tone doesn't feel exactly right, that just means that you haven't hit on your specific sound yet.

Once you've found your tone, you'll also discover that there are times when you need to use it but can't, because you're at work or doing something where making your tonal pitch would be deemed inappropriate. In these cases, make it in your mind. You know what it sounds like and you can achieve the same results by making the sound of it in your mind instead of out loud. To fine-tune your tonal pitch and use it to increase your vibration as it moves through you, imagine the tone resonating just a little bit faster. The effect of this slight change in speed will raise your own frequency.

I intuitively knew when I hit upon my tonal pitch. It moved easily through me and felt natural, strong, and vibrant, not forced. If you're forcing the pitch, then you haven't discovered your true soul tone yet. That's okay, just keep trying until you do. Sometimes my pitch will rise slightly at the end of "ommm" as my frequency rises. I do this boosting exercise any time that I feel low. Using your personal pitch is a great way to ground yourself while connecting to your core spiritual being.

> *Sound connects the
> spiritual soul to the physical
> body, allowing the spirit to
> shine through.*

27. Becoming Aware of Your Own Awareness

As you walk the path of increased vibration, you will find that you are more aware of the world around you and of your own energy levels every day. At some point, you will suddenly realize that you are now "aware of your own awareness," which means that you've become more cognizant of when you're aware of your own energy, the energy of others, and of the things around you; whether they're plants, animals, or inanimate objects. This quite often happens suddenly without any warning. You just realize that you're conscious of your own awareness. It feels as if you're awake and are living completely in the moment. It's an amazing feeling that will propel you forward on your spiritual path. When you reach this awareness, you are now consistently working at a higher level within your own energy fields. Each step along this path can be thought of as a ladder, with each rung representing a new permanent increase associated with your spirituality. While it's quite normal to have fluctuations in your energy levels because you exist as a human on the earthly plane, you have the ability, through your thoughts and actions, to move forward constantly and permanently raising your vibration by degrees, just as you would climb each step on a ladder to reach the rooftop.

> *Enlightenment is walking
> within your own awareness
> to find justification and
> explanation.

28. Be Responsible For Your Own Actions

One of the most important lessons you can learn on the earthly plane is to take responsibility for your actions. Think about how you behave for a minute. Do you face the consequences of your actions, or do you run and hide? Running and hiding is the easy way out. Owning up to what you've done is much more difficult because it requires you to really look at what you're doing and the effects on yourself and others. Taking responsibility is a positive upward shift in frequency. Don't put blame on another when you know in your heart you're the one who may be at fault. Playing the blame game is negative and will lower your vibration. It isn't easy to say you did something wrong or to admit when the blame falls squarely on your shoulders and no one else's. It's difficult to get past the embarrassment and shame that may be associated with taking responsibility for your wrong actions. When you blame another or allow another to accept blame that doesn't belong to them, that lowers your frequency. It's a lose-lose situation unless a person is consciously taking blame to save someone else from dire consequences, which is a self-sacrificing act that raises energy.

There's nothing worse than trying to carry on a conversation with someone who always blames everyone else for their actions or the things that they say. When you run into someone like this, it's obvious to you what is going on. You find that instead of talking openly with this person, you're on guard and watching your words. You don't want to give them any reason to blame you for something they did! When people are locked into this type of behavior, they're stuck in a pattern of negativity. Seeing this conduct in others can help you recognize it in yourself and can spur you to change your own behavior.

Here's an example: If someone told you to go ahead and eat the left-over snack in the refrigerator at work because it wouldn't be missed, even though it wasn't theirs to give to you, and then you ate it, upsetting the real owner of the food, simply say you ate it and offer to replace it. Telling the coworker that someone else said you could have the snack isn't going to change the fact that you ate the food. Face up to what you did and offer to replace it or pay for it. Don't say it's the fault of whoever told you to eat it. It's not. It was your choice to shove that snack in your mouth, no one else's. Take responsibility for all of your behaviors, good or bad.

*Be honest and accept
responsibility for the things
you do and say.
Admit your mistakes.*

Part Two

---*---

Your
Spiritual
Path

29. Finding your Life Purpose

Two age old questions are "Why am I here?" and "What's my purpose in life?" There are as many answers to these questions as there are people who ask them. It's important to understand your life purpose; when you know that purpose, you can move forward in a clear path of spiritual development. Understanding why you've decided to be on the earthly plane and the lessons you want to learn during this experience increases your vibration and energy levels. If you aren't clear in your life purpose, stop right now and consider the following:

Think about the things you do in your life. Are you a teacher—not just an educator in school, but an instructor of life? If you are, then teaching is one of your life purposes. Do you often share your knowledge just because you feel the need to help other people and not because you're bragging about how much you know? Or maybe you're a caregiver in this lifetime and it's your purpose to take care of others. Think about what you do on a daily basis. You may discover that you have more than one reason for being here. Whatever reason or reasons you find for living your life, you'll know it is right because it will resonate within you as a Universal Truth and you'll feel complete.

> * *Your objective is to*
> *discover the reason for*
> *your existence and fulfill*
> *your life purpose.*

30. Develop Your Psychic Ability

Each of us is born with psychic abilities, but not all of us choose to develop those abilities. To live at higher rates of vibration, purposefully work on expanding your psychic abilities by pushing them further than you thought possible. Don't allow fear of the unknown to stop you from learning more about yourself. You're intuitive by nature, and you have gut instincts and innate knowledge. The more you learn, the more you practice, and the more you understand what you're doing and why, the higher your soul will elevate. This happens because the act of increasing your internal fortitude is spiritual in nature. It connects to your intuition, the Other Side, and an understanding of all things metaphysical.

Where do you start? That depends on your current level of psychic development. If you're just beginning to notice your psychic abilities, then everything you read and every exercise you complete will raise your levels. If you've been working on your psychic abilities for years, push yourself to discover fresh and unique ideas; even if those ideas are hundreds of years old, they are still new to you. Move outside of what you already know to find new information that you've never considered before. There's an old saying that when the student is ready, the teacher will come. Consider that as you seek new knowledge.

> * Knowledge is power,
> and powerful knowledge
> increases your spirituality.

31. Do a Reading
for Someone

As you develop your psychic abilities and become more comfortable with them, share your talents with other people. You may feel that you aren't ready or that you aren't qualified to do readings, but you'll never know what you're capable of doing until you try. Being able to connect to Universal Energy, to realize that you're getting impressions that another may find helpful, is a sign of a higher frequency. Sharing this knowledge will also increase your vibration. Start with someone you trust to give you honest feedback on your reading, so you'll feel comfortable sharing your ability. As your confidence grows, you'll feel better about giving readings to people you don't know.

That said, not everyone wants to do readings for other people, so you may never move past doing a reading for a friend just to see how accurate you are—that's okay. Sometimes developing psychic abilities is something you only need to do for yourself, and it takes doing a few readings for others to realize that fact. But if you feel comfortable sharing your talents with other people after you've done several readings, you will move forward on your spiritual path. Doing public readings isn't for everyone. There's a lot of responsibility that goes along with it but you never know … it just may be right for you.

> *Tune in, trust, and try to*
> *discover a new path.*

32. Recognize Past Lives

Have you ever visited a place and felt as if you've been there before? Maybe you knew your way around the streets or recognized buildings, bridges, or elements of nature such as a waterfall or massive oak tree. But the strange thing is, you've never been to this location. Are you connecting with a past life? It's very possible.

Past lives can give you positive experiences, but they can also cause negative emotions such as fear. Let's say you are afraid of flying. Have you had a bad experience flying? If not, then you should look deeper by having a past-life reading or past-life regression done by a recommended professional. It could be revealed during the session that your fear stems from a past lifetime where you were a pilot who was shot down during war and died a fiery death. That past-life memory is still attached to you, causing an irrational fear of flying in your present life. By learning about past lives and then releasing any negative energy associated with them, you raise your frequency in two ways: first, by learning about yourself on a soul level and second, by taking positive action to release any negativity from your past life that is causing unnecessary stress and negative emotions in your current lifetime.

*Look to the soul's past to
enhance your life now.*

33. Create a Sand Jar with Intention

When you create something with intention, you are putting part of your own energy into that creation. Try this activity to raise your frequency. You'll need some multicolored sand, a glass jar with a lid, and a spoon. Now add sand to the jar, layering one color over the other, being careful not to mix the colors together until the jar is full. As you build your column of colored sand, give intention to the project. This intention should be something that you will think of every time you look at the colorful display you've created with your own hands. Your specific intention could be something as simple as "calm feelings," "positive emotions," or "warm, loving actions." You can also give the creation a very exact and complicated intention such as, "When I gaze at this colored sand, I will feel positive and sure about the decisions I'm making in my life. I will know in my soul that I'm doing the right things for me and for my own spirituality. This rightness of being will be reflected in my actions and reactions with each and every situation I encounter in my life." Whatever intention you give to the sand jar, be it simple or complicated, make it one that resonates within you, thereby increasing your vibration whenever you look at it or handle it.

> * Create with intent,
> live with purpose, and
> commit to the self.

34. Listen to Your
Intuition When Shopping

To give your energy a positive infusion, find a new item that draws you to it. Metaphysical stores are great places to find items that can raise your frequency because they're made with the intention of connecting to someone on a spiritual path. It doesn't matter if the object is made by machines or if handmade by an artisan, though it's okay if you have a personal preference. Visit a metaphysical store to look for a new piece of jewelry, book, or art. Before you enter the store, ask your guides to show you the item that will help you raise your personal vibration just by owning it. Walk through the store at a leisurely pace, looking at all the different items available while opening your energy to the item that is yours. Pick up the items to see how they feel to you. Sometimes they'll feel warm and inviting; other times they'll feel cold, with no personal connection. You'll feel drawn to specific areas in the store where the energy feels more intense and focused. Or you may notice an item that draws you to it, as if it's calling to you. This may happen as soon as you walk through the door, or it may get stronger as you walk around. Listen to your instincts and notice how the feeling increases as you get closer to the item that is meant to be yours. When you find it, you'll know instinctively that this item is meant for you. Sometimes all it takes to know that the item is supposed to be yours is a single glance. You see it and you know. Purchase it and use it with positive intention.

This happens in bookstores, too. You may be casually looking at titles and suddenly feel drawn to pick up a specific book out of the hundreds on the shelf. Or you may be looking in one area and then feel the need to go to an entirely different section, maybe even one that you never browse. Then you might feel drawn to pick up a specific book in that section. That's because there is something in that book that will help you in some way. You may open the book to a random page and specific words seem to jump right out at you with a message that answers a question or is a sign that you're on the right track. Or you may get a feeling that you need to buy the title, and when you get home and start reading, you'll discover the reason you had to have that particular book.

Just the simple act of following your instincts brings about a change of thought, causes an increase in your spiritual connection to the soul, and is a confirmation for you.

> *Connection to your
> spiritual energy brings about
> clarity of purpose through
> unexpected means.*

35. A Little Goes a Long Way

Even the smallest increases in the rate at which your energy vibrates can have a positive effect on you. One of the things that may cause you problems is trying to rush the process and increase your vibration too quickly. You may feel that you need to be at the top of your game immediately. Slow down; don't be in a hurry. This is a lifelong process where you can always reach higher and higher levels over time. Remember, there isn't really a "top of the chart," like there is a top forty hit list for music. You have unlimited levels of energy that you can tap into to increase your vibration. This energy is in a state of constant fluctuation, so every little step you make is a positive movement along your path. It isn't a competition to see who can raise their vibration the fastest. This is your soul's quest—your personal journey—and on this passage, it only takes a little to give you lot of enlightenment. Increasing frequency is equivalent to your enlightenment, your happiness, and joy in life; it's the freedom you feel when you connect to nature or to another person. It's the little things that widen your eyes and make your heart fill to bursting with love, joy, and amazement.

*Every small
accomplishment moves
you forward on your
spiritual path.*

36. Don't Leave Decisions to Chance

Choose to consciously make firm, positive decisions in your life. When you leave decisions to chance, you lose control over that aspect of your life. Let's look at a workplace example. Imagine that a new project came up at work, one at which you would excel and that you'd enjoy, but you're undecided about talking to your supervisor and saying you'd like to head the project. You can choose to have that conversation, or you can leave it up to chance and hope that your boss has noticed how well you work and decides to give you the project. If you talk to your boss and let your ideas, enthusiasm, and desire for the project be known, then you've given a good effort to obtain the responsibility, even if the final outcome isn't up to you. If you just wait to see if you're selected for the position without taking any positive action, then you're assuming your boss will just know what you want. Meanwhile, a coworker tells the supervisor he or she wants to head the project. If you express your desires as well, the supervisor has two people to choose between; if you don't say anything, you eliminate yourself through indecision. By not speaking up, you actually made the decision to leave it up to chance.

> *Always take positive
> actions, even if final
> decisions aren't yours
> to make.*

37. INSPIRATION

When normal levels of inspiration feel "off," it's likely that your energy levels are low and out of balance. If you can't put your finger on how you got out of sync and there's no stimulus to get anything done, then it's time to look for a little inspiration. Encouragement is all around you, but sometimes it can be difficult to find.

When we say we feel inspired, what we really mean is that we feel influenced in some way to rise to higher levels of expectations. When looking for inspiration, you want to seek out things that will stimulate your mind and increase your energy—things that make you more aware, creative, and joyful. What could inspire you? Maybe it's being with a friend or the memory of a joyful time in your life. You may feel inspired when looking at a peaceful scene or being with like-minded people. Reading an encouraging quote at the beginning of every day might work well for you. Once you're inspired, your creativity will soar and you will feel like you can accomplish anything you set your mind to. And you can. You only need to focus on coming back to center and finding the things that will give you the inspiration you need, so you can then use your enthusiasm to inspire others.

> * You can find inspiration
> in the most unexpected
> places if you'll only take a
> moment to look.

38. Harmony

Harmony is when all parts of your being are fluid and in tune with Universal Energy. You feel like life is going smoothly, as if everything you do works out well. You may even feel that you have the golden touch. Every opportunity turns into a success and good things come to you in abundance. Harmony is a consistent and orderly rhythm within your being that affects everything you do.

When your energy flow is not harmonious with your spiritual being, you may find that you have to force yourself to carry out your daily routine. Or you may feel like no matter what you do, you're repeating the same pattern. You can't get past a certain point, you're making no headway, and just feel stuck. To bring yourself back into harmony, use creative visualization to focus on your entire being and then imagine that you're connecting with the stream of Universal Energy, letting it move through you, bringing balance and releasing any blockages that are keeping you from feeling in sync with your spiritual self. As you do this exercise, you may feel as if a great weight is being lifted from you, freeing your mind, body, and soul. When this weight is gone, you will feel more synchronicity in your life, allowing you to soar to greater heights.

> ∗ With peace, calmness,
> and consistency in your life,
> all parts of the whole flow
> together as one.

39. Trusting
Inner Wisdom

Sometimes trusting someone can be difficult, especially if that person is you. But real problems can crop up when you don't trust in your own inner wisdom. Everyone has individual and unique life experiences that form how they think of the world, their role in it, and how they relate to those they interact with every day. If you don't trust in yourself—if you don't believe and know that you are a wise and wonderful person inside—then it's difficult to relate well to others. You may have to release negativity surrounding past experiences before you can connect to your own inner wisdom. Take it one step at a time by recognizing what's holding you back and then consciously choosing to let go of those feelings.

Trusting your inner wisdom is following your instincts, believing in yourself, and knowing that while you may make mistakes in life, you always do what you feel is right. If you follow this philosophy, you will find that connections with others come more easily and you have fewer trust issues and doubts about the motives or behaviors of those in your life. Doubt is a negative energy that can lower your frequency. Try not to doubt yourself. Know that on a soul level you always recognize the wisest solutions to problems. It's listening to those solutions, believing in yourself, and acting on that knowledge, which can be difficult.

> *You are a wise spiritual
> entity; believe and have faith
> in your core essence.*

40. Your Frequency
Alarm Clock

Your energy comes off you in waves, affecting everyone around you, even when you're not aware that it's happening. Positive waves will bring a lot of positivity back to you, and lower levels will bring less. Do you realize when your energy levels are high and when they're low? When you're in tune with your own levels, you can raise them even higher.

A good way to increase your awareness of times of high frequency is to use the idea of an internal alarm clock. It's similar to waking up minutes before the alarm goes off. Your body somehow knows what it's supposed to do. To make yourself more aware of times of high frequency that you may unconsciously ignore, set your internal alarm clock by purposefully raising your vibration and then, when it is high, use creative visualization to register the levels. Tell yourself that every time you are at this intense energy level, you'll receive a sign that you can't ignore, just like you can't ignore the noise of your alarm clock in the morning. The sign may be a certain buzz word, a butterfly, a specific noise—anything that feels right to you and will get your attention. Your body will take care of activating this alarm when you're at a high frequency. Then, when you notice your "alarm" signal, you will know to pay attention to whatever brought you to an increased frequency.

*Monitor yourself, take
notice, and be aware of the
energy within you.*

41. Connect to the Akashic Records

The Akashic Records is the Hall of Knowledge held within the Universal Energy flow. These records contain all knowledge about everything and everyone throughout all time. When you connect to the Akashic Records, you can discover things about yourself that you may have been suppressing simply by being on the earthly plane. Through these discoveries, you're raising your frequency.

To enter the Akashic Records, find a place to sit or lie down and then use creative visualization to become one with Universal Energy by imagining that you are part of this natural flow of energy. You are absorbed into it and its knowledge becomes yours; you cannot be separated from the Universal Energy because you are part of it. Now ask your guides to escort you to the Hall of Records. I see the Akashic Records as a huge library filled with books, with a gatekeeper who retrieves the required book for me, allows me to read it, and then returns it to the shelf. You may have to try several times before you can visit the Akashic Records, so don't give up too soon. The information you receive from reading the Akashic Records may be very philosophical. It may even seem vague, but upon further thought, it will become clear. If you are lucky, the message may be specific and detailed.

> *Knowledge contained
> in the Akashic Records
> can greatly affect you in a
> positive way on every level
> of your being.

42. Attend a Psychic Fair

If you've never attended a psychic fair, you may not know what to expect. And what you'll experience all depends on the quality of the vendors and your frame of mind when you attend. Some psychic fairs are full to bursting with the positive energy of the people, teachers, and vendors in attendance. Being surrounded by high levels of energy can inadvertently raise your own. (This doesn't mean you're turning into a psychic vampire and feeding off the energy of the people in attendance; I'm talking about drawing on the general energy of the event.) It can take you to higher levels simply because a gathering of high frequencies tends to overflow and spread throughout the space. Have you ever been in a bad mood but around someone who was happy and laughing? The next thing you know, your bad mood is gone and you're happy too. It's the same idea. The positive energy just rubs off on you.

Other psychic fairs may not contain this same vibrant energy, or it may be spotty because the attendees aren't in a positive energy flow. It's important to note that the size of the psychic fair doesn't matter. You can have a small psychic fair that is pulsating with energy or a large one that doesn't seem like anything special. When you attend any type of psychic event, just go with the flow.

> *Go to a psychic fair
> without any specific
> expectations, but enter
> with an open mind.

43. Visit an Energy Vortex Area

There are certain areas around the world, called "energy vortexes," that emit high levels of electric, magnetic, and electromagnetic energy from Earth.

In ancient times, people considered these areas to be sacred, and many people still do today. These areas are calculated by looking at Earth as an energy grid. Ley lines are thought to be Earth's natural energy lines that run along geographical places of interest, including holy places and ancient sites that can be connected and are considered to have powerful energy. You can often find energy vortexes in the areas where ley lines intersect. Visiting these areas can make you feel rejuvenated, more energetic, and more in tune with your psychic abilities.

Stonehenge, the Bermuda Triangle, and Sedona, Arizona, are thought to be energy vortexes. But you can also find vortexes in your own backyard. You will recognize them by noticing the bark on trees. If the bark appears to have grown in a spiral around the trunk, that's a good indication of a vortex. Another clue is the vegetation: look for an area where the plants have grown in a nearly perfect circle. That's the outline of the vortex. Vortexes are also thought to come in pairs, a male and female, with the female always being barren and the male containing impressive vegetation growth.

> *Look for a vortex in your
> local area and visit it often
> to increase your energy.

44. Read about Metaphysics, Soul, and New Age Topics

Learning about the soul and spirituality, anything metaphysical, and New Age ideas is a surefire way to get your energy levels on the rise. Read as much as you can on these topics from a variety of authors. Take what feels right to you and make it your own. If a certain book or genre doesn't feel like it is connecting to you right now—if it is difficult to understand or just sounds out-and-out ridiculous—then it's either not part of your life lesson or you're not yet at the place on your spiritual path where you can connect to these ideas. Set aside that information for now; when the time is right and you're ready for these ideas, they'll come back around to you and make sense.

Just the act of seeking out something brings it to you. If you're searching for ways to become a more spiritual person, if you want to learn more about New Age thought and ideals, or if you are just curious as to what other philosophies and thoughts are out there, then finding answers through research will bring you enlightenment. You may find that one simple idea catapults you to another plane on your spiritual path. And unless you are looking for it, you might never discover that gem of truth.

> *Increase your knowledge
> to access greater realms
> of spirituality.*

45. Pendulums

A pendulum is a tool used to receive answers to situations and questions that are concerning you at specific times in your life. Some people use their pendulums daily to receive guidance from the higher realms or their higher self. The answers you receive to your questions are guided in two ways: The first method connects to answers within yourself, while the second connects to answers from other realms.

When looking within, you are connecting with your higher self, and since every answer to every question lies deep within each of us, the pendulum acts as a conduit of energy between your inner self—your soul—and the pendulum. When you ask a question, you release a certain energy, which runs through your body like an impulse through your nervous system and connects to your core spiritual self to retrieve the answer. Then, the energy released from your spiritual self reacts with the pendulum, causing it to move in whatever pattern you've designated for Yes, No, or Maybe. When used as an energy detector, the pendulum can show you if your frequency is high or low simply by the questions you ask and the responses you receive. The important thing to do in order to ensure accurate answers is be centered and focused on the task at hand when using this tool to ask questions. If you're scattered and not really paying attention, you're not going to get accurate results, and you may even see this in the way the pendulum moves. If you notice the movement isn't smooth but is kind of all over the place, jerky and unstable, take a few minutes to focus and center your own energy and then try again.

The second way to use a pendulum is as a spiritual communication device. You can ask questions of your guides or angels and receive responses from other realms. The process for this is pretty much the same as using a pendulum for seeking inner wisdom.

Prior to using your pendulum, cleanse it with white light to rid it of any negative leftover energy from people who may have handled it prior to you. To do this, use creative visualization to imagine white light, which is the purest energy that flows from God (or whatever higher being you believe in) and the Universe. Imagine this white light flowing through you and into the pendulum. As the white light moves into the pendulum, it eliminates the energy of everyone else who has previously handled it and cleanses it, leaving it pure and in tune with only your energy. Once it is cleansed, you can give the pendulum the intention of working for the higher good and with positivity. Some people prefer that no one else touch their pendulum once it's been cleansed; others will share their pendulum and then cleanse it again afterwards. It's completely up to you and what you prefer.

> *Pendulum energy can
> connect to the core of your
> spiritual being or to
> your guides.*

46. Be Curious

Curiosity killed the cat, but that cat has nine lives, right? Today, be as curious as the cat. Look for the reasons why things happen, even if you're skeptical about that which can't be seen. You can't see the wind, but it's there isn't it? You can see its effect by the movement of the trees, the ripples over a pond, or in the way it whips your hair around your face. There's more than we can see with our two eyes; you simply need to pay attention to the things around you. Maybe you felt as if someone whispered in your ear but you were alone at the time. Was it your imagination or could it have been a spirit? Investigate. Think of what you heard—could it have been a message from someone that has passed? Or maybe it's communication from your guides. If you're not curious, you're not going to seek deeper answers. Have a burning desire to know more and more about yourself and your spirituality.

Having said all that, a healthy dose of skepticism is a good thing. Some people can get so caught up in the "woo-woo" of metaphysical and psychic phenomena that they lose sight of the lessons they're supposed to learn. Be curious, stay grounded in reality, and search for the deeper meanings of life. This will bring you a greater enlightenment, knowledge, and truth.

> *Ask questions, be
> inquisitive, and revel in
> your discoveries.*

47. Learn I Ching

I Ching, also known as the *Book of Changes*, is one of the world's oldest oracles. It's a divination system based on sixty-four hexagrams with each hexagram containing six lines, either broken or solid. The broken lines are called yin and the solid lines are yang. *I Ching* is quite detailed and involved because it not only gives divination meanings based on the hexagrams formed, but there are also number values associated with each symbol. *I Ching* readings also incorporate various elements within nature into the spread. *I Ching* is usually done by tossing coins or yarrow stalks and then, depending upon the way these items lay and form hexagrams, you determine the answer to your questions based upon each hexagram's specific meaning. It is most often consulted for changing conditions in a person's life, especially during times of crisis, impending change, or when you're feeling uncertain about a big issue. It's also used to gain greater insight into personal questions or current situations encountered during daily life, since it shows you your options and not just your current state.

Today, do a simple search for the hexagram symbols online and see if the method of *I Ching* divination calls to you. If so, ask several questions and practice the divination using coins (the fastest method). Whether you're using *I Ching* for a big or small problem, this method of divination holds the potential to raise your energy by causing you to look deeper within yourself. It offers possible solutions and guidance. Ultimately, as with all methods of divination, it's up to you to put that guidance to work in your life.

> *Discover solutions through*
> *the deliberation of old-*
> *world divination.*

48. Tarot

While many psychics don't need to use tools such as the Tarot, this ancient method of divination can be a good tool to use when you're facing confusion or when you need a different perspective on your dilemma. It can offer insight into situations and problems that you're too close to and can't see clearly. Tarot increases your frequency because it connects with your spiritual energy and gives insight through the lay of the cards that can help you make decisions.

If you don't know how to read the Tarot, find a deck and dive into studying the cards and their meanings. Many Tarot books even offer quick keywords to get you started. Soon you'll be able to read for yourself and others, as it doesn't take long to develop a familiarity with the Tarot. Some Tarot readers know the cards and their traditional associations as well as they know their own names. Others use the unique, detailed meanings given by the inventor of a particular deck to determine how the reading applies to them. Both ways are fine. You do not have to have psychic abilities to do a Tarot reading, but many people who use the Tarot do receive psychic impressions while using the cards and connecting to specific energy. If you're doing the reading for yourself or just learning the Tarot, use the author's meanings but also listen to any impressions you receive during the reading (even if you think you're not psychic) because the two combined can offer great insight.

> * The lay of the cards can
> offer unforeseen options.

49. Reiki

Reiki is a Japanese technique where one person uses the laying on of hands to attune the unseen life-force energy of another person. It is often used to reduce stress that you're holding in your body, which in turn aids in relaxation. It is also used to help promote healing. Reiki practitioners do not usually touch the person receiving treatment; the hands transmit energy by hovering above the physical body.

The basic principle of reiki is that low life-force energy causes problems and illness. Reiki is used to treat you as a whole being, not just your physical body, so it also benefits you emotionally, mentally, and spiritually. Having high life-force energy will allow you to be happier, healthier, and live stress-free. To me, the energy tapped into during a reiki session is similar to tapping into your own personal vibration to increase it. A reiki practitioner helps you balance and increase your soul energy as you find peace, security, and relaxation through the harmonious passage of healing energy from God and the Universe to you. There are certain symbols used during a reiki session that only certified reiki masters are allowed to use. Training to use reiki consists of four levels, and the ability to use reiki is passed from one person to another. Reiki can be used to help you find balance because it brings healing energy into your own soul energy, which raises it.

Today, consider contacting a local reiki practitioner for a healing session. For a more simplistic connection to the power of reiki, lightly run your hands along your limbs while concentrating on drawing life-force energy from the Universe through your hands and into yourself.

> *Tap into the Universal
> Energy through the
> laying on of hands.*

50. Worry Stone Amulet

Worry is a natural reaction to stress in your life. Excessive worry can lead to physical problems and illness, such as anxiety and panic attacks. When you find that worry is a constant companion or you're feeling stressed and frustrated but can't seem to release the negativity that is keeping you in a constant state of unease, a worry stone or amulet is just what's needed.

Find a small stone, piece of wood, or other smooth object that is small enough to hold between your fingers. It doesn't necessarily have to be smooth but that will make it easier to rub your worries away. If the object is rough, it will become smooth over time as you use it. Some people prefer to use a small piece of certain fabric, like satin or velvet, as their worry amulet. You may want to keep your worry stone or amulet in your pocket, make it into a pendant that you can wear around your neck, keep it on a key chain, or make it into a bracelet. It's important that it's close by you or on your person so when negative energy such as stress and worry starts overwhelming you, bringing your energy down, you can reverse the effect by rubbing the amulet and allowing the negative energy to flow into it and out of you.

*Don't let worry turn your
life upside down; create an
outlet for this negativity.*

51. Wind Chimes

Have you every really listened to the sound of wind chimes? The light, airy tone and pitch has an almost ethereal quality that can resonate with your spiritual self. Get a set of wind chimes and hang them where you can sit nearby and close your eyes, listening as the wind gently moves the chimes, creating their unique musical sound. Feel yourself connecting to the flow of the melody the chimes make. Focus on their unique tone. Allow yourself to feel your soul energy rising, becoming one with the harmonious energy of the chimes. Connect to this energy and feel it move through you as the chimes sing their ethereal songs. As you listen, use creative visualization to let your energy flow with the sounds. Listen to any messages that you hear or images that you see, for as you become in tune with the chimes, you'll often find that you're releasing constraints you've put on your own psychic abilities. Don't be surprised if you begin receiving impressions.

Not at home right now? There is another option when you're away from your chimes but need a quick connection. Go online and search for places that sell chimes. Many of them give you the option to listen to their sounds on your computer. I've discovered a few in this manner that I really love and have even found chime earrings that I can take with me anywhere I go.

> *Pure tones and melodies*
> *flitter on the air, embracing*
> *you in otherworldly charms.*

52. Prisms

A prism is a three-dimensional object that reflects light as an array of colors. Using a prism adds color energy to your life, which can be utilized to increase your own spirituality. To benefit from the effects of this array of color, obtain a hanging prism and put it in a window where it can catch the light of the sun and reflect colors throughout your home. Then sit quietly and focus on the colors—feel their energy and, as you do, feel your own energy increase. See if you can feel a difference in the energy of one color from the next. Is it warmer, cooler, or more vibrant?

If you can't find a prism, you can also use stained glass for a similar effect. Another alternative is to get several clear glass bottles with lids, fill them with water and food coloring, and place them in the sun. Regardless of the approach you take, the results will be the same. The energy flow created by the reflection of colors within the home brings positive energy into your living space. Pay attention to the colors and let yourself feel the connection with the Universal Energy that flows from the sun and through the glass, resulting in wondrous color schemes all around you.

*Let the Universe shower
its colors throughout
your life.*

53. Triangle-Tone
to Harmonize

Just as listening to wind chimes or finding your personal tonal pitch can raise frequency, harmonizing your energy with the tone of a triangle can achieve the same result. If you're unsure about purchasing a triangle, you can visit a music store and try this exercise before making your decision. Start by holding the triangle and striking it, letting its clear tonal frequency resonate through you in two ways. First, you will hear the sound. As you hear it, let the musical note flow through you, filling you with its unique tonal energy. Harmonize with the sound. Don't cut off your connection to it before the tone completely disappears. Even then, once the sound is gone, notice whether you can still feel the pitch within your own energy. Second, you will feel the energy vibrate through your hands, up your arms, and into your body. As the triangle's tonal energy merges within your body, feel your own energy rising to meet its pitch and tone. Once you see how effective this can be, you may decide to take the triangle home with you.

For portable tone-tuning, try a very small bell or even finger cymbals. You can carry these with you and use them for quick results when you need to connect to your higher spiritual energy.

> *Flow as one with the
> tones of triangles, bells,
> or finger cymbals.

54. RUNES

According to the *American Heritage Dictionary*, the word *rune* describes "Any of the characters in several alphabets used by ancient Germanic peoples from the 3rd to the 13th century," and the root word meant to "whisper, to talk in secret." It goes on to describe the use of runes in casting spells, identifying material possessions, and making calendars.

People often carved rune messages into rocks on the sides of popular thoroughfares. They picked specific rune letters as protection symbols, and these were placed on their homes, woven into their clothing, worn as metal pendants, or even etched onto their weapons. As Christianity spread, runes became regarded as Pagan symbols associated with communication, mysteries, and magic.

Today, runes are used for divination to help you find answers to problems in your life. Try constructing your own simple set of runes on scraps of paper and doing a reading or two to see if this method of divination strikes a chord within you. You can find many online sources that explain various rune systems. Rune readings are complex. They make you look deeper into your spirituality and behaviors, and the rune definitions really make you think outside the box about yourself. When using runes as a divination tool, you will consider the meaning of the rune as given in whatever source you are referencing (a website or book, or a booklet if you purchase a ready-made rune set), but you'll also want to personally connect to the rune so that the energy of the rune combines with your own energy. This connection allows you to choose the correct runes as you address your specific area of concern.

> * *The symbols of the past*
> *can give information*
> *about the future.*

55. Scrying

Scrying is the process of looking, gazing, or staring into an object and using divination to see a future event. Many times you'll hear of psychics using a crystal ball, tea leaves, mirrors, a dark bowl of water or dark ink, coffee grinds, a pendulum, or a room filled with candles to practice scrying. Some people also prepare and enact an entire ritual when they scry.

You can scry to enhance your own psychic abilities. First, choose the object you want to use as a scrying tool. I have a water bottle on my desk right now. If I want to use it for scrying, I stare into it until I start to receive images. It's the staring and focused concentration that allows you to see images, not the actual thing you're staring at; the scrying tool is simply a medium to help you focus and connect to your own psychic abilities. Once the images begin, you may see only one image or you may see a scene unfold as if you're watching a movie. Make note of the images you see, as you'll need to determine how you will use the information. Will you act upon what you see? Share it with others? Or simply be more aware? It's important to pay attention to the details you receive and then determine how those parts relate to and affect the whole situation.

Eventually, you'll fine-tune your abilities so you don't need tools to obtain impressions. Instead, you'll tap into your own intuition, Universal Knowledge, or you'll receive messages from guides. While you may sometimes prefer to use tools, you will not require them. When scrying, you open yourself to the energy of the Universe, which allows you to increase your spiritual energy and obtain information.

> *See into the beyond and
> become one with Universal
> Energy to find wisdom.

56. Dowsing

I remember my grandmother teaching me to dowse when I was a child. She gave me a divining rod made out of a willow branch and told me to go find water. You can use dowsing to locate underground water by using a wooden stick or a tree branch that's shaped like a Y. Walk around holding the stick by the double end. When you feel the single end bending down toward the ground, that's where you'll find water. You can also use dowsing to find oil, metals, gemstones, minerals, or lost objects.

Many dowsers use a dowsing rod, also called a divining rod, while some dowsers can just walk around and feel where the water is underground, simply because their connection to Earth is so strong. In this case, the person's body acts as the divining rod. You can also use pendulums, metals, and crystals as divining rods. I still prefer a willow stick because it is part of nature and already has a connection to Earth's energy. When dowsing, you're connecting your energy to the energy of Earth. When you make that connection, it is going to affect you even more because it's positive energy. When you feel that dowsing rod start to move, it connects with you and raises your energy. It's all about the energy passing between Earth, the divining rod, and you as a spiritual entity.

*Seek and find when the
rod becomes divine.

57. Chanting
and Drumming

Chanting and drumming are good ways to get in touch with your own spiritual energy. Chanting is repeating a prayer, affirmation, or mantra over and over. By saying it repeatedly, you align yourself to higher levels of energy within the cosmic universe. The tones used in chanting and drumming are also important. They are monotonous, said in the same droning way. Consider the ancient Gregorian chants—they are a variety of tones, some lower and some higher, but when you hear the overall tonal energy of the chant and you feel its energy flowing through you, you're experiencing oneness with Universal Energy.

The same concept applies to drumming. The tone of the drum, striking it in a repetitive manner—which may be fast or slow or a combination of speeds—and the action and movement of drumming increases your energy to match that of Universal Energy flow. You're making a connection between the Universal Energy surrounding the drums and your personal frequency. This practice works well because people have done the exact same thing in the same way for hundreds of years; they've carved a pathway into the Universe Energy flow so all you have to do is simply walk upon that path to access this same knowledge.

> ✳ *The path may be narrow*
> *or steep, but if you repeat*
> *each step along the way, you*
> *will rise to greater heights.*

58. Fifth-
Dimensional Energy

I believe that the fifth dimension is when you, as an individual, realize that everyone is connected at a Universal level. It is when you begin to believe in past lives or other metaphysical theories, and you may push away things that you have learned in the past because they no longer feel right to you on a soul level. These negative past beliefs now seem to conflict with your energy because they no longer mesh with how you see and feel the world. I know that happened for me when I was a teenager because I had issues with the difference between the way people behaved in church and the way they acted outside of church. It seemed hypocritical to me that people could be so duplicitous, even though we were all connected within the Universe. As you move into elevated dimensions, you'll find you no longer cling to old ways of thinking but instead look for newer concepts and ideals that mesh well with your higher self. Many people consider the fifth dimension to be a realm where space and time are fluid, not set as they are in our dimension. This is true, but I believe it goes much deeper and is a step into higher Universal Knowledge.

*When you grow
spiritually, you begin to see a
wider view of the Universe.*

59. Immerse Your
Hands in Water

Because we're mainly made up of water and we need it to function, it only stands to reason that we can increase our frequency with water. You need to drink lots of water to stave off dehydration, and this in and of itself raises your energy. Taking a shower or hot bath at the end of a long day can make you feel calmer and more relaxed. When you don't have time for that long, hot bath where you can soak and become one with the power of water, but you need a quick pick-me-up throughout the day, you can still purposefully connect to water to achieve the same results. You can also intentionally use water to raise your energy by quickly immersing your hands in it.

When you wash your hands, hold them still and let the water flow over them. You're not submerging them in water, but immersing them, letting the water run freely over your hands. Feel the fluid texture of the water, the warm or cool temperature of it, and its invigorating life force. Now imagine that energy flowing into your hands, up your arms, and into your body as the water flows over your palms, the back of your hands, and between your fingers. Feel its movement flowing through you, to the core of your being.

Just as you can use the power of water to invigorate yourself, it can also be used to release negativity. If you've had an argument with someone or things aren't going well in your day and you are feeling low, frustrated, or depressed, take a few minutes of alone time near a sink. Turn on the water, picking the temperature that feels right for you at that moment in time. Perhaps cool water will soothe your temper, or hot water will relax away your tension. As the water flows over your hands, imagine all the negative emotions and stress you are feeling leaving your body through your hands and washing away with the water. Once the negativity is released, allow the positivity of the water's energy to flow back into you through your hands and bring balance to your soul.

You're accomplishing two things with this exercise: you're releasing the negative and increasing the positive in your energy, bringing balance to your core spiritual self. The next time you feel that your frequency is low, head to the bathroom or kitchen sink and immerse your hands in water. If you're near an outside fountain, a pond, or stream, submerge your hands in that water for a few minutes. Any water will accomplish the same results in your energy simply by connecting to it for a short time.

> * *Water is a powerful*
> *element that can increase*
> *your life force and bring*
> *balance on many levels.*

60. Burn Incense

Some incense has a nice pleasant scent and some is pungent and strong. Incense is often used to relax—to give you feelings of peacefulness and calm. It is used during meditation and in connecting with the higher self, your spirit guides, and the masters on the Other Side. It is also used to purify the areas of your home and your spiritual being. Incense can help you concentrate, become more focused, and boost your creativity and motivation, which in turn can make you feel more confident. It can make you feel happier and more in tune with yourself. The wonderful aromas of incense can help you feel better in almost any situation.

If you're going use incense—especially if you've never tried it before—go to the store and ask if they can burn a sample of the scent you're interested in purchasing before you buy it. If you're adventurous, just take a chance, knowing that you may not like the aroma when you get the incense home and burn it. I know in the past I've purchased incense only to discover that it sent me into sneezing fits when I actually used it.

The way to maximize the use of incense is to light it and then sit quietly; really enjoy the smell, breathe it in, and let it flow through you. Ask yourself what the scent reminds you of and think of the different ways that this scent affects you. It may affect you in a positive light, it may remind you of negative situations in your life; but however it affects you, you will use those feeling to raise your vibration. For example, say the incense you've purchased smells like fresh dew in the morning. Or it smells like fresh-cut grass or the smell in the air after a summer's rain. Now use that imagery and think about how you feel when you connect this scent to your thoughts and inner nature. Do you feel calm? Do you feel happy? Are you giddy inside? However it makes you feel, connect to that feeling as you breathe in the scent of the incense and then allow your energy to elevate as you think of these things. If the scent reminds you of a negative experience, closely examine that situation and find just one positive thing that resulted from it. Use that thought to allow your energy to rise to higher levels.

When using incense, you can also connect to your guides and feel yourself in a plane of existence with them. Allow your mind to wander and allow the scent to flow through you and envelop you as you sense the connection to your own spirituality.

> * *The wonderful, flavorful*
> *aromas of incense can*
> *awaken you to feelings you*
> *may be ignoring.*

61. Numerology:
Finding Your High-
Frequency Number

Numerology is a system where you use numbers to determine your strengths, talents, and emotional reactions to things—including the way you react to people—based on the meanings of the numbers. There are several different number systems used today in numerology.

You can tell a lot about yourself by the numbers associated with your name. Pick the method that feels right to you, write your full name, and write the corresponding number underneath each letter. Next, add these numbers up and reduce them down. If I look at my name—Melissa Alvarez—using Chaldean numerology, the corresponding numbers to each letter are 4531331 1361257. Added together they total 45, which further reduces down to 9. That means 9 is my name number. I could learn about characteristics associated with the number 9 by reading the meanings of the number according to the method I'm using, which in my case it means that I am original, take initiative, am determined, and I get to the heart of the matter.

To determine your high frequency number, you're going to make a chart. Make three rows of numbers across the page. Leave space around them because you're going to add circles around the numbers. The top row, moving left to right, will list the numbers 7, 8 and 9. The next row will contain 4, 5, and 6, and the bottom row will contain 1, 2, and 3. Now you're going to look at each individual number in your name and for each number you will place a circle around the number on your chart. For example, in my name I have the number 1 four times, the number 2 one time, the number 3 four times, etc. When I look at my chart circles, the numbers 1 and 3 are the highest with four circles each. The number

1 is the basis for all other numbers and means that I'm creative and tend to be protective. The number 3 means that I look on the bright side of things, I look for the truth of the matter, and I'm never neutral—either I like something and agree with it, or I really don't. When I consider these meanings with my personality, it truly does fit. You can do this with your birth name or your married name, if you're female, and it's interesting to notice the differences between the two. Usually they always mesh with your core self. You can find your high-frequency number by making a chart like this for yourself.

Learning about the numerology surrounding your name will increase your vibration because you're gaining knowledge about yourself through this ancient system.

> *Consider the numbers
> that surround you, and
> look deeper to unveil the
> mysteries of your inner
> self that lie within.

62. Astral Travel,
Astral Journey

The astral plane is another dimension of life that is accessible every time you go to sleep or whenever you purposefully astral travel. You will feel as if you're leaving your body and are able to move around freely on the astral plane. You will be able to see things on both the astral plane and the earthly plane simultaneously. By visiting the astral plane and leaving your body—even just temporarily—you're raising your vibration by connecting to your true spirituality and your soul energy. There is a silver cord that connects your astral body to your physical body at all times. Through this silver cord, you are able to return to your body at any given moment during astral travel if you feel uncomfortable.

Try this exercise. Lie down, find your center, then imagine that you're leaving your body and traveling on the astral plane. You may have to do this several times before you feel that you're moving from your body and into the astral plane. As you journey, if you ever feel frightened, you may feel yourself jerk back into your body very quickly; it's nothing to be alarmed about and is quite normal. Any time you want to increase your personal vibration, astral travel will elevate you to greater heights.

> * Take flight to dimensions
> outside the physical realm
> of existence to embrace
> your inner light.

63. Ascension

Typically, ascension is the conversion of matter into spirit; it is the actual transformation of the highest order, moving from the physical realm into the spiritual realm without experiencing death. Ascended beings have the ability to manipulate matter and can take any physical form whenever they so desire, but their true state of being is pure energy.

I have a somewhat different view of ascension. I don't believe it's only for a select few or that you can only ascend by bypassing death and turning to spirit. I believe that when you're raising your soul's spiritual frequency by changing the way you think about the Universe, the world, religions, or any other type of belief that makes you look at life in a new manner, you are taking steps toward ascension. For example, when you're learning about your psychic abilities—how to tap into your spiritual self and enable yourself to grow on a spiritual level—then you are ascending, since your beliefs grow stronger within these realms. You're constantly opening new doors and windows and climbing higher along your spiritual path. You're accepting new ideas that you may not have considered before; you're making them your own and developing or expanding upon your own core spiritual beliefs. To me, ascension is about spirituality and connecting to your soul energy as you move forward on your chosen path. When I talk about dimensions, I mean our state of consciousness at any given time in addition to the physical dimensions. Believe in your unique ideas or a collective consciousness of ideas shared by many people, then ascend into higher dimensions.

How do you move through the levels of ascension? All the ways we've discussed so far about increasing frequency can be used to help you ascend to higher levels, because in doing the exercises you're changing the way you feel about things while increasing your personal vibration.

When you clear blockages from your path, when you're releasing negativity, you're ascending. You're growing closer and closer to God. Your conscious levels will shift as you ascend, but you have to be willing to move those blockages out of your path. One of the key things to do during this process is to face any fears you may have, try to understand where they originate, and then eliminate them. Fear will only hold you back from reaching your goals. It is also important to search for deeper meanings in all of the aspects of your life. Living a shallow existence will not get you to where you want to go, but looking deeper and experiencing thought-provoking ideals will. My view is not traditional, but then again, it fits my life path.

> *Change your beliefs,
> expand your horizons, and
> believe in order to ascend to
> higher dimensions.

64. What Does Enlightenment Mean To You?

One of the most important ways you can meet your goals is to identify what enlightenment means to you. Do you consider yourself a beginner starting out on the path of enlightenment? Do you consider yourself to already be enlightened and furthering your spiritual growth by increasing your personal vibration? Either way is fine because it is right for you; every person is on their own unique spiritual pathway.

We each have our own definition of enlightenment, but the general sense of the term means that we are awakened to Universal Truths in order to return to the source of Creation and cease reincarnating in the earthly plane. Being enlightened means that you are profoundly conscious of your true inner nature and you achieved this consciousness through your own personal experiences. It means that you have looked beyond your intellect and have embraced possibilities through your senses—including your sixth sense—that the intellect could not fully explain. It is recognizing that your true essence, your core spiritual self, is made up of energy that transcends both time and space. You recognize that everything and everyone shares this interchanging, living energy and that you are but one small part of the whole. When you actively seek enlightenment, you're taking positive steps toward reaching your spiritual goals.

> * To become enlightened
> is to know yourself deeply,
> spiritually, and completely.

65. Going with the Flow

When you're making your way through life, it's easier to go with the flow around you instead of fighting it. What I mean by "going with the flow" is that you don't get upset over things you cannot change, no matter how disruptive they can be in your life. Have you ever noticed that when you're having problems, you no longer feel as if you're moving in the same direction as the energy around you? I know that I can feel blocked at every turn at times, and there is usually a reason or lesson in the situation. The awareness of noticing that I'm blocked enables me to see where I'm no longer moving in the same way as the positive energy around me. I certainly don't want to be moving in sync with a river of negative energy! To keep my life as easy and drama-free as possible, I look for the reasons behind these blocks and remove them to bring myself back into balance and go with the flow. Driving is a good metaphor for how this idea can manifest on the earthly plane. When you're driving, you can't control what others do, but you can maintain an even keel instead of getting angry and frustrated at their actions. If you do get upset, you just need to pull over and release the anger and frustration before driving again.

This doesn't mean you simply do whatever seems easiest in any given situation, but that you try to follow the most harmonious path to your goal. The right choice may be a difficult one on some levels, but you will be able to see how it really fits with the flow of Universal Energy.

> *In times of trouble,
> determine whether you're
> going against the flow
> or with it.

66. Willpower and Flow

Willpower is your ability to follow through on the things you set out to do in life. For example, if you're on a diet, willpower is what keeps you from cheating on the diet because you really want to lose weight. If you're in a relationship, it's your willpower that keeps you from two-timing the person you're with because you love them and you'd never do anything to hurt them, regardless of how much you're tempted. Flow is when you are fully immersed in your energy. Allow your energy to move through you to accomplish goals you've set for yourself. It will be easier to achieve success in your endeavors.

Willpower can be difficult to maintain, while flow never is. Flow is going through life moving with the rhythm of music, in sync with the positivity around you, moving easily through negativity to get back to the positive. You're connecting to energy, which is different from just having willpower and saying, "I'm going to do this," or "I'm not going to do that." Flow is doing something on an emotional, soul level. If you can make it part of your regular flow of energy, then you'll find that it's much easier to achieve high energy levels than if you try to use willpower to force yourself to raise your frequency. Both willpower and flow are necessary, but you must discern the difference between the two.

> *Let Universal Energy*
> *flow through you, move you,*
> *and lift you higher.*

67. Today Is Today, Tomorrow Is Tomorrow: Take One Day at a Time

Are you always planning and organizing until your schedule is bursting at the seams? There's nothing wrong with living a full life, but to raise your personal vibrational rate, try a different approach. Instead of planning every little detail, try living one day at a time without planning for tomorrow. It's okay! Take a deep breath—you can do this. You *can* relinquish control for a short time and just be—just see what happens if you have a day without plans.

In letting go of your need to control every aspect of your life, you'll find that new things will come to you that you weren't even expecting. When your day is chock-full of things to do, you don't have any room for the unexpected to appear—and if it does, you may not notice it. If you only consider what is happening in the moment and let go of control issues, then tomorrow is only tomorrow and you'll face what comes as it appears. If you can keep the mindset that today is today and tomorrow is tomorrow and just take one day at a time, you will give your soul energy a break from the hectic pace it's always in, allowing it to grow. You may even find that you're able to relax a little along the way.

> *Live today as if you'll
> never have another, and
> tomorrow will take care
> of itself.*

Part Three

*

Releasing Negativity

68. Detach Yourself
from Negativity

Negativity can integrate into your life in ways that you might not even imagine. When you're feeling stressed, depressed, or just off-kilter, try this exercise to detach from negative thoughts and feelings.

Imagine that you are in a big field, desert, or valley surrounded by mountains on all sides. Look at your life and gather negative situations, people, and emotions that are affecting you and put them all together in a group, stack them in a big pile or pen them in a corral in front of you. Now mentally push them away from you. Send them to the other side of the field, across the desert, or up into the mountains. Once the negative things are far, far away from you, look at them one at a time, really considering each situation or person and how it relates to you and affects you. Does the situation look less bleak from this distance? Is the person that's bringing you down just full of hot air because they feel small and worthless themselves? When you push negativity away to a place where you can see it for what it truly is, you are destroying its attachment to your life. This exercise can be done at any time in any place, and it will always challenge you to see the people and situations in your life as they truly are.

> *Push negativity into the
> distance to see it clearly.*

69. Release
Defensiveness

When people start knocking you down and acting negatively toward you, when it feels like everyone is out to get you or is constantly berating you, it's really easy to get defensive. That's normal. Putting up a defense is human nature and an important way that we protect ourselves from outside forces. However, acting defensively lowers frequency, so it's better to find a positive way to handle people and situations that make you feel defensive.

One way to do this is to imagine a positive outcome that you'd like to happen. When someone is giving you a hard time, focus on that positive result. Imagine that they suddenly become positive and upbeat and their negativity falls away from them and is absorbed into the ground under their feet. Let your responses to them remain positive and soon, even if they don't change, you will feel differently about the situation because you're looking at it from a positive angle instead of a negative one. Maybe it's their life lesson to learn patience and positivity from you, even if they don't understand it at that moment. Maybe it's your life lesson to see the good in the situation even if it totally sucks while you're going through it. Your belief in creating a positive result is what ultimately creates that result.

> *Let go of a defensive
> attitude by believing in a
> positive outcome.

70. Take Action Only
When You Are in Balance

Negativity can be an overwhelming force around you. If you're surrounded by negativity—whether it's coming from within you or from outside of you—do not make any decisions or take action until you've brought yourself back into balance.

If you make decisions when your energy is low and negative, you may regret them later. Take the time to use creative visualization to clear yourself of all negativity prior to taking action. Imagine your energy vibrating faster and faster until it's moving quickly within you. As your energy increases, feel yourself becoming lighter and clearer of mind. Once you feel that you're back at center, that you are in balance, and that your energy is at a higher rate than it was when you were overwhelmed with negativity, *then* you are in a better place to make decisions and take action. You will see the situation clearly and feel comfortable with what you decide to do.

Acting on impulse in the heat of the moment or in anger can stifle positive energy flow if your actions aren't reflective of your spiritual self. This happens because in the middle of the situation, emotions are soaring and you lose control of yourself, saying things that you may not really mean and that you'll later regret. In the middle of chaos, take a deep breath and be true to yourself.

> *Avoid impulsive, negative*
> *actions; wait until you're*
> *surrounded by positivity.*

71. Learn To Let Go

Holding on too tightly to anything is a negative, controlling action. Maintaining control over your life is a good thing so you're not scattered and unfocused; however, when you become obsessed with being in control and hold on too tightly as a result, you suffocate any positive influences that may be coming to you, simply because you can't relinquish control.

To learn to let go of things you don't need to control, first you have to recognize what those things are. Do you always need for people to do what *you* want them to do instead of allowing them to do what *they* want to do? Do you insist on taking particular actions time and time again, even if it's making someone in your life miserable? Think about your actions; if you are forcing your will on everyone else, it's time to change this behavior and let go. Not only will this raise your frequency, it will also make your life much more joyful and stress-free. We are each our own person, and when you try to hold on too tightly in an effort to gain control, it has an opposite effect: you actually lose control. While you may get what you want in the short-term, in the long-term you'll find that holding on too tightly never turns out in a positive way.

> * Release that which
> binds you in order to
> find the freedom and
> balance you need to be
> spiritually fulfilled.

72. Turn off the
Electronics for a Week

In today's world of technology, cell phones, GPS systems, televisions, Xboxes, Nintendos, Playstations, iPods, iPads, Nooks, and Kindles are part of everyday life for a lot of people.

You may think that you can't live without your cell phone, your television, your gaming devices, or your music, but you can. If you unplug for only a week, you'll find that you will have increased your vibration and will look at life with less stress or anxiety. In today's world, we're too accessible to everyone else; we want instant gratification and get upset when we don't receive it. However, what we truly need is to learn calmness and patience.

Television programming is full of negative energy because tragedy sells advertising. While there's nothing wrong with staying informed with what's going on in the world, try not to become so caught up in the negativity that you begin to look at the world through a negative lens. This brings your energy down. Sometimes, you need to take a break from all electronics just so you can find your balance and come back to center within your own energy flow. Let everyone who is important to you know that you'll be unavailable for a week. Then turn off all the gadgets, pack them away so you won't be tempted to use them, and then find your true self. Take time to just be you.

*In the quiet you will
learn great secrets.*

73. Self-Pity and Frequency

Poor, poor, pitiful me! Is that something you think about yourself? Do you believe that everything is always going wrong for you no matter what you do? Do you think that everyone is personally against you or that you can never do anything right? Are you often comparing what you have or don't have to what your friends, family, neighbors, and acquaintances have? Do you pity yourself because you don't have what others have?

That's a lot to consider, but give those questions some thought. Pity will drag your energy vibration down so fast it'll make your head spin. Stop feeling sorry for yourself, pull yourself up by your bootstraps, and consider all the positive things you have accomplished and achieved. Quit thinking that others are out to get you and that life is inherently unfair. You're right, life isn't fair sometimes and that's just the way it is. Stop comparing yourself to other people and embrace the wonderful person that you are. Sure, it's fine to feel sorry for yourself now and again, but don't get absorbed in it and carry on for days on end or make it a regular part of your life. Let it last for a few minutes and then release the feelings. Not only will self-pity bring down your energy, but it will negatively affect those around you.

> *If you feel self-pity at
> times, have a short pity
> party and let it go.*

74. STOP COMPLAINING

Can you go one day without complaining about something? How about an hour? Thirty minutes? Some days it just seems that you need to complain about everything, doesn't it? It's a normal part of being human, but when you're actively trying to raise your energy, you have to put the complaining aside. Words have power whether you're saying them out loud or chattering away inside your head. Your thoughts flow into the Universal Energy just as your words do. Everything you say is put out into the Universe and can come back to you at some point in your life. This is why it's so important to only say what you mean and mean what you say, to not participate in gossip or keep secrets. You do not need to speak out loud everything that you know, nor do you need to complain constantly in your mind. Even if you're not saying the words out loud, it's still a destructive action that gives your thoughts and words negative energy. Instead of complaining, try to look at what you want to grumble about in a different light. Can you find the silver lining? Look closer. It's there, just waiting for you to find it. Once you see it, you'll have something positive to say, which will bring positivity to your path.

> *If you can't say something
> positive, don't say
> anything at all.*

75. Poor Concentration

If you are having problems focusing and often find that you're daydreaming or staring at the page in front of you without comprehending what you're reading, it's probable that your concentration has gone on the fritz. Bring your focus back to center and increase your energy with snow quartz or amazonite. Snow quartz boosts clarity of thought and helps clear extraneous thoughts from your mind. It helps to remove negativity and brings wisdom and purity. Amazonite is usually an opaque green stone but ranges from yellow-green to blue-green. It's soothing, calming, relieves stress, eases your mind, and boosts the nervous system. Start with snow quartz and then try amazonite to see which works best for you. You should carry the crystal with you at all times in your pocket or wear it close to your body as a necklace, bracelet, or earrings.

A loss of concentration is often caused by avoidance (because you really don't want to do the project) or boredom, which leads to being easily distracted. When you find that you're bored or avoiding what you're supposed to be concentrating on, stand up, stretch to wake up your muscles, then sit back down and do at least three more things that will get you closer to completion. Then take a break. You'll make yourself work further and give yourself a reward, which is always a positive thing!

*Push yourself harder when
your focus is distracted.*

76. Bury Your Problems

Problems, problems, problems. Sometimes it seems that everything you touch turns to crud, not gold. Nothing goes right, you're frustrated, and your energy is in the gutter. What to do? I like to bury my problems in the ground. The energy of the earth will absorb the negative energy of the problems, bring me back into balance, and increase my energy.

I live near the beach, so I like to bury problems on the surf so the energy is absorbed in the sand and the tide can wash away any negativity that remains. I take my kid's shovel and pail and pick a spot where the water will wash over my buried not-treasure. In the sand I make a circle, square, or other shape—whatever feels right in that moment. I dig down a little, place my palms in the center of the area and imagine all negativity flowing out of me and into the sand, taking all my problems with it. Then I imagine the positive energy of the earth flowing back into me through my palms, bringing balance and an increase in my frequency. When I am finished, I cover the hole with the sand I removed and watch until the waves move over the area. I imagine the waves are gathering any residues of negative energy, cleansing them as they're washed out to sea.

If you don't live near the ocean, you can do this exercise by finding a spot of earth that feels right to you, using the above steps, and then pouring a bucket of salt water—salt is an important cleansing tool here—over the area to wash away negativity. You may even choose a spot in your yard that you use repeatedly. Give it a name like the Cleansing Corner, to connect with what you're doing.

> *Release problems and
> negativity into the earth,
> then absorb its positive
> energy to restore balance.*

77. Ego

When your ego is elevated, it can create obstructions along your spiritual path, block the flow of your energy, and cause you to be judgmental. An elevated ego is when someone has too much pride, sees themselves as more than they actually are, or thinks they are better than everyone else. We've all met people who think very highly of themselves. You're going to run into people like this throughout life, maybe even on a daily basis. While they probably just need to put a pin in it and deflate themselves a little bit, it's not in their nature to do so. It's easier to understand these types of people if you acknowledge that it's part of their life path to be this way. There is a lesson to be learned either by them or by the people with whom they're interacting.

If you allow your ego to get in the way, you aren't going to attain the best results in energy work because you'll think you're already at high frequencies when, in fact, you may be at the lower realms. Move your ego out of the way and then forget about it.

If your ego is too low, you'll run into an opposite set of problems. You may think that you don't deserve success, that you're not good enough, or that it's too difficult to attain your goals. In this case, you need to look at yourself honestly, find the cause of your low self-esteem, and realize that you do deserve to live at higher frequencies. Having a faulty ego is just as detrimental to your spiritual growth as having an overinflated one. Finding balance, being humble, and looking at your situation honestly is the best way to forge ahead.

> *Check an inflated ego at
> the door, or open that door
> of self-worth to allow a
> small ego to grow.

78. Dispel Interference from the Physical and Spiritual World

Our everyday lives can cause a great deal of interference in our energy work. What this means is that you allow people on the physical plane to stop you from connecting to your true spiritual nature. What do you do when everyone needs you and you can't get any spiritual work done? You have to deal with situations as they arise and try to block interference. For example, go to a room that no one else in your family is occupying. Yes, you're temporarily isolating yourself from your family, but you need some alone time to focus on increasing your frequency without interruption.

Physical interference is pretty straightforward, but what about interference from the spiritual plane? If you're psychic, you can ask your guides and those with messages for you to come back later, because you're very busy right now. They'll generally accommodate you. Sometimes energy from the other side can connect to you and keep you from meeting your goals. Just as you'd isolate yourself from people on the earthly plane, do the same thing with the spiritual plane: isolate yourself spiritually from any kind of spirit contact that may be detrimental to you accomplishing your goals. Use creative visualization to create a wall or boundary around yourself, sealing out all intrusive influences. By temporarily isolating yourself, you're increasing your energy and keeping away interruptions while doing work that will enhance your personal and spiritual growth.

> *Isolation can open you to possibilities that you cannot see when you're amid chaos.

79. Illness

When you're ill, it's difficult to do work on a spiritual plane because you simply don't feel well. Illness can lower your energy; if you aren't physically at the top of your game, it's hard to be spiritually at the top of your game. But you can also use times of illness as a way to move forward on your spiritual path.

Let's pretend (because I don't want you to *really* be sick) that you have the flu. You feel horrible and just want to lie in the bed and sleep. If that's what you feel you need, then by all means, sleep. Follow your body's instructions—that's the only way you'll get well faster. During the times you are awake, stay in bed but let your mind work. Think about the positive flow of energy moving through you and helping your body to heal. Imagine white light flowing to every cell in your body, invigorating those cells and energizing you at the molecular level. Imagine your energy levels soaring, filling you with positivity. As you do this, imagine the illness going away or being shorter in duration so that you're helping yourself along the road to recovery. Use God's white light, light energy, light consciousness, and an increase of your own personal vibration to heal yourself from within. Thinking about the positive effects of energy on your physical body can bring tangible results.

> *Miracles can happen*
> *when you use God's white*
> *light to heal what ails you.*

80. Cry

When you cry, you release a sudden, overwhelming amount of energy that is in direct relationship to your emotions and feelings. You may be crying out of happiness, loss, joy, or despair. Whatever the cause, an occasional cry is good for the soul. It is cleansing. It releases energy that, if held inside, could cause a buildup of emotion that will eventually come out in the form of a meltdown or explosion. If you tend to hold back and not allow yourself to experience a good cry, try this: the next time you feel that burning sensation at the back of your eyes, the tightness in your throat, and that overwhelming emotion rising up inside you—let it go. Find a private space or a bathroom if you are out in public and feel uncomfortable. Let the tears flow forth like rain, let your body be wracked with sobs, and feel every ounce of the emotion that's causing you to cry. Afterwards you'll be surprised at how much better you feel and how much clearer the world looks.

Holding strong emotions inside can do one of two things to your energy level: it will either sink lower and lower until you find yourself in a state of depression, or it'll get wound up so tight with no way to be expressed that you'll eventually blow. To keep yourself in a constantly upward state of movement, release emotions by experiencing them fully.

> ＊ *It's okay to cry. Even if*
> *you sob hysterically, it will*
> *help you heal.*

81. Release
Negativity Balloons

The simpler you can make the process of releasing negative energy from your life, the greater results you'll achieve. The next time you are having a problem that is bogging you down, buy a helium balloon that reflects your problem. If it's a big problem, buy a big balloon; if it's a small problem, get a small one. Remove any ribbons or other ties, then use a marker to write your problem on the surface. Don't include any personal information (your name, address, etc.) that may be found by someone later if the balloon pops. Get your problem out of your system and onto the balloon. You could write a paragraph or just one word—it's up to you. Now, release that balloon. Watch it drift away, taking the problem's negativity away from you. Feel your own soul energy rise as high as the balloon rises into the sky.

A greener alternative is blow up your own balloon (without helium), write your problem on it, and then drop it from a high place. As the balloon drifts on the breezes, imagine it pulling all of your negative energy away from you. When it hits the ground, the negativity is absorbed into the ground. If you can see your balloon hit the ground, be sure to retrieve it and throw it away.

> *Allow negativity to float
> away from you, freeing you
> from its clutches.*

82. DRAMA

Are you a dramatic person who turns everything that happens to you into a life-or-death situation? We all have times of high drama in our lives, but being addicted to drama—needing it in your daily existence—is something you should eliminate. Don't add drama just to raise more awareness of difficult times you may be going through or to give yourself some grand mystique by making the people around you miserable with your exploits. Turning your spiritual lesson into a dramatic episode just to become the center of attention will lower your personal vibration. That doesn't mean you should dismiss your feelings or any pain you're experiencing; you should embrace these things because they are part of your soul's path and growth. Just don't blow them out of proportion in order to bring attention to yourself, and don't discuss your problems without considering the feelings of the person you're talking to. Otherwise, you're only using them as a sounding board. You can also turn to friends and family for support. If you deal with the situation on your own or with a close friend or family member, in a quiet, calm manner where you connect to yourself on a soul level, then you are solving the problem, getting your feelings out, and increasing your energy.

> *Participating in high
> drama or avoiding it is
> your choice to make.*

83. Put Pride in Your Back Pocket

Being proud of yourself and your accomplishments is a good thing. Being proud of the people in your family, your coworkers, or others that you know is also great. But to be so proud of yourself that you come across as arrogant and snobbish is a problem. When you are so prideful that you put yourself above others or talk constantly about your accomplishments instead of being balanced in your approach to life, then you're emitting negativity and lowering your energy levels. Being too prideful means that you think you're beyond following the rules or that you deserve to have everything you want given to you. Signs of too much pride include being smug, refusing to see your own weaknesses, and acting sarcastically to those you think are beneath you. You believe that you know it all and do it all perfectly and that you have nothing left to learn or no growth left to experience.

If you discover that you're letting pride keep you from being your true spiritual self, then shove it in your back pocket. Put it behind you, out of the way. You'll still know it's there, you'll still be proud of yourself, but now pride is not ruling your life as it would be if you were wearing it on your shirtsleeve.

> *Take the opportunity to*
> *see pride as it really is, then*
> *be humble and release it to*
> *find a new truth.*

84. Don't Engage in Gossip

When I was growing up, I was always told that if you couldn't say something nice about someone, you shouldn't say anything at all. In some situations, it's difficult to keep your mouth shut, but shut it you must. When it comes to raising your spiritual vibration, this is a rule to live by. Gossip in any form is negative. If you engage in gossip, people will be wary of trusting you because they'll never know if you'll spread around what they tell you in confidence.

When you're talking about someone else and what they're doing, who they're seeing, and passing along information that someone may have wanted to keep quiet, you are lowering your vibration. I found out in high school that gossip is usually going to come back around to you in one of two ways: you find that you're the subject of gossip and the things said may be totally untrue, or you get called out about the things you passed on. When you find yourself in the hot seat, will you tell the truth or lie? Lying will only make it worse—it's better to just admit responsibility for what you said and refrain from gossiping in the future. If you're able to do this, you'll find that you've permanently raised your energy a few degrees.

> *Lies spread quickly, like
> a flame; unless truth is its
> name, refrain.

85. Forgive Someone and Forgive Yourself

Forgiving someone else is hard; forgiving yourself is even harder. Even when you've been able to find it in your heart to forgive someone, you may never forget the events that happened. That's human nature. Sometimes, it can take a long time to forgive someone. It has to come when the time is right for you. This timing also depends on the actions of the other person or people involved and whether or not they're trying to seek your forgiveness. If they have tried to make things right with you but you're still holding onto your negative feelings, then give the situation some extra thought. Can you get past the hurt? If you can, even if you no longer want that person in your life, then offering your forgiveness will help you move past the negative emotions that you're harboring, bringing you feelings of peace and resolution. Offering forgiveness allows you to heal. It is a show of inner strength, a sign that you have moved past the pain of the situation and released it. This same thing applies to the way you feel about yourself and the things you've done in life. We all have to take responsibility for our own behavior. If you can forgive yourself for past actions, then you can move into a higher, more positive energy.

> * Let go of pain and
> emotional agony by forgiving
> those who hurt you.

86. Raise the Roof

There's nothing more enjoyable than getting your body moving to increase your overall energy. While there are a variety of exercises you can do, here is one that I think is fun, exhilarating, and a fantastic way to get your energy soaring higher.

First you're going to kneel on the floor on one knee or both (I kneel on one knee), then you'll start making your unique tonal pitch. Repeat it several times as you connect to your core self. Once you're solidly into your tonal pitch, keep repeating it and slowly stand up, raising your hands over your head until they're as high as you can get them. Now stretch and reach as far as you can toward the heavens. When you think you can stretch no farther, push yourself just a little more. You can stand on your tiptoes if that helps you. When you're as stretched out as possible, quickly pull yourself back down to the kneeling position. Repeat this motion again, only this time, move a little faster as you stand and when you fall back down to a kneeling position. With the next repetition, go even faster. Keep this up until you are moving without any pause. Continue this until your energy is soaring.

*Energy is pace, sound,
and a body in motion.
Energize yourself by
combining all three.

87. Fear and Frequency

What are you afraid of? Maybe it's the dark, loss of loved ones, failure, inadequacies, snakes, storms, or another person. It doesn't matter what it is you're afraid of, fear can negatively affect your life. I used to be deathly afraid of two things: ants and false teeth. You may be thinking that these are irrational fears, and I tend to agree now, but until I got over this fear, I'd get hysterical if an ant got on me or if I saw false teeth. You must face your fears if you're going to reach your goals. Look for reasons why you're afraid, whether in this world or from a past life. My fear of false teeth was from an incident in my present life. The fear of ants ran much deeper. While I had an episode as a baby with ants, it wasn't enough to cause the extreme fear I felt about them. Then, when looking into past lives, I discovered a reason for the fear, one that rang true on a soul level. I won't go into details, but I released the situation and now ants no longer terrify me. Consider your fears and how you can release them. See if you can discover the root cause, because if you can, releasing them will be much easier.

> *Fear is a negative force
> that can adversely affect all
> aspects of your life. Let it go.*

88. Discard Negative
Second-Nature Feelings

Do you ever feel like you can't do a particular job, act in a specific way, or succeed in something you want to accomplish? Think about why you feel this way. Is it because someone told you these things? Maybe someone didn't come right out and say so, but they hinted with snide little remarks that made you feel about an inch tall. It happens a lot. People don't always realize how the little remarks they make in passing will affect someone emotionally. The best thing to do is ignore the person and let their words slide off your back. Don't accept others' comments as fact, because someone else's opinion isn't your soul truth. You can do whatever you want to do in life. You can be successful. All you have to do is believe in yourself, your drive, and your ambition. Know in your heart that what other people think is simply their opinion, which shouldn't affect your life dramatically. You don't have to listen to them. When you let other people's words make you feel second-rate, then you're missing an opportunity to feel positive and sure about yourself at your spiritual core. Words have power, but that doesn't mean you have to allow negative words to have power over you.

> *Don't believe those who
> judge you negatively. They
> may need to look in the
> mirror before they speak.

89. MISPERCEPTION
REVERSAL

Misperception is when you don't correctly interpret what you're seeing, hearing, sensing, feeling, or being told. This often happens when people are learning about the paranormal or spirituality. As you progress along your spiritual path, you want to be honest with yourself both mentally and emotionally. If you don't understand something, talk to someone who does understand it—someone in your circle of friends or a person who specializes in the field. Do research and make sure you're interpreting the concepts correctly to reverse misperception. You have to turn it around and look at it in a different light. There's nothing worse than thinking you're doing something right only to find out much later that you've been doing it all wrong for a long time. Do your research in the beginning so you start out on the right foot and without misperceptions of the work you want to learn about. If you're able to turn around any misperceptions, you'll make great gains. Don't get upset and say you know you're right when you may not be; listen to others and pursue information with an open mind. Know that sometimes you may misunderstand, and that's okay. By taking positive steps to be clear in your studies, you're opening yourself to a deeper understanding of information that you may have previously misinterpreted.

> *Ask questions in order
> to stay clear in purpose
> as you move along your
> spiritual path.

90. Put the Bite on Emotional Vampires

We've all met emotional vampires—people who can literally suck your energy dry. An emotional vampire is someone who leaves you feeling drained after you've spent some time with them. Some emotional vampires don't even realize what they're doing, while others intentionally use episodes of emotional upset to make you feel guilty. They often come across as needy, helpless, or depressed individuals. They feel your positive light and high energy levels, so they attach themselves to you because you make them feel better about themselves through your caring words and actions. Maybe you've shared an event or crisis with them and they feel bonded to you, as though no one other than you can ever understand them. Even people you tend to ignore can attach themselves to your energy without you even realizing it. To put the bite on these emotional vampires, you have to disconnect their energy from your own.

Here's a creative visualization technique you can use any time your energy feels drained. By cutting loose any negative attachments, you will feel lighter and free your energy of the emotional vampire's ties on you. Start by sitting quietly and closing your eyes. Now look all over your body for any kind of attachments you may find. They may appear as thick pink cords, a tangle of webby-looking connections, or even as strings or ropes. However you see these attachments in your mind's eye, recognize them for what they are: negative connections placed on your energy by others. Now, use the first and middle fingers of your dominant hand as scissors and start cutting away all of the attachments. If some appear to have roots, pull them out. As you cut and pull, imagine holding the ends in your opposite hand. Look for these connections everywhere: on your back, under your toenails, in your armpits, in your hair, even in private places where you wouldn't expect to find them. Once you're sure that you've found all the negative attachments, release them. Imagine them springing back to where they originated. This isn't a negative action. You're simply giving the attachment back to the person to whom it belongs. You can also imagine the connections flying into outer space, where they can never attach to you again.

Once you've gotten rid of all the attachments, put a bubble of white light around you. Place mirrors on the outside of the bubble so that any new attachments will bounce right off of your energy and return to the person who wants to attach to you. Any time you feel that you may have emotional vampires attaching to you, do this exercise to eliminate their bite.

> *Removing negative energy*
> *attachments keeps you clear,*
> *invigorated, and light.*

91. LOCATE LOW-FREQUENCY HOLDING PATTERNS

No one knows the internal workings of your body as well as you do. Have you ever felt that you knew something was medically wrong (or right) and no one would listen to you? Then, after seeing a doctor, it turned out you were correct? It's this ability to know your body that can help you locate low-frequency holding patterns and increase the energy in those areas by releasing negativity around them.

For instance, maybe you often feel like you're carrying the weight of the world on your shoulders. You feel like a heaviness is pushing down on you and you're experiencing pain and tension in your shoulders and neck. This is an indication of an area of low energy and high stress in your body. To fix this problem area, imagine that you're stepping out from underneath the problems and stress, that you're releasing tension from your shoulders, neck, and upper back. Roll your shoulders and stretch your neck until you feel loose and supple. Imagine an increased blood flow to your upper body that stimulates the nerve endings and increases the flow of energy movement within the muscles. As the tension leaves the area and the energy increases, you're releasing the holding pattern in this area. Do this exercise whenever you feel a buildup of pressure in your muscles anywhere in your body.

> *Release tension in your
> body to alleviate low energy,
> soreness, and stress.*

92. Ease Your Grief

We all face times of grief in our lives. It may be the loss of a family member, friend, coworker, or family pet. Grief can be difficult to bear. Your heart aches, and you feel overwhelmed by sadness and despair. It's important to recognize the five stages of grief: denial, anger, bargaining, depression, and acceptance. You may move back and forth between the stages quite a bit before transitioning into acceptance, but you should know that all these emotions are normal.

Regardless of the stage of grief you're in, you can help yourself by carrying certain crystals with you. Keep them in a pocket where you can touch them often, rubbing them with your fingers to absorb their energy, especially when you feel overcome with your grief. Apache tear, smoky quartz, spirit quartz, and angelite can help ease the pain you're feeling as you deal with loss of your loved one or other life-changing news. While the crystals aren't going to completely take away your pain, they can shorten the length of time you grieve. You'll never forget your loss, but the pain will eventually ease and give way to acceptance. When we grieve, our energy drops; using crystals can restore frequency. There are times in your life when you'll need more help than a crystal can provide to move through the grieving process. In these instances, rely on members of the medical field, clergy, family, and friends to help you through your time of need.

> * Find joy in your memories
> as you grieve your loss.

93. Eliminate Worry

Releasing all the worry in your life is no easy task. If fact, you'll probably never be able to eliminate it completely. There's always someone or something that will cause you moments of worry. Maybe you're waiting on test results from your doctor or your child is driving alone for the first time. What you don't want is to be constantly and consistently worrying about every little thing that happens. I can speak from experience here: I used to be a complete worrywart. I didn't realize that it wasn't fun until after I'd changed my perspective. By looking at the bigger picture and my spiritual pathway within the Universe, I no longer worried about every little thing; I could see what was important and what was not.

Perspective is the most important and the easiest way that you can eliminate worry from your life. While the things that cause you worry may seem huge to you at the moment, if you look at the bigger picture and consider those same things on a Universal scale, then they're not such a big issue anymore. This is an especially challenging lesson for the young; since their view of the world is limited by their experiences, small problems seem larger in comparison. Remember to practice compassion with children and teenagers when they profess to worrying about what you know to be a trivial thing. Use this same idea of perspective and compassion to curb your own worrying tendencies.

When you're in a constant state of worry, the feelings of stress that go with it will bring your energy down. You'll get the opposite effect when you eliminate worry from your life.

> *Keep your worries
> in perspective.*

94. Get Out of
Your Own Way

We live in a society where we're always on the go, always have plans and schedules and agendas to uphold. When problems arise in life, we try to fix them by whatever means necessary so we can get back to our schedules and lists. However, this isn't always the best course of action to take. Sometimes we get so wrapped up in what we need to *do* that we forget what we need to *be*.

Instead of constantly doing something to stay busy, try stepping out of your own way. Perhaps you just need to wait a while for the answer to come and the situation to resolve itself. When you get actively involved in "fixing" a situation, especially one that is out of your control, you're just getting in your own way, blocking yourself from obtaining a resolution. It's difficult to sit back and not do anything when you can imagine all sorts of ways to "help." Evaluate each situation and notice when you're just getting in your own way by being overly involved. You don't always have to be moving at the speed of sound to accomplish goals or learn lessons. Sometimes you just need to let the dish simmer for a while instead of rushing around adding spices and stirring and tasting and ruining the flavor with your extra efforts. It could be that facing a situation head on is as simple as looking at it with a clear, relaxed mind and doing nothing.

** First, determine the
action needed, even if
that is inaction.*

95. Defuse Situations with Kindness

If you're confronted with someone who has lost their temper, try your best not to fall into the low patterns of their anger by getting mad as well. Keep your cool; neutralize their anger by expressing words of kindness, caring, and understanding. These emotions come from a higher plane and will help to counterbalance their angry emotions. As their anger subsides, your words will help that person to come to a place where they too increase their energy levels by leaving the negative emotion behind. This strategy may not work in every situation, so you'll have to play it by ear. But more often than not, this practice can keep an angry situation from turning into an uncontrollable rage.

When you do get pulled into an argument and lose your own temper, recognize that you're playing into the other person's emotions and walk away from the situation. This will give you time to regain control, find balance, and come to the situation from a place of high vibrations instead of staying on their level. When you're calm, go back to the person and try to resolve the problem. If it's an encounter with someone you don't know, then just release those feelings; let it go and move on with your life. Dwelling on what you should have done or could have done will not resolve anything.

> *Kind words can often keep
> negative situations from
> getting out of control.*

96. Calming
the Inner Critic

Who's the inner critic? You know who I mean, the little voice in your mind that goes on and on and on, weighing out possibilities, telling you that you can't do something, and listing all the reasons why you will not be successful. If your inner critic is being negative all the time, tell that nagging motor mouth to just tone it down for a while. Just who is that rambling on in your head? It's you, of course! You can be your own worst enemy by talking yourself to death internally, doubting yourself, or over-analyzing everything. Find time to calm down the chatter. It is in this quiet place that you can reconnect with your true self.

While it's a good thing to try to achieve temporary quiet in your mind, you don't want to completely shut up your inner critic forever. You wouldn't be able to do that anyway, because weighing decisions and thinking things out in your mind is a positive action. Your inner critic is a part of you that is connected to you on a soul level and knows you better than you may know yourself, so sometimes listening to these thoughts can be very helpful. It's when it your thoughts turn more negative than positive that you need to bring your inner critic back into balance.

> *Don't sabotage yourself by*
> *listening to negativity from*
> *your inner critic.*

97. Anxiety

Anxiety is when you feel fearful or worried without knowing why. Maybe you focus on one thing that you're afraid of and think negatively about it until you work yourself into a state of constant nervous tension. Anxiety can cause you to feel unsettled, apprehensive, and on edge until you're waiting for the worst to happen in any given situation, fueling yet more anxious feelings. It can cause very real physical symptoms like muscle tension, stomach upset, and sweating or cold chills. When you are under intense stress or fear, your body misinterprets this as a real physical threat and reacts accordingly: increased heart rate, decreased digestion, and heightened senses. That ancient instinct may help you run away from a predator, but it doesn't do much in today's world. Anxiety is a negative emotion that can interfere with you functioning at your best during your daily activities.

If you are feeling anxious, grab a rose quartz and hold it close to your heart. Anxiety is one of those emotions that creates a heavy, slow-moving energy pattern within you. Using a rose quartz to alleviate anxiety will also release the blocks that are keeping your frequency down. You can carry the rose quartz or wear it as a long pendant. When anxiety starts coming on, hold the quartz in your hand over your heart. Imagine your body surrounded by a vibrant yet soothing pink energy. Let the quartz's calming effect flow through you, releasing the anxious feelings and filling you with a lightness of heart. Imagine the tightness in your chest gently flowing away as you breathe deeply. Using rose quartz can help ease your anxious feelings.

> * *Turn negatives into*
> *positives to keep*
> *anxiety at bay.*

98. Mindful Breathing
to Release Negativity

We don't normally pay attention to our breathing. You might notice that it's difficult to catch your breath if you've been sprinting, but most of the time, we don't think about how fast or slow we're breathing at any given time. I once saw a show on television that discussed how some people could slow down their breathing and heart rate. Of course, I had to try it. I practiced until I could lower my heart rate and breathing repetitions on demand. What if we were to apply this principle to our breathing to release negativity from our bodies? Let's do this exercise. Lie down somewhere comfortable and close your eyes, only focusing on the air coming in and going out of your lungs. Notice the speed of your inhalations and exhalations. Breathe slower. Take deeper, longer breaths until you feel your body relaxing. As you physically slow down your breathing, begin using creative visualization to locate any negative energy stored in your body. On the next exhalation, send the negative energy out with the breath; when you inhale, imagine positive white light filling the spot where the negativity once was. Keep doing this until you're taking very few breaths in a minute and until you feel all the negativity has been replaced by positive white light.

> * Mindful breathing is being
> aware of each breath you
> take, giving it purpose.

99. Pressure Points
to Release Negativity

There are hundreds of pressure points throughout the body—bundles of nerves that can cause pleasure or pain. Some people say there are eleven, some say there are a hundred, and others say there are several hundred of them. It all depends on who you're talking to and their philosophy. You can use pressure points to release negativity within the body.

Pain is trapped heat. If you were to cut yourself, the pain is caused by heat rushing to the site of the wound during its creation and while it heals. That's why wounds are often warm. If you were to touch a pressure point close to an area of pain and use creative visualization to draw the heat from the painful area down into the pressure point, you could expel it through the pressure point by pressing down on it. If you have a headache, you can press the dip in the fatty area between your thumb and forefinger to release the pain of the headache. By utilizing pressure points throughout the body, you can let go of pain and bring about relief.

Search the Internet to find individual charts that indicate all of the pressure points in the feet and in the rest of the body. Search under "pressure points in the body" to find a chart that will work specifically for you. Try releasing a pain through a pressure point today and record your results.

Unlock the self-healing
power of your body.

Part Four

*

Self-Transformation

100. Be Fully Engaged and Transparent

If you're not fully engaged in life, then you're not living life to its greatest potential. You're just meandering along and may miss opportunities as they come your way. If you're fully engaged, you're willing to go that extra mile, put forth more effort, and accomplish more than someone who isn't living life openly and transparently. This means you're always doing positive things that are bringing you more joy, you're living in the moment, you love with your whole heart and soul. You're not hiding in the shadows or questioning your actions. Regardless of what you're doing, if you're giving it 110 percent and are living in the moment, you will get more out of it.

The other part of this is to be fully transparent. Don't lie, don't make things up, and don't do things that people may question. When you're fully transparent, engaged, and are living your life full of honesty and truth, you are operating at a high frequency. If you realize that you're not living this way, now is the time to determine how you can do things differently so you can be fully engaged and transparent. Not only does this benefit those who know you and interact with you, but it benefits you on a soul level as you become more aware and involved in your own life.

> *Give your all with honesty
> to be more spiritually aware.

101. Tolerance

If you looked up the definition of *tolerance*, it roughly means the capacity to be sympathetic to the beliefs and practices that others engage in that are different from your own beliefs. It means to not be judgmental, to put up with difficult people, hard situations, and unpleasantness. Just because someone believes or does something differently than you do doesn't mean it's wrong; it just means it's different. This includes the way people dress, act, or live their lives. Everyone is unique and has their own way of doing things. You're not their judge and jury. By being tolerant of people and not judging or forcing your thoughts and feelings on them, you are raising your energy while learning about people and their different approaches to life. We all have our own life lessons to learn, so if you're trying to say that someone else's life lesson is wrong, well that's not your place because it's not your lesson. We're all here to learn from one another; we all mapped out our own lives before birth, so it's not up to individuals to say what's right and what's wrong in someone else's journey. By practicing tolerance and understanding, you'll develop a greater understanding of yourself and those around you.

> *The way is not fixed in stone; only we can walk our personal road with all its stops, starts, and turns.*

102. Appreciate
What You Receive

Have you ever gotten something and couldn't enjoy it because you felt that you didn't deserve it or that you should have spent the money on something else? What if it was a gift and you kept questioning the reason it was given to you, looking for ulterior motives? Assuming you're not a thief, you worked hard to obtain the things you own in this lifetime, so don't feel guilty about them—but don't brag about them either. These things are what they are. You may not understand why you received some of the things you have, especially when it comes to someone else's generosity, when they give or do things for you that you totally don't expect. Just appreciate the fact that a gift or help was given, say "thank you," and mean it. Try not to question why you're receiving things in your life. Maybe you manifested it a while back and it's just now getting to you. It's always better to be appreciative and to acknowledge gifts instead of questioning why you're being gifted. There's a reason for it. Appreciate the gifts and the people in your life more and ask why less.

> *Gifts aren't only material
> possessions; they can also
> be spiritual, psychic, or
> paranormal in nature.
> The people in your life are
> gifts—appreciate them.

103. Snow

Depending upon where you live, winter can be mild with little snow or it can be harsh with below-freezing temperatures and one blizzard after another. If you live in a climate that has snow, you can use it to connect to your soul energy. Go outside and make a snow angel. Lie down in the snow and feel its cold softness all around you. If you've been outside for a while, your toes and fingers may tingle; let this tingling sensation move upward until your entire body is tingling, gathering all the negativity within you. (Just don't stay out too long for safety.) The snow around you may feel less cold now because of your body heat. Imagine that the cold snow is protecting you on a spiritual level, insulating you from any negativity in your life. Now let it cleanse you. Start to move slowly and breathe deeply as you make the snow angel. On each exhale, release all the negativity captured by the tingling sensation until the tingling stops. Now imagine that the snow is creating an invisible shield of protection that will keep negativity at bay. If you live in a tropical climate, you'll need to take a trip to a cold climate or—more likely—turn your air conditioning all the way down to do this exercise using creative visualization.

> *Let the crystallized flakes
> of purity insulate your spirit.

104. Feel the
Heat and Shiver

There is a definite feeling that goes along with increasing your frequency, and that feeling is a sensation of warmth. As you do different exercises that allow you to live a more positive and meaningful life, you'll notice specific signs associated with the higher levels of energy within you. When I am successful in these energy exercises, I feel heat as the molecules within my body move faster and faster. I'll often feel warmth radiating from within me, flowing out from my core to my extremities. It's associated with a feeling of happiness and contentment. This is not a painful heat, as around a wound; this warmth reminds me of sitting in front of a fireplace bundled up in a blanket on a cold winter's day. It's a feeling of coziness, happiness, and warmth. You may feel an increase in your personal energy in a different manner, as tingling sensation or a glowing awareness. Another sign that you've hit on a Universal Truth on a soul level is a cold chill that radiates through your body, causing the hairs on your arm and the back of your neck to rise in goosebumps. In addition to the cold chill, you have a feeling of just "knowing" that whatever just happened or was said to cause the chill is the absolute truth on a soul level. Acknowledging this truth will cause an internal feeling of warmth.

> * Whether warm or cold,
> internal temperature
> changes signal an
> awareness of truth.

105. Calm Yourself

Some days, everything that can go wrong will go wrong. If you're tired, anxious, and easily frustrated, then it just makes the day worse. How in the world can you focus on raising your frequency when you're having a disastrous day? You have to take a moment for yourself, to find balance and come back to center, even if you have to lock yourself in the bathroom away from the kids and family responsibilities to calm yourself down. Count to ten—or to one hundred, if you must—either out loud or in your mind. As you say each number, imagine the stress leaving your body with the word, eliminating your upset feelings and replacing them with positivity.

If you're in the middle of an intense confrontation, you still have to calm yourself before reacting. Next time you're in this situation, try this: Just as actors imagine their audience in their underwear to calm stage fright, when you're in a heated discussion, imagine the other person is wearing a skin-tight pink leotard and tights with a big ruffled tutu, humongous fairy wings and antennae on their head. When you have this silly thought, you'll change your mood from one of anger to one of light-hearted observation and it will be easier to either walk away from the situation or change tactics to come to a satisfactory resolution.

> *Find calmness in
> the middle of a storm
> of emotions.*

106. The Difference
between Being Alone
and being lonely

Being alone means spending time by yourself for a short or long period of time. Some people can be alone for months and never feel lonely, while others feel lonely even when they have a lot of people around them on a daily basis. Being alone is a good thing because you can connect with your spiritual self; you can feel your core spiritual energy and accomplish tasks that others may disrupt you from doing. You can really get to know the many different dimensions of your spiritual self. You can do exercises that promote an increase in energy. Spending time alone gives you the ability to do the things you want to do to progress along your spiritual path without interruption. Taking time to be alone can be a welcome change of pace from the hustle and bustle of the outside world so that when you do return to the regular pace of your life, you'll find more positivity in it. Being alone gives you time to recharge and reenergize yourself on a soul level.

Loneliness, however, means that you're craving interaction with another person and not getting it. You may feel as if you have no one to talk to, that no one cares about you, and you are missing human contact. Loneliness is often one of the first signs of depression, so if you're feeling lonely, now is the time to go out and do something. Go to the gym and talk to people. Go to a retail store and talk to the clerk. Go out and do anything you can do to interact with people. There is a deeper degree of loneliness for single people who aren't in relationships. You may feel that you have no one to come home to. If you're not looking to be in a relationship right now, then take a class so you can interact with others to satisfy the human need for company. There's nothing wrong with having a huge group of friends instead of being in a relationship. Romantic relationships come and go in our lives. Sometimes you just have to accept that now is not the time for a romance and find other ways to meet those natural desires for interaction. Make the best of the situation you are in and try not to feel lonely when you're alone. Being proactive in fighting loneliness will help you keep depression at bay. If you're having a difficult time getting rid of your lonely feelings—if you feel misunderstood or like there's something wrong with you—then you should see a medical professional. Doctors can assist in cases where loneliness is more than you can handle. It's not a sign of weakness to seek help; it is a sign of inner strength. Loneliness never lasts forever.

> ＊ *The path we walk, we*
> *walk alone—find solitude*
> *and comfort along the way.*

107. Talking and Sharing Emotions

When you share your emotions, you're giving a deep part of yourself to another, which raises your soul energy. Sometimes sharing not only increases your personal vibration but can also positively affect the person you're talking to. You may not even realize that you're doing it because it is an internal process. When you're able to talk things out, share events in your life, and discuss belief systems and ideas, you are making positive strides on a soul level.

While we're discussing discussions, I want to point out that sometimes being quiet is the right thing to do. When you can listen and let someone else talk, then you're allowing that person to get things off their chest and bring balance within themselves by releasing things that are bothering them. Sometimes people need an ear and it doesn't matter who you are to them (they may not even know you) because they just need to vent. It's great to have friends that you can vent with because you're able to get feelings out in the open and cleanse yourself of stress. If no one is around, talk to yourself; speak out loud, really feel your emotions, and then release them to get everything out in the open, even if no one is listening but you.

> *We need the interaction
> with others that sharing
> gives in order to cope
> with our lives.*

108. Internal Feng Shui

Just as external Feng Shui changes the pattern of furniture and accessories to free up the flow of energy within your home, office, or any place you spend time in on a regular basis, you can use internal Feng Shui for rearrangement on a spiritual level to increase your internal energy flow.

To do internal Feng Shui, sit quietly and ask yourself questions. Imagine you have rooms or boxes within your mind for different types of questions and issues. You may have one room or box for work, another for relationships, family and home life, spiritual topics, friends, recreation, and so forth. The idea here is to categorize your thoughts, ideas, and priorities. Some you'll put into rooms or boxes to address later, while others need to remain at the forefront so you can work on them now. This prioritization will help to align the energy flow through your body so it's working at a more efficient and smooth pace.

Some spiritual topics to consider are how to increase your frequency, your spiritual path, your purpose in life, and developing your psychic abilities (are you recognizing and accepting them, or questioning if your abilities are real or not?). Consider the paranormal and anything of a metaphysical or spiritual nature. How about your family life? Is there total chaos all the time, or is it settled and happy? What are some things you can do to make sure your family life is stable and progressing in forward motion? How about work? Is it going well without problems, or is there a coworker who makes your life miserable day after day? What can you do to change this? Can you transfer out of that department or do something differently? Considering these situations will help you come to decisions and compartmentalize items in your mind.

You'll also want to think about the good things you're doing in life. Are you helping others? Are you successful in all areas of your life? Are you at peace within yourself? If you're having problems, you need to look at those too. If you're having money problems, is there a way you can increase your finances? Get creative but stay honest. Are there problems with relationships? How can you fix them? By considering the not-so-good aspects of your life, you can think of ways to flip a negative into a positive. When you're doing internal Feng Shui, you're moving things around in your mind, considering them in a different manner, clearing space and freeing up the flow of energy within your body. Go through the different areas of your life to obtain answers and organize that information as you look at your internal situations in a different light.

*Internal reorganization
and an honest look at
yourself at a core level will
bring about peace of mind.*

109. Stretch

When you stretch your muscles, you're lengthening and elongating them. This has many advantages, including keeping your body young and flexible. It also helps you to reduce muscle tension that can accumulate due to stress, which brings down your energy. When you stretch, you release the muscle tension and increase energy at the same time. You will feel more invigorated and in tune with yourself if you keep your body flexible. If you don't stretch, you can get tired more easily and feel heavy and stiff. Stretching helps you to relax on a mental level too. How does stretching help you on a spiritual level? When you stretch you can focus on your soul purpose and your energy. With every movement, consciously send invigorating energy into your muscles. Feel the connection between mind, body, and soul. Know that your movements are taking your mind to greater understanding of your physical being. Stretching increases circulation within the muscles, which raises your energy level overall but it also raises your personal vibration. You're bringing all of these parts of your being together—mind, body and spirit—while relaxing your mind and clearing your thoughts.

Today, establish a morning or evening stretching routine. It need only last a few minutes, but you're likely to want more once you get started. Push yourself to greater limits; let the mundane task of stretching free your mind to explore the concepts of spirituality during your exercise.

* Movement of the body
makes you physically fit
and gives mental focus.

110. I Never
Thought About…

As you move along this path, look at things that you've never considered before. Maybe you have never thought about your purpose in life or why you are here. These are things that should be goals for you to accomplish during this quest. Think of something that you've never had an interest in. Perhaps you've never been interested in chemical engineering. Because you've never been interested in this subject, you've never given much thought to chemicals. Think about how chemicals work. You can apply this to the things in your home, like the chemicals you use to clean the bathroom or kitchen. How do these products work to make the surfaces clean? What are the intricate chemical reactions that take place to make your house sparkle? Are the reactions making the chemicals' molecules move at a faster rate, similar to what happens when you raise your energy?

When you consider something new, you cause your mind to expand and your brainwaves to work in a manner they haven't before, which in turn raises your own internal energy patterns. If you're having trouble thinking of something new, visit the library and go to a section you never visit. Grab a book and start reading. Take a few minutes each day to think about something that you've never even wondered about before, then use that information to create something new in your life.

> *If you don't know it, learn
> it. As you learn, you'll grow.

111. Wind Frequency

Have you ever considered the frequency of wind? Wind can be a violent, devastating storm if it's in the middle of a hurricane or tornado. It can also be a gentle breeze that graces your face with little tendrils of feeling as you stand outside under a tree. The feel of the wind across your face and the way it swirls around your body, moving your hair and clothing, can be a powerful catalyst in increasing your energy.

The next time you're outside, be aware of the wind. Is it a slight breeze, or is it of an intensity that lets you know a storm is approaching? When you're aware of the wind, stop what you're doing and just feel it. Notice how it moves over your skin, how its energy affects your body and your own energy. As the wind picks up, can you feel your energy rising with it? Let yourself go into a trance state and become one with the force of the wind. Let it move against you, flow around you, and notice how you feel about its effect. Even if it's a strong wind, allow yourself to feel calm and assured that its power will have a positive effect on your core spiritual self. Think of the power of the wind. If the wind is stronger, does that mean its energy is higher? Not necessarily. The strength of wind can affect you and cause you to feel the connection with its energy.

Let's imagine that you're standing on a balcony and you feel a gentle breeze across your face. You've had a hectic day at work, and you are weary. Focus on it; allow it to bring you back to center. Now imagine that your frequency is connecting to the frequency of the wind. As it absorbs the energy of the wind, feel your energy increase. Even a stronger wind can accomplish the same goal. You have to feel the connection to the wind in order to allow your own energy to increase.

> * *The power of the wind*
> *can energize your soul.*

112. Crisscross
Applesauce

In elementary school, this is the way kids sit with their legs crossed in front of them, hands on their knees to keep them out of trouble. This way of sitting allows you to sit up straight and fit in your personal space without being distracting to other people. This position is often used in yoga as well. It's a neutral position that you can use to connect with your inner self or to elevate your energy flow. Because it helps you align your body, this position also helps you align your energy at the same time. To use this way of sitting to bring alignment to your core spiritual energy, imagine that you have a steel rod for a spine. You can't slump forward or lean backward but are perfectly aligned. Now, imagine your energy as it vibrates within you. Feel the vibration beginning at your toes. Move through your crisscrossed legs and notice how the vibration increases as you get to the base of your spine. Now move up the steel rod, allowing the energy that is your frequency to move faster as it connects with the steel rod, until it's moving at the fastest rate possible where the rod connects with your skull. Now you can really feel your personal vibration within your mind. Become one with the fast vibration of your unique energy.

> *Perfection is attained
> through the flow of self.*

113. Wear a Fun Hat, Outfit, Socks, or Underwear

When you wear the same types of clothing every day, it can become routine and boring. You may be required to wear a uniform or suit for your job, but every once in a while you can kick-start your energy by adding color and fun items to your wardrobe. Sometimes raising your vibration can be as simple as wearing a vibrant piece of clothing or an accessory that brightens your mood, makes you feel adventurous, or is simply a secret that no one else can see. By adding this element of fun, you're elevating your energy and bringing happiness to yourself. Choose colors that are vivacious and energetic in various shades like yellow, green, red, or purple or multicolored patterns that are engaging and entertaining. You may decide to wear a big floppy hat, a cowboy hat, a baseball cap, or any other headgear that you normally wouldn't wear. Maybe your outfit is a little more flamboyant than your normal attire or your socks light up or glow in the dark. And no one has to know about that sexy underwear unless you want them to know. By purposefully livening up your attire, you're filling your energy with lightness and fun. The bright colors will attract a faster vibration to match the vibration of the colors, which in turn causes your own frequency to increase.

*Jazz up your wardrobe
to add an element of fun
and excitement.*

114. Write down One Positive Thing about Yourself Every Day

Today you may have encountered someone who was mad at the world, a kid driving in an unsafe manner, or a rude clerk at the grocery store, which may have left you exhausted, irritated, and on edge. When life gives you nothing but lemons, make it a habit to remember what's good in your life and in yourself. Every day, write down one positive item that reflects your personality, family life, work ethic, or anything else that makes you who you are. Are you in high demand at work because you're a fantastic organizer? Have you gone years without a traffic incident because you're a safe driver? Did you react to the rude clerk with love and kindness in the face of her bad temper? All of these are excellent positive attributes that should make you proud. If you start your day by writing down a positive point, you can reflect on it all day, using it to raising your energy throughout the day. Alternatively, write it down at the end of the day to balance out any negativity you've encountered before you go to sleep. Or you can do both! The important thing with this exercise is to make a habit of writing down at least one positive aspect of your life or yourself on a daily basis.

*By noting your positive
attributes, you will
appreciate your true nature.*

115. WRITE WITH BOTH HANDS

Can you write fluently with both hands? Have you ever tried? Most of us write a lot better with one hand or the other, but practicing writing with both hands is an excellent exercise. It will be challenging at first because it's a difficult task unless you're already ambidextrous. When you use your nondominant hand to write, you're causing your brain to work in a different way. Start with printing your name. Practice doing it over and over again until it's legible. You'll notice that your handwriting may lean in one direction or the other, or you'll write uphill or downhill on the page. Make a point to try to write in a straight line. This will be easier if you use lined notebook paper, but eventually try to do this exercise on unlined paper. Don't get frustrated. Just remember that as you're focusing on your handwriting, you're making energy move at a faster rate. Once you are able to print your name in a straight line and it's legible, then move on to cursive writing. You may have to position your hand in a different manner than you normally do when writing with your dominant hand. Keep at it until you are able to write clearly and legibly in both print and script. Make a list or journal entry using on your nondominant hand to write. The more you practice, the more legible your writing will become.

*Boost your brainpower
with different and
unusual tasks.*

116. Find Meaning
in the Little Things

When was the last time you looked for the meanings in random events throughout your day? Maybe you struck up a conversation with a total stranger, or maybe you had a butterfly land on your arm. Maybe you drove down the road and someone waved to you that you didn't know. Is there meaning in that? There is always meaning in the little things that happen in our lives if we will only pay attention. Too often we overlook the meanings of the things we experience simply because we're too busy, not paying attention, or don't notice them. There are great lessons to be learned in the fact that every small thing we experience has some meaning to us on some level. As you go through your day and are working on increasing your energy, try thinking about the reasons behind these little things. Perhaps you find a penny that's heads up and your grandmother always said to you "find a penny, pick it up, all day long you'll have good luck" and finding the penny reminds you of your deceased grandmother. This little thing, the penny, is a sign from your grandmother to let you know that she's around, watching over you, even if she can no longer be with you on the physical plane. Imagine how much joy that little penny has brought you when you look for a deeper meaning. Don't ignore the little things in life.

*Consider that which you
normally overlook.*

117. ACT ON A WHIM

Acting on a whim can be called impulsive, reckless, or a number of other negative-sounding things. When you act on a whim, what are you really doing? You're taking a moment in time, embracing that moment, and running with whatever idea you have at that instant. Say you're on a long road trip and you decide to change your route and go somewhere that you hadn't planned on going. That's acting on a whim. Being impulsive and acting on a whim can have positive results. You're sitting home alone and remember that there is an art festival downtown, so you hop in your car and go. When you get there, you run into a close friend that you haven't seen in a while, so the two of you hang out and enjoy each other's company. Today, act on at least one whim and see where it takes you.

By taking action on the spur of the moment, you're embracing your energy on the spot because you're doing something that you really want to do at that moment. In the past, the layers of yourself—the "you" the world sees and that you use for protection—may have blocked your internal soul's spiritual energy. By acting on a whim and reconnecting to this energy at your core essence, you're raising your frequency and are having fun along the way too.

> *Fulfill your desires by
> being true to yourself.

118. GET A FULL
BODY MASSAGE

There are many benefits to getting a massage. It increases the circulation through your body, increases your energy, and allows you to relax. It's often used by hospitals and clinics to reduce stress and relieve anxiety or depression. It is also used in sports injuries, for pain and stiffness, and is now even being used in cancer and blood-pressure treatments. If you're ill, you should always discuss massage with your physician prior to getting one. A massage can leave you feeling sore, especially in the case of deep muscle massage.

As you receive a massage, your blood is moving faster through your body and more oxygen is going to your cells, tissues, and organs. As you experience these things on a cellular level, you can connect to the sensations of the massage and the feelings of relaxation. During a massage is the perfect time to think about the next steps to take in your spiritual growth. You may decide to try something you've never tried before. Massage can help with flexibility and release endorphins, which act like a natural painkiller. The key point in having a massage is to experience relaxation through tissue work, to connect the body with the spirit, and to allow you to focus on your spirituality during the massage. Massage should never be used as a replacement for medical care.

*Experience massage to
connect to your spiritual self
and because it feels good.*

119. STEP OUT OF YOUR COMFORT ZONE

It's easy to stay in your zone where everything is nice and comfy and you don't have to worry about who's doing what or who's saying what. You just do your thing and that's that. Still, sometimes it's good for you to take a little hop out of that comfort zone and move in a different direction by doing something unique that's not a normal part of your day.

Say you normally go to the park to walk or work out. Maybe today you should choose a different park. Why? Well, who knows? Maybe it's because you need the connection to the different energy in the other park. Maybe you'll run into people there that you've never met before. You could make a new best friend simply by visiting a different park. You never know what great things will happen to you until you step outside your comfort zone. If you're staying in your comfort zone and you're not pushing yourself past that same old energy, then you're not going to move forward on your path. By forcing yourself to do something different, you're awakening yourself on a spiritual level and you're forcing yourself to do something that will benefit you in the long run. As they say, variety is the spice of life.

*The decision is yours:
make a change and have
new experiences.*

120. Leading and Following

For some of us, leading is a regular part of life; for others, following comes naturally. You've got to do what is right for you. However, to increase your energy, try to be a leader. Step out in front, take a stand, make a decision, and pave the way for new and innovative ideas and processes. As a leader, you're responsible for sharing your knowledge. Maybe you're the head of an organization. You're doing things that put you out in the front, and that's going to help people understand the message you're trying to get across or the purpose behind the work you're doing. What if you don't always feel like being a leader? It can be a heavy responsibility to always be in charge. Maybe you're normally a leader and you're always working toward something, but you just need to be a follower for a little while. You don't *always* have to be a leader in *every* situation. Choose and pick the times when you have the strength of character to show the way. Remember that sometimes you have to let go and give someone else the reins while you step into the role of follower. And that's totally fine. Whether you're leading or following, you're expanding your knowledge base, interacting with people, and affecting them in some way.

> *Step forward or step back
> to utilize the power of your
> energy for good.*

121. Write down Weaknesses and Work to Strengthen them

When was the last time you thought about your weaknesses? Our own weaknesses aren't something we normally like to dwell on because we consider them to be negative attributes that are easier to just ignore. Yet if you become aware of what your weaknesses are, you can work on them and turn them into strengths. As you do this, you're making a positive change to a personality trait or characteristic within you. Identifying your weaknesses isn't the same as your inner critic's voice telling you what your weaknesses are; I'm talking about when you make a conscious effort to identify areas where you can improve.

Start by making a list of your weaknesses. Are you stubborn, nosey, or always need to be in control? Maybe you think negatively about yourself, never accept compliments, or don't give yourself the credit you deserve. These are all weaknesses. Now in a second column on the page, write down the opposite of the weakness. Actively practice the opposite of one weakness today and see how you feel. Record the results in your journal. If your weakness is that you procrastinate too much, then the strength would be to do things right away instead of putting them off. If you never accept compliments, then make it a point to accept every compliment that comes your way for a day.

By acknowledging your weaknesses, you will be able to increase your frequency and make changes that will last a lifetime, not just for a day or two.

> * *Weakness is strength*
> *in disguise.*

122. Acknowledge and Embrace Your Strengths

Just as you acknowledge your weaknesses, it's also good to acknowledge your strengths. People like to think about their strengths—the qualities that make them unique—because these are positive attributes. As you're considering your strengths, write them down and think about how you can make them even stronger. You can use your strengths to fortify your weaknesses.

As you reflect on the positive things about your being, don't think that you're being conceited or that you're looking at yourself as better than others. Those are negative traits, and unless you're a conceited person, you probably wouldn't think this way at all. Look at your positive traits as a piece of your whole spiritual being. Imagine how you can use these traits to help others, to move further along your spiritual path, or to complete good deeds. If you are a good organizer, you could use this quality to help out in an animal shelter by organizing adoption events. If you have a voice that would make the angels weep in happiness, then take that talent to a nursing home and brighten the day of someone who is near the end of their journey on the physical realm.

Look at yourself and come up with ways that you can improve upon or utilize your current strengths as you do your energy work.

> * *You are stronger than*
> *you may imagine.*

123. Examine Old Assumptions

Assumptions are when we believe something to be true with little or no evidence that it is true. What if I assume that all people who ride bikes will get in the way and make automobile drivers weave to the side to go around them? This would be an assumption that would need to be examined because not everyone who rides a bike causes problems for drivers. There are many people who do stay in the bike lane and follow the rules. By assuming that *all* bikers ride incorrectly, then I am the one who is wrong.

By assuming something, you are determining that you're correct without having proof. Look at the things you always assume. Ketchup on eggs will taste horrible, so you'll never try them. What if you were to try this combination and realize that you absolutely love ketchup on eggs? Then your old assumption was incorrect. Whatever assumptions you have in your life, take a close look at them today and decide if you were wrong about any of them. Are there assumptions you can now discard because they no longer fit into your beliefs? Are there any new assumptions you've made that you could be wrong about? By examining your old assumptions, you can make changes in your beliefs. You'll no longer be stuck with old assumptions that you held in the past.

** Assumptions aren't
always correct. Find the
facts instead.*

124. Dance, Dance, Dance

There's nothing like dance to get your frequency flying. You can go out and dance the night away with a partner in the clubs, or you can stay home and dance by yourself. Put on some music and turn it up! Feel the beat of the drums pounding in your chest. Let the rhythm of the guitar and other instruments invigorate you as the reverberations of the music move through you. Don't worry about what you look like when you're dancing. The point is to raise your vibration by connecting with the melody of the music, not to look great on a surface level. Move those hips, spin on your toes, do some jazz steps, add some ballet moves, or even throw in some chicken dancing. Have fun! Release all of your inhibitions and do whatever comes naturally in time with the music. There's no one watching, you don't have to worry that you'll look odd or stupid or that you're not in the best physical shape. Just dance. Pretend you won an award for creating the most unique and popular dance in the world. Make up a routine that fits the song or act out a scene that fits the words. If there are words, sing along. Belt out those words with strong emotion, even if you can't carry a tune. Feel your energy surge and soar as you become one with the music. If you can't dance due to physical limitations, dance in your mind and heart to receive the same benefits.

*Dance only for yourself
and feel the freedom that
only music can give.*

125. Remember a Happy Time and Relive It

Happy memories are a fantastic way to connect to your true spiritual self. Think of a time when you were really happy. Were you surrounded by loved ones? Were you sitting alone on a park bench communing with nature? Remembering happy times is different then always living in the past; when you can't let go of the past and live your life based on the things you've previously accomplished, without trying to further your growth in the present; that is a negative action. Today, remember your memories instead of getting stuck in them.

There are many times in our lives when we are truly happy: a marriage, the birth of a child, or receiving a career promotion that you worked really hard to obtain. Maybe you threw someone a surprise party and your happiness was a direct result of doing something for someone else. As you think of a happy time in your life, remember the emotions associated with it, the people and things around you at the time, and really allow your senses to relive the event in your mind. As you remember, allow yourself to enjoy the memory, smile as you recall specific details, even laugh out loud, because in doing so, you're allowing the happiness of this past event to positively affect you in the present.

** Do not remain seated in
the past but allow memories
to bring joy to your day.*

126. Move into Your Imagination

You can use your imagination in many different ways. Kids play games and create elaborate worlds with only blocks and toys as their tools. As adults we sometimes lose the ability to just *play*. Think back to when you were a kid. How did you play? How did using your imagination make you feel? Being imaginative gives us feelings of happiness, adds excitement to our lives, and makes us feel more carefree. It's time to get back to those emotions. If you can return to the joyful feelings that you had through play, you'll find that you feel happier about yourself and more at peace as an adult. As a child you may have played with dolls, cars, or building blocks. As an adult you can use your imagination to write books, comics, music, or even invent something the world needs. There is no end to how creative you can be when you move into your imagination. It will also keep you focused on completing the tasks at hand because imagination makes mundane tasks more interesting. The more you use your creativity, the more your energy will grow. You'll become focused on your creative venture because your thinking will be in a different light. If you're imagination feels stuck, take a walk or do something that is a change of pace to activate it again.

> *If you can imagine it,
> you can achieve it.*

127. FIND ENJOYMENT
IN DAILY LIFE

Life can keep you really busy, which means it's easy to forget to look for joy throughout your day. It's important for our emotional well-being to always find ways to be happy. Maybe it's your dog or cat greeting you when you get home from work that brings you a sense of happiness and pleasure. Or maybe it's a starting your day with a cup of quality coffee or freshly steeped tea.

What are some ways you can look to everyday things to feel more joyful? Make a craft, learn a new skill that you've always wanted to know how to do, get in touch with an old friend. Sit in front of the mirror and brush your hair, or buy a new item for your wardrobe. Just pay attention to the things you do today and see which ones give you a special little lift.

When you notice the individual things in your experiences that make you happy, no matter how small, then you can tap into that energy to increase your overall joy. The more enjoyment you have in your daily life, the more your personal energy rises. When you don't find enjoyment in your life, you can end up feeling sad, lonely, or depressed. Look for the good people in your life and the good events that happen and let them bring you joy.

> *If you think there isn't anything enjoyable in your day, look again—you're missing it.*

128. Purify Your Body

To get your energy to the highest rate possible, you should occasionally purify your body—cleanse it and get rid of any impurities. I'm not talking about on a spiritual level but on a physical level. Detoxing is a way to give your internal organs a rest while allowing the liver to eliminate toxins through the body via the skin, kidneys, and intestines. Before you do any type of internal body cleansing, make sure you get an okay from your medical doctor, especially if you have any health conditions that would prevent you from doing this exercise.

Chemicals can build up inside us, causing a decrease in our energy levels, which can lead to more frequent colds or make us more susceptible to any viruses going around. To cleanse yourself of impurities, once in a while you need to do a detoxification of your body. It's simple to achieve this by cleansing your internal organs through a detox plan. Before you do a detox you'll want to stop any intake of chemicals that cause toxic buildup. Caffeine, nicotine, alcohol, sugar, salt, and fat are just a few of the things that can cause chemical overload within your system. Try to stop the intake of chemicals at least a day before you detox. Eat healthy selections or organic groceries instead of processed foods. Be careful of the chemicals that you use to clean your home because they can add to chemical buildup too. Eliminate synthetic chemicals as much as you can.

Remember to consult your doctor about any big changes in diet before starting a detox plan. If you're doing a two-day detox, you can try fasting. You have to have water to live, so you can try a natural water detox where you only drink water for a day or two. If you think that will be too boring, use juice instead of water. Many people also do a seven-day detox, which begins with two days of liquids followed by a specific diet that will continue to give your internal organs time to rest.

Another detox method is to spend time in a sauna, which opens the pores and cleanses the skin. There are many different ways to detox; pick a way that is safe and is something you can stick with for twenty-four or forty-eight hours. If you're not big on fasting, you can also eat certain foods that will naturally detoxify your body: eat a lot of leafy vegetables and add black pepper, garlic, lemon juice, or honey to your diet to cleanse yourself. Once you purify your body either through fasting or by adding new, healthier foods to your diet, you'll experience a sense of renewal.

> *A physical cleansing will
> make you feel lighter in
> mind, body, and spirit.*

129. Quiet Your Mind

How busy is your mind? Sometimes I feel as if my mind is running ninety miles an hour and it's hard to control my thoughts. I find myself thinking about the things I have to do in the day, keeping a running checklist of what still needs to be done, the order I have to do things in, what needs to be done first, what I can put off until later … I'm not talking about my inner critic. I'm talking about me making to-do lists in my head that are pages long and include scores of deadlines. When your mind is constantly going like this, it can feel like you're zipping through the day without enough time. I'm often told to "slow it down," although I don't even realize that I'm moving at top speed. It feels normal for me. This can bog down your energy without even trying.

Each day I make sure to find time to just take a few moments to quiet my mind—to just stop what I'm doing and just be me, without thinking of the zillion things I seem to always have on my plate. I often do this when I'm sitting at my desk, in the middle of writing or designing. I stop what I'm doing, lean back in my chair, close my eyes, and breathe deeply. Then I imagine that I'm moving all of the thoughts out of my mind into a separate room that I've created in my mind's eye. I put all the thoughts in there and shut the door. Then I focus on my breathing and imagine that I'm sitting in a room full of white light. I allow the light to wash over me, energizing me, lifting me into its brilliance. When I feel that my mind is truly quiet, I open the door to my thoughts, and you know what? They don't come running out to overwhelm me again. I can pick and choose what issues I want to address. This slows me down when I'm thinking of everything at once.

*Quiet your mind in order
to move forward.*

130. Floating Down a Stream

Finding unique ways to connect to your soul—your spiritual core self—will raise your energy and engage your creativity. Here's a fun creative visualization exercise you can do to restore any disconnect with your spiritual self.

Lie down and imagine that it's a hot summer day. You have a big rubber raft and are embarking on a lazy journey down a calm stream. Feel the coolness of the water against your legs as you place the raft into the stream and climb on board. Let your fingers dip into the refreshing water as the slow current floats you gently down the stream. Look around at the speckles of sunlight filtering through the leaves on nearby trees. Hear the gurgle of the stream as it flows smoothly beneath you. Feel the rubber of the raft against your skin. Listen to the sounds of nature: the crickets chirping and the birds singing. Smell the earthy scent of the forest as you drift toward some unknown destination. Take this time to feel your soul's energy flowing through you. Once you are reconnected with your spiritual self, roll off the raft and into the water, imagining its silky smoothness invigorating your being. If you are lucky enough to live near a stream that you can float down, try this exercise for real!

*Let the energy of an easy
flowing stream reconnect you
with your spiritual self.*

131. Find Your Power Vortex

Each of us has an internal and external power vortex. Do you know yours? The power vortex is where you feel the most connection to your spiritual self. First search internally. Do you feel the most connected in the soles of your feet because they ground you to Earth? Maybe it's the top of your head or the center of your chest. There's no right or wrong answer. Your internal vortex is the place inside you where you can literally feel energy flowing though you, making your conscious self one with your spiritual self.

Now think of an area outside yourself. Do you feel the most connected with your spiritual self when you're in the mountains? Or when you're sitting under a tree considering your spirituality? Maybe it's a certain path you walk every day that is your power vortex. When I lived in North Carolina, I often walked on a path from our apartment to a huge lake. There was just something about that greenway, as it was called, that enabled me to connect to my inner self on a soul level. Where I currently live, my place is the beach. There's just something about walking along the hardened sand with the water lapping about my feet or staring out into that big expanse of water that energizes, stabilizes, and connects me to my spiritual self.

> * Discover your power
> vortexes to connect to
> your spirituality.

132. ATTUNE TO FREQUENCY

Pay special attention to the changes you feel in your body and in your mind and soul as you work to increase your personal vibration. As I sit here typing this, writing about ways to increase frequency, I feel that my own energy is elevated. I'm searching within myself, looking for ways that I've used in the past. But what exactly does it feel like? How can you attune to frequency if you don't know what you should be feeling?

Let me explain. Right now, I'm tired. We've had rain for days and the turnouts at our barn are completely flooded. Today we cleaned all the stalls, put down shavings, bathed all six horses, and cleaned all twenty-four hooves. Physically, I'm tired. I also had to deal with some upsetting news, which made me feel a bit depressed. My energy was low. But as I've been sitting here working on this book, becoming more aware of my current energy as I write, I've noticed a few things. I feel an internal humming as my frequency increases. Imagine the sound of an air conditioner running—now imagine that sound in your chest and feel its vibration pulsating through you. That's what I'm feeling. With this increase in my internal energy, I no longer feel saddened over the news I received. It'll work out the way it's supposed to. I'm still physically tired but no longer on edge. I feel a quiet comfort. All because I'm attuned to my frequency.

You can do the same thing by simply noticing the intricacies within your body as you do frequency work. It is important that you're aware; when you're aware, you can attune.

> *Pay specific attention to
> the little changes in your
> mind, body, and spirit
> as you attune.*

133. Tap into Your Own Uniqueness

Have you ever really thought about the things that make you different from everyone else? Maybe you have a flair for fashion, or you can give a mean haircut. Are you taller than everyone else? I know many people who look at their uniqueness as a negative attribute. When you do this, you're lowering your energy; if you look at the things that are unique to you in a positive manner, you'll increase your vibration.

I'm a redhead. As a kid I always wished that my hair was a different color. I was the only girl in my class who had auburn hair and I was teased big time because of it, which was not fun. As a young adult, I decided that my hair was one of the things that made me unique. I was still teased but instead of letting it affect me negatively, I decided people did this simply because I was unique, so their actions no longer made me feel bad. I just ignored them. Analyze what makes you unique. Make a list of your qualities, physical attributes, and the things you can do that make you stand out from the crowd. Then appreciate yourself as the wonderful person that you are regardless of others who may want to push you into a mold of their own creation.

> *Embrace your uniqueness.
> There isn't anyone else like
> you on the planet.

134. Examine Your
Physical Strength

Your physical strength is important as you travel your spiritual path. If you're out of shape, then you're physically not functioning at your fullest potential and this can be reflected internally through your reactions and actions toward others. Take note of any issues you have when it comes to your activity levels. If you're physically strong but overweight, maybe now is the time to start a weight-loss program. If you're slim but weak, start a weight-training program. You don't have to join a paid facility to enhance your physical attributes unless that is your preferred method. You can just start eating more healthfully, take a walk, or ride a bike.

Becoming aware of your physical strengths and weaknesses enables you to become more in tune with your core energy and spiritual nature. It makes you become more disciplined and focused. As you become physically stronger, more flexible, and better toned through exercise, you'll also notice that you are emotionally different. Where you once may have been short-tempered and stuck in your ways, you will become more flexible and less rigid. This makes you a stronger person overall. Once you are aware that physical strength and emotional strength go hand-in-hand, you can take positive action to make changes that will spur even more positive growth.

Strength—both inner and outer—will change your perception of yourself and your world.

135. Just Move

Sometimes you just have to move to empower your body, mind, and spirit. Turn off the television, get up out of the chair, and move your body! When you sit around a lot, your energy levels slow down. Have you ever been sitting and your legs just feel like they're full of tension? They may ache, be jittery, or have little muscle spasms. You may stretch your legs out but the feeling just doesn't go away. If you were to get up and move around, you'll notice the tension dissipates and your legs no longer feel so antsy. It's because you gave them what they needed: activity. There are some days that you're just so exhausted that moving is unappealing. But if you make it a habit to take a walk after dinner, you'll find that this time spent just moving clears your mind and invigorates and cleanses your muscles and any tension held in them, which raises your energy levels. Sitting around becoming a couch potato will not only adversely affect your physical fitness, it can negatively affect your spirituality and your emotional balance. When you do nothing but sit around and watch television or play video games, you lose your motivation for anything else. You tire easily and get yourself into a rut that's hard to get out of.

** Make yourself move, even
when you don't feel like it.*

136. Be Extraordinary

Choose to be an extraordinary person to increase your frequency. It's easy to be ordinary—to do what's expected of you, to never strive to go above and beyond the normal day-to-day existence. Each day, try to do something extraordinary. Push yourself past the limits of what you expect out of yourself. Don't do this for anyone else; do it for yourself, because you want to help others and be an example of positive energy in action. Help someone who doesn't expect it. Let someone go ahead of you in line. Buy a firefighter, soldier, policeman, or EMT their lunch because you appreciate what they do for the public. Give the waitress who's obviously having a bad day a bigger tip than you'd normally leave. Instead of thinking that you shouldn't get involved in a situation that you encounter, jump in and help. It may just make a world of difference to someone else and it will raise your energy from that of ordinary to extraordinary.

Leave behind feelings that you are special because you're being such a great, giving person. When you counter your positive actions with ego-based thoughts, you're really not meeting your goal. Leave all thoughts of personal gain for yourself, even inflated egotistical emotions, out of this exercise. Then you will truly be an extraordinary individual.

> *Step up to the plate and be
> the extraordinary spiritual
> person you were born to be.

137. Invest In You

People often demand a lot of your time, asking you to do this or that, expecting more from you than you think you can give. While it's wonderful to invest in others and aid them when they need it, you also have to invest in yourself. When you try to be everything to everyone, your energy can dwindle down into nothingness. If you start to feel this happening to you, it's time to invest in yourself more. Escape into a lingering hot bath and read the new novel you just bought. Take a time-out from your busy schedule to do something that you *want* to do and not something that's expected of you. Raising your frequency is all about feeling an inner increase in your soul's energy as you feel happiness, an increase in self-worth, or just a calm peacefulness. Don't feel guilty about taking time for yourself; you need it and you deserve it. If the local community college is offering a cool cooking class that you'd love to enroll in but feel that you can't take the time away from your other obligations, go ahead and sign up for the class. This is investing in yourself by doing something that you'll enjoy, and enjoyment makes for the greatest increases in your personal vibrational rate.

*⁎ Life is too short not
to invest in yourself.*

138. Change
Your Attitude

Projecting a negative, angry, or know-it-all attitude is not only bad for your energy, it can make you appear to be an unlikable, intolerable person to be around. Are you really this way, or are you letting the negativity around you or your unhappiness make you come across as a big ol' jerk? By making changes within yourself, which inadvertently affects your attitude toward others, you will raise your energy and change the way others see you. It's no fun to be mad—or depressed, upset, anxious, or worried—all the time, is it? It's within your power to rise above these types of feelings, to seek out their cause and then eliminate them from your life. Don't wallow in despair, don't feel sorry for yourself. Realize that you are the only one who can change your life, and then do it. Only you can take the bull by the horns and say, "That's it, I don't have to be this way." Look at your attitude, decide what you need to change, and then just do it. You don't know everything; no one does. You can release anger, deal with sadness, and move forward along your spiritual path just by making a positive decision to do so. Every time you confront attitudes and make changes, you're increasing your frequency.

*Give yourself an
attitude adjustment.*

139. Transform
Your Thoughts

What you put out to the Universe is what inevitably comes back to you, whether you're striving for material things or balance on a soul level. Transform your thoughts from negative to positive, and then apply this new positivity to all aspects of your life. Thoughts can turn to doubt even if you're not trying to let them move toward the negative—that's just human nature. You can push the negativity aside and replace pessimistic thoughts with positive ones as long as you're conscious of those less-than-helpful ruminations. Today, try to recognize a contagious bad mood, then make sure to keep your thoughts positive to counteract that negativity.

Maybe your day at work as been hectic and stressful and your boss yelled at you for something you didn't even do. That's his path, his negativity showing through. It doesn't have to be your path. Instead of allowing his actions to rub off on you, recognize the actions for what they are: his negative choices. Then purposefully choose to keep your own optimistic focus without letting his bad day affect you. If you do allow his negativity to influence you in this manner, you'll just pass that negative energy on to someone else, probably your family or friends. Instead, use creative visualization and imagine that his harsh words are turning to mist and dissipating in the air, unable to affect you in any way whatsoever.

** Think in a positive
manner and you'll find that
you can manifest all sorts of
positivity in your life.*

140. Slow Down

Today's society is a fast-moving jumble of instantaneous gratification. It doesn't matter what you need to do, you can probably do it quickly. You can get your meals at a drive-thru and eat in your car, or call out for delivery and have your meals brought to your home in thirty minutes or less. You can talk to whomever you want at any time on your cell phone, or send a text message or email wherever you are. You can participate in many social networking sites via your phone so you're never out of touch in this electronic network. Instead of taking time to pick out a personal gift for someone, you can buy a gift card. While there's nothing wrong with any of this, your mind is working more and relaxing less.

Our world is more convenient than ever so you'll never miss anything again, right? But wait...did you miss that smile the drive-thru worker gave you? Did you notice the lady you cut off in traffic while you were talking on the phone? Sometimes, you just need to put on the brakes to tap into your own spirituality. When you slow down and focus on feeling every aspect of the wondrous life you've been given instead of speeding through it and missing parts of it, then you are acting on a more spiritual level.

> *Slow down your life to
> enjoy just being in it.*

141. Gain New Knowledge, Grow and Learn

Going to school gave you many opportunities to learn and grow as an individual. Once you graduate from school—be it high school or college—you should continue to study and learn different things about the world you live in, even if you're not doing it in a formal educational setting. Reading is the best way to gain knowledge. The more you know and the more you learn, the more you grow as an intellectual person. Today, pick a topic that you're not familiar with and read as much as you can on the subject. Knowledge is power. It is something that can never be taken away from you. Your internal energy, your core essence, is related to spiritual and personal growth. If you take the time to study and learn about spirituality or any self-improvement subjects and put what you learn into practice, you will surely increase your vibration. For instance, if you've always been interested in real estate, then take a course, even if you don't plan to become a real estate agent. Or perhaps you've always wanted to go skydiving—learn all you can about the sport in case you decide to don that parachute one day. If you have an interest in something, pursue that interest! Don't limit yourself by thinking that you can't do it.

*Challenge yourself to
discover one new fact
every day.*

Part Five

*

Your Higher
Self, Soul
Responsibility

142. Know Yourself, Understand Your Wants and Desires

You must know yourself and understand your wants and desires in order to obtain growth of any kind during this lifetime on the earthly plane. If you don't know yourself, you are walking through life in a daze, unaware of how you relate to people and situations or how you look at life. You may not have set goals, or you may feel lost because you don't understand your life purpose or know what you want to achieve in your career or personal life. If you understand what you want out of life, you can move forward with purpose. You can set goals and strive to achieve them, work to be proud of your accomplishments, and view yourself in a positive light. In turn this will make people look at you with high regard or be proud of you. By building on a strong foundation of goals and achievements, you will continue to succeed.

Knowing yourself is important in your interactions with others. If you know certain people or situations will set you off or make you feel poorly, then you can take steps to avoid them. If you know that you prefer working outside to sitting behind a desk all day, that understanding of yourself will help you in your job search. Knowing yourself enables you to grow as a complete spiritual being. Today, spend a few minutes contemplating what you want out of life.

> *Know what it is you want
> in order to get it.*

143. Discover Who You Are At Your Spiritual Core

Do you know who you are at your core? Or are you trying to be what someone else wants you to be? When you focus on truly knowing yourself at the very basis of your being, you can grow personally, spiritually, and with divine purpose. If you're always living your life trying to be what someone else wants you to be, you're not really embracing the real you. You're ignoring your basic instincts, your true nature, to be something or someone that you're not, just because another person thinks you should be or act in a specific way. By following their instructions and fitting into their mold, you may eventually lose your true self, your essence, and your energy. Controlling people can snuff out your light, but if you're strong at your spiritual core, they'll have a much harder time extinguishing your brilliance. Know yourself.

If people don't accept you for who you are and what you believe, those aren't the kind of people you want in your life. Think about if there is anyone in your life who tries to fit you into a category you don't belong in. Release these people and find others who will appreciate and love you for who you truly are at the deepest levels, faults and all. Doing this means you're realizing the truth of your soul, raising your energy, and moving forward on your spiritual path.

> *Don't let others determine
> who you are or what you
> shall become.*

144. Meditate to Meet Your Higher Self

Your higher self is your soul being, the core part of you in all your completeness. Your physical being on the earthly plane is just a projection of your higher self. Your higher self is in command of the life plan you created before being born, and it is through your higher self that you can make sure you are following that plan.

While you are always subconsciously connected to your higher self, there are several ways to consciously make this connection and communicate. You can use extended meditation, journaling, or a quick method of sitting quietly for only a few minutes to connect with your spiritual essence if you need a fast answer. You may see a vision of yourself as you are now, as you appeared in your youth, as a spiritual being, or as pure energy. Ask your higher self questions. How can you do better in life? How can you be a more spiritual person? What is your soul purpose in this lifetime? The answers you receive will not be based on fear (that's your ego talking) but will instead be wise and knowledgeable. This raises your energy because you're more connected to all of the parts of yourself as a spiritual entity.

*Make a date with your
higher self to get to know
the real you.*

145. Listen to
Your Gut Instinct

How many times have you had a feeling, deep down in your gut, that something was wrong, yet you couldn't say what it was exactly? When you don't listen to your gut instinct, you run into problems or situations that probably could have been avoided. Gut instinct is also a reflection of your psychic abilities, although most people don't call it that. We're all instinctual because we're animals; if you listen to your gut then you're in tune with your primal urges and instinctual nature. The next time you get a feeling that you should or shouldn't do something, follow that urge—yes, even if everyone around you disagrees or doesn't understand. If you get a negative gut feeling about a person who you think may not be what they say they are, listen to it. If you don't, that person could cause you problems down the road. Whether you call it gut instinct or psychic ability, you're listening to your internal self. Trust in yourself. Trust your first impressions. These messages come from a deep core place in your soul. If you ignore your instincts, you're lowering your energy. By paying attention to these urges, you will probably prevent problems for yourself in the long run.

*Instincts are a natural
protection. When you
listen, you connect to your
instinctual nature.*

146. Find Your Soul Energy

In this exercise you'll use a candle's flame as a tool to look into yourself and connect to your soul energy.

Light a candle and focus on the flame. As the flame flickers in front of you, use creative visualization to connect to the energy of the flame, then reflect that energy back into yourself to tune into the essence of your soul energy. Compare your energy to that of the flame. Is yours lower, the same, or higher? The flame is simply a tool to help you focus and turn your attention inward. The way the flame moves gives you different indications on how its energy varies in form. By noticing these fluctuations, you can mirror this to your own internal energy. Is your energy irregular? Is it moving like the flame, or is it solid and steady? If your energy is moving in irregular patterns, you may need to do work to strengthen it.

As you study the flame and consider your own energy's frequency, you'll be able to sense internally the rate at which it is vibrating. When you are aware of your current frequency status, you can take steps to raise it to even higher levels.

*For the flame flickers
in response to its energy,
just as your light brightens
or dims in response to your
internal vibration.*

147. Oppose Yourself

Facing opposition can be a fearful event, especially if what you're opposing is negative in nature, such as an angry person. But opposing yourself isn't a negative action—it is positive because you're using an opposite action to achieve constructive results.

When you give yourself oppositions in life, those are prime times for increasing your core energy. Doing something totally opposite of what you normally do is a chance to feel the differences in your energy and to raise it. If it is low and you normally stay in this type of pattern, do something completely different to give it a jump-start. This acts as a catalyst and can move you from one level to another relatively quickly. For example, if you're in a situation when your normal reaction would be to stay quiet and not say anything, responding and getting involved will change this low-energy pattern to a higher vibration. In any situation in life, if you can do something opposite—something outside of your normal patterns—that's a positive step because you're taking action. Challenge yourself today: pick an opposite activity, strategy, or reaction to change your daily routine and make positive things happen.

*Opposition makes you
stronger, both emotionally
and spiritually.

148. Look into the Window of Your Soul

It's often said that the eyes are the window to the soul, and if you look into your own soul, you can see the true spiritual nature of your being. To do this exercise, stand in front of a mirror or hold a mirror in your hand and look at yourself. Don't consider anything about your looks, just look directly into your eyes. Look deep within yourself to connect with your own spiritual truth and core energy. By doing this, you bring focus to your essence.

What do you do if you don't like what you see? Maybe you see someone who is a touch selfish or who isn't living to their fullest potential. Maybe you see someone who could be more than they are at this point in time if they would only take the time to obtain personal and spiritual growth through an increase in frequency. As you look into your eyes, imagine that you are raising your energy. Envision the molecules within you moving at a faster rate. As you do this with purpose and intention, and as you feel an internal increase in your energy, do you see a change in your eyes? Can you sense a change in the way you feel about yourself?

> *Look into the window*
> *of your soul to discover*
> *spiritual truth.*

149. Sleep

Sleep raises your energy because you need it to function. It gives your body time to rest and restore itself so you can start each day on a positive note. Some people need less sleep than others to have an optimal day. If you're not getting enough rest while you're trying to increase your frequency levels, it's going to be difficult because your body isn't operating at full capacity. Have you ever noticed the appearance of new mothers? They often look zoned out, with a glazed look in their eyes, sort of scatterbrained and frazzled and exhausted. They are sleep-deprived. Taking care of a baby is difficult, and it takes a toll on your body.

If you're not getting enough sleep for whatever reason, try to work in time where you can grab a power nap in the afternoon, or even in the morning. Adjust your schedule so you can go to bed earlier or wake later. Create a setting that is conducive to a good night's sleep. Sometimes creating a nightly routine helps you sleep better. You may need to add white noise to your room so you can get uninterrupted sleep during the night. Waking up a lot during the night can be a sign of spiritual growth, but it can also be a weak bladder; if that could be the culprit, stop drinking liquids earlier in the evening. What you're lying on could be disrupting your sleep; if you normally sleep on a bed, try the couch, the floor, or a recliner. Turn off the phone, the television—everything that could wake you. If you are a new parent, see if your partner or a friend is willing to give you a night of uninterrupted sleep as a gift. Waking up repeatedly during the night disrupts your sleep patterns. You can still do work to raise your frequency if you're tired, but it will be more difficult. The more rested you are, the more success you'll have.

*Soft background music
can be a helpful sleep aid.*

150. A Morning Ritual

Every morning when you wake up, before you get out of bed, take a moment to greet yourself, give yourself a hug, and say "I love you" to yourself. We greet people in our lives with smiles and open arms, so why not do the same thing for yourself? It gives you a moment to appreciate your spiritual being, connect with your soul, and raise your energy before you rise. When you awaken, take a few minutes to stretch. Really feel the stretch through your muscles. Wake them up, energize them. Wrap your arms across your chest, grasping each upper arm and then squeeze, hugging yourself. Now say, "Good morning (insert your name), I love you, and I will have a great day. I will be positive and upbeat, I will not allow negativity to lead me astray, and I will be a beacon of light." Once you're fully awake and prepared to start your day, get out of the bed. Keep this feeling of increased energy and love moving through you as you shower and dress for the day. When you have breakfast, be aware that the food is also aiding your positive beginning.

*Loving yourself is just
as important as loving
other people.*

151. Pray

I'm a big fan of prayer. I think that everyone should pray to whatever entity they believe in, not only during times of need but as a regular part of their spiritual or religious practices. Praying helps you to connect to your spiritual self. It helps you to communicate within another dimension, moving past the mundane day-to-day experiences into the Divine. It allows you to ask for help from a heavenly deity and to offer thanks for the people and things that are in your life. Prayer is often done alone but it can be done in groups, during song, or in verse. There are many prayer circles where people in the circle pray for others during times of need. Prayer has the power to heal you spiritually, emotionally, and (some claim) even physically.

By opening yourself to the spiritual during prayer, you're opening your heart and soul to a power and energy that is much greater than you. In doing so, you're raising your own personal frequency. Prayer doesn't have to be formal; it can be as simple as a few words spoken out loud in a time of need—"Help me, God"—or it can be a long formal prayer said in a house of worship. It is up to you and your beliefs how you proceed with prayer.

> *Pray from the soul to
> touch the heart of God.*

152. Meet Your Angels

Each one of us has angels that watch over us. You may have already met your angels or felt their presence around you. They can appear in many forms: a loud, powerful, disembodied voice; a strong fragrance; or a human offering help or delivering a cryptic message. The first time I met one of my angels, I was driving at five in the morning. I was headed toward a curve in the road where I couldn't see around the bend. I wasn't speeding because it was very dark and deer are a problem in that area. Suddenly, the interior of my car filled with the overpowering scent of various flowers. I smelled roses, honeysuckle, lilacs, wisteria, gardenia, and jasmine all at once. I heard a shouted "STOP!" so I braked and went around the curve very slowly. Then I saw a car backing out into the road. If my angels hadn't warned me through scent and sound, I would have hit that car. By connecting with my angels, I avoided a car accident, and this experience permanently increased my frequency. Whenever I smell that particular scent, I always know my angels are nearby.

You can consciously choose to connect with your angels rather than waiting for them to contact you. Spend a few minutes today relaxing, then ask your angels for a specific sign to let you know they are with you, or ask to meet them during meditation.

> *Angels watch over you,
> offering protection and love.

153. Look Past
This Dimension

How do you look beyond what you can see with your physical eyes, beyond the physical plane of existence and into the next dimension? When you talk with your spirit guides, you will often see them in your mind's eye, which means that you are looking into their dimension and seeing them as they are on the Other Side. You can experience the astral plane during astral travel. During astral travel, you go out of this dimension into the next one. You can journey between dimensions—between the earthly plane and the astral plane—when you're asleep or dreaming as well. You have to be focused and relaxed in order to see into these other dimensions, so meditation is an excellent method to use. Creative visualization also works well.

When you look beyond the earthly dimension and into other realms, you're connecting to the energy of that dimension, which in turn will raise your own personal energy vibration. You make a connection with that reality and are able to understand that there are a lot more possibilities in the Universe than you can see with your physical eyes. New plants and animals are constantly being discovered on our planet, so who's to say there aren't undiscovered things in the spiritual dimension? Just take a peek. Become aware of the existence of other dimensions to enhance your spiritual growth.

> *Obtain assistance for your
> spiritual needs from outside
> this realm of existence.

154. LOVE

Love is the one thing in this world that will always bring you joy. When you feel as though you aren't loved or that love is lacking in your life, you may find yourself surrounded by feelings of inadequacy or sadness. Finding love doesn't mean you have to be in a romantic relationship; it can be the love of family, friends, or even a pet that satisfies this human need. When you have love in your life, you'll always be able to tap into the feelings of happiness that love gives you. Do you love yourself? If you don't—if you're not happy with your spiritual being—you need to determine what you don't love about yourself and use that information to make changes so you can love the special person you are. Think about the love in your life that you may not even realize is there. Love comes in all different shapes and forms; you just have to know who and what you love and who and what loves you back. Pets give unconditional love every single day regardless of your faults and mistakes. They are forgiving, honest, and will love you with every fiber of their being. If you don't have a pet, consider getting one. If you're not able to care for a pet, consider volunteering at an animal shelter to walk or play with unclaimed pets to expose yourself to their simple brand of love.

> ∗ *Give love like there's*
> *no tomorrow.*

155. Live the Life
you Planned

Before your birth, you mapped out a plan to have specific experiences in your life that would teach you the lessons you needed to learn. While still in the spiritual realm, you made agreements with others who may or may not have incarnated during the same time frame as you. These lessons are experienced as you live and interact with people on the earthly plane.

As the creator, planner, and instigator of your earthly experience, you set your purpose and are striving to reach those objectives. You have to be spiritually aware of your own essence so that you can clearly see the goals and lessons that you planned. Sometimes fear can cause you to approach life in a bit of a fog because you really don't want to move forward with the lessons you're supposed to learn. You're either afraid or you just don't want to learn the lesson. You need to embrace your earthly experience with clear vision. Doing so allows your energy to grow so you'll be fully awake, aware, and participating in your premade plans. As your frequency builds within you, you'll have no choice but to acknowledge your plans because you're more open-minded and connected to your true spiritual self.

> *Only you know your
> true spiritual self at your
> core. Embrace life as an
> opportunity for growth.

156. Enlighten
another Person

As you move down your path of enlightenment, you will learn many things about yourself, the world you live in, and the spiritual planes of existence. You will learn about your soul's spirituality, psychic abilities, the paranormal, and/or metaphysics. One way that you can give back to the Universe as you grow spiritually is to use your knowledge to enlighten another person. As I learned what I now know about metaphysics, the spiritual, the paranormal, and how psychic abilities work, I didn't have anyone to teach me about these things. I learned it all through my own experiences, which often sent me to books to do more research. One thing I do now to give back is to enlighten others through teaching and by offering the material that I have learned in various formats. I write books, I teach workshops, and I talk to people one-on-one so they can gain a better understanding of what they're going through as they're going through it. Sometimes it's difficult to understand what is going on in your life, especially when there is a lot of forward motion with your energy and on a spiritual, psychic, or paranormal level. Being a guide or mentor to others by sharing your experiences and teaching with your knowledge will allow you more growth while helping others. How can you enlighten someone in your circle today?

*Knowledge is power but
it's meant to be shared.*

157. Connect To
Your Guides

One of the first things you can do to connect to your spirit guides is sit down in a quiet place—well, it doesn't really have to be a quiet place and you don't even have to be sitting down, you could be standing up—the point is, you just want to talk to your guides. You don't have to make a huge time commitment in order to meet these helpers. You could be standing in line at a fast food restaurant, ask your guide a question, and get an answer before you even reach the register to place your order. You should be sincere in your approach to raising your consciousness so you can easily talk with your guides. It may take you several attempts to reach your guides the first time, but if you keep at it, you will be successful.

Have a conversation with them (either out loud or in your mind) and tell your guides that you'd like to meet them and get to know them better. Ask their names, what they look like, and anything they could tell you about themselves. One of your questions may be "Why are you guiding me?" or "What is our spiritual connection?" Once you ask your questions, you should trust the first impression you receive; the first thing you see or hear after asking the question is your guide's or guides' response.

When you meet your guides, you may see someone of a different race or from a different background than yourself, and that's fine. Your guides will appear to you in a way that you can easily connect with, or they may appear as they were in a past life the two of you shared. If your guides are telling you something and you can hear them (clairaudience), pay attention to what they're saying. Don't doubt what you're hearing because your first impression is going to be right 99.9 percent of the time.

You can connect to your guides when meditating, but not everyone has time to sit quietly and meditate, so you can also learn to talk to your guides when you're busy during your daily activities. The key point is that you ask, listen, and trust that what you're receiving is their helpful input. Give your guides free rein to pop in whenever they need to tell you something. If it's important, they'll do so anyway, but when you give them permission to contact you more often, you have more opportunities to connect with their higher frequency.

Once you are able to see and communicate with your guides, contact them regularly. They are here to help you understand your purpose and lessons in this lifetime, to help you through difficult times, and to celebrate with you during happy times.

> ✳ *Your guides want to help*
> *you, if you'll only let them.*

158. United Care
of the Soul

As spiritual beings, it is our responsibility to take care of our souls during the human existence on the earthly plane. It is our duty to take care of every facet of our being, including the subconscious and conscious mind, the higher self, our spiritual knowledge base, our spiritual being, and our soul energy. This includes every aspect of ourselves that makes us a complete spiritual entity.

As you exist on the earthly plane, it is your responsibility to become enlightened, to become awakened, to look for more than you can see with your two eyes. You know on a spiritual level that there is more to you than flesh and bones or life and death. By understanding that you are a deeper spiritual being and by making an agreement with yourself, which is the United Care of the Soul, you are taking care of your spirituality. You're looking for more information, striving to be a more complete person, and you're incorporating all the energy that is a part of you into an elevated state. You're not just assuming you can raise your frequency; you know that it's your right and responsibility to take care of your entire spiritual being on a deeply spiritual level because you are a spiritual entity first, human second.

*Make a United Care of
the Soul agreement with
yourself today to stay on the
path of enlightenment.*

159. Keep a Promise

For me, a promise is my word. I try very hard to always keep the promises I make. The feeling of disappointment that is associated with a broken promise is something I do everything I can to avoid. For some people, making a promise is just a way to shut someone up or to get out of a situation; they may make a promise without having any intention of following through. These are negative actions. When you keep promises that you make, whether it's a promise to yourself or to someone else, you're increasing your vibration because you're keeping your word.

Think back on times when you didn't keep a promise to someone else. Were they disappointed, sad, or upset because you didn't do what you said you'd do? Did you feel small because you didn't follow through on your promise, or couldn't you have cared less? Remember that words hold a lot of power; when you associate a promise with words, you're giving those words even more power.

Now, think of times that you did do what you promised. How did the other person feel? Were they happy and proud of you for what you did? Did you make someone else's job easier because you delivered? How did you feel? Were you proud of yourself, or happy that you made someone smile?

> *If you can't keep your
> word and follow through,
> don't make promises.

160. Embrace Adversity

There are plenty of times in life when you face adversity: when things don't go the way you want them to, when you encounter disagreements, or when life is just difficult and you're experiencing setbacks at every turn. It always happens, because this is your life and tough times often accompany life lessons. The harder the lesson, the more difficult it may be to get through it. Even if you feel like your world is falling apart, don't give up! Look at the situation as something that you have to rise above and resolve to come out of it on a positive note. I've always heard (and often found it to be true) that if a bad situation doesn't kill you, it will make you stronger. You gain a sense of strength in your soul by embracing adversity. You may not feel it while you're in the middle of the situation, but you are becoming a stronger person because of what you are going through. Embracing adversity isn't easy by any means, but it will allow you to see different possibilities within your life and examine your reactions to those situations. Adversity is a teacher; there is an opportunity to learn from the trials and tribulations you're experiencing. Adversity often shows its face right before you're about to make a major breakthrough of some kind.

> * Look at adversity as soul-
> strengthening exercises.

161. Go Beyond Skepticism

I'm a firm believer that seeing is believing. I'm skeptical, so for me learning to go beyond what I could see with my own eyes was difficult. When you have things happen to you repeatedly and you can't physically see why it happened, it makes you examine the situation in a different light and consider possibilities that you aren't sure even exist.

There have been times when I've felt someone tug on my shirt, but no one was there when I turned around. Other times I experienced manifestations in my peripheral vision and when I looked directly at what I saw, there wasn't anything there. When this happened, I searched for logical, reasonable reasons for what I had seen. Once I had ruled out every possible logical possibility, I was left with ones that I wasn't sure I wanted to even consider. After you've begun feeling what is beyond this realm, you have to start looking past what you see with the physical eyes and look with your third eye.

Let's say, for instance, that your spirit guide manifests in front of you to deliver an important message. If you see the spirit guide but you're skeptical, then you're not going to believe what you're seeing is really there; you will not receive the message. Maybe you're trying to connect with your spirit guide and in your mind's eye you see a lady with long dark brown hair, a light blue shirt, and khaki pants and she's telling you her name is Alison and that she's your spirit guide. Are you going to believe that? Set aside your skepticism. Try to look at things a little differently when it comes to embracing your psychic abilities and the things you see and experience. When you're dealing with metaphysical experiences, fear often plays a big role in keeping you from discovering the extent of the realms we can't see with our physical eyes. If you can release this fear as you study and have experiences, you'll be better able to determine your own truth. It's not easy to let go of fear, but if you at least try, then you're making a good start on the road of discovery.

Being skeptical is a good thing. You don't want to always be jumping on a bandwagon and not paying attention to your core beliefs. You should always rule out logical explanations for events before you put it down to spirituality, or psychic or paranormal experiences. However, when mundane explanations won't account for something, release your skepticism to see if you can find a deeper meaning.

> * Look beyond, see what
> you see—you might
> be surprised.

162. Behave and Act With Grace

There's nothing worse than running into someone who is constantly acting in horrendous and silly ways. To raise your personal frequency, act with grace and kindness when you're dealing with difficult people. You'll find that your energy increases quickly when you're gracious and act as the bigger person in difficult situations by simply giving in, or at least not fighting against whatever the situation is and allowing the difficult person to have their way. Don't see your actions as "giving up"; you're simply looking at the situation from a different point of view and not holding onto any negativity surrounding the scene or the people involved. You are rising above pettiness. When you act with grace, you're letting go of control and stepping beyond what is expected of you, especially if someone is expecting one type of behavior and you give them a different, more graceful response. Your actions may throw them off-kilter a little bit and make them wonder why your reaction was different than expected. This indirectly helps them to increase their own frequency. There are many people who always react with a "what's in it for me" attitude when acting with grace could very well bring them more than they hoped.

> *Live your life with grace
> and, more often than not,
> you will receive grace
> in return.*

163. Look for Rainbows

Rainbows are a beautiful sign that all is well after a thunderstorm or shower. Such beauty can stop us in our tracks, causing us to gaze into the sky at one of nature's wonders. Have you seen the rare double rainbow? The next time you do, recognize its unique beauty and apply how you feel about it to yourself on a soul level. Do you feel awe, wonder, or amazement? Your feelings are tied to your true essence and your connection with the spiritual realm. Can you feel these same emotions about yourself? You are just as rare and unique as that double rainbow. Reflect upon your own spirituality when you see a rainbow. Maybe you like to drive around searching for rainbows. It's fun to do this every now and again after a rain shower.

However, looking for rainbows doesn't always mean scanning the sky to find one of these brightly colored arches. There are plenty of "rainbows" in our daily life if we'd just pay attention to them. Have you heard the laughter of an infant? Or, after a hectic day at work, felt a cool breeze wrapping around you, settling and calming you? These are rainbows of a different sort—natural wonders that highlight the beauty that is all around us. Embrace all of the rainbows in your life with a sense of wonder.

> * *The beauty of a rainbow is*
> *as radiant and powerful as*
> *the beauty of your soul.*

164. Be a Good Person
(Be Bad Sometimes Too)

We've all been told at some point in our lives to "be good." We're supposed to be good people with high ideals and morals. We're supposed to take the high road, to be the better person in times of adversity, to stand out from the crowd. Being a good person means that you go above and beyond the norm to act in kind ways, to help others, and to live your life with integrity. In today's society, this seems to be forgotten more and more. Don't become a statistic without a good moral code of conduct. Your spiritual being deserves to shine with the goodness within you.

But what if we want to be a little bad? Can that raise frequency too? It depends. If you're going to rob a store and hurt someone just to get your kicks, then no, that will most definitely not raise your frequency. But if you want to dress up, flirt, and act a little naughty once in a while, that will raise your vibration because you're boosting your self-confidence. You're not doing anything wrong and you're not hurting anyone. It's great to take the higher road, but sometimes we need the excitement of being a little bit bad too.

Be a good person overall
with a little spice
of naughtiness.

165. Release Something that's Holding You Back

Do you feel like you're running from morning to night and are so exhausted that you even have trouble falling asleep? When life has gotten this hectic, you need to make changes. The first thing you should do is take a look at everything occupying your time. What can you release? As you progress along your spiritual path, you'll discover that some things you once felt you needed to do are now holding you back. Think of it as graduating from one level to another. When you graduate from school you don't continue to attend those classes, do you? It's the same in life. When you do something that is helping your spiritual growth, but then you learn what you need and graduate from that lesson, you need to release it and move forward to the next lesson. There are also times when we take on certain projects but they end up holding us back instead of aiding us in meeting our goals. Such dead projects take up time that could be spent on something new. When this happens, you begin to dislike what you're doing and you'll start to feel that it's a waste of time. These are clear signs that it's time to release that project or practice and move on. You have to let that project go for something new to come into your life. Today, examine your exercises, projects, and practices to see if you have outgrown any; decide to let go of any that doesn't help to better you.

*Release that which
no longer serves you.*

166. Recognize and Appreciate the Gifts in Your Life

When you consider the gifts in your life, what comes to mind? Is it a family member, a friend, a job, or a home? Did you think about love and happiness? It could be your psychic, mediumistic, or healing abilities. Gifts come in many shapes and sizes, tangible and intangible. You can recognize the gifts in your life by considering what brings you the most joy. Try not to take the gifts you've been given in this life for granted. They may not always be with you, so appreciate them while they're in your life. People move away, life changes, and things happen that will alter your gifts. The gift you have today may become someone else's gift tomorrow so that you are open to receive a new gift to appreciate.

Gifts are the manifestation of positive energy that will allow you to move further along your spiritual path through sharing something with another person, learning, or becoming enlightened. Too often we don't recognize the gifts in our lives until they're gone. You may be so bogged down in other things that you take the gifts you're given for granted. Begin today by appreciating and acknowledging the gifts in your life. If your number one gift is a person, let them know today how much they mean to you.

Take inventory of the gifts
you've been honored
to receive.

167. Mortality and Death

The idea of death is very scary for many people, whether it's your own or that of someone you love. This initial reaction to death lowers your vibration; it makes you sad and upset, sometimes devastatingly so, which is a normal human reaction because you're going to miss the person you've lost. You'll miss the relationship and interaction you had with them. This also applies to pets, as they can be an important part of our lives.

How can you use the idea of mortality to raise your energy levels? Through belief. The first thing you can do is believe that death is not the end. Death is a transition from this world back home, to the place we came from—call it Heaven, the Other Side, or any other name. Death is only the end of the physical body. Death releases the soul from its limitations so that it can continue on its infinite journey toward learning life lessons, finding ultimate happiness and joy, and eventually returning to its source of Creation. Knowing that we're only on one plane of existence at this time can help us to understand that our mortality in the physical body is not the end of our soul; it's a continuation of our soul's path in the grand scheme of things. The soul is immortal, made of pure energy, and it lives on. If you believe this, you can better understand your feelings about mortality. Looking at death in a positive way will bring you peace. You will still grieve after the loss of a loved one, you will still miss the person who has passed, but you will also find solace in knowing that they have continued on their path and eventually you will see them again on the spiritual plane.

> *Release the fear of death
> to experience all the earthly
> plane has to offer.*

168. Surrender, Don't Force Your Will

It's a hard thing to surrender to someone else's will. It's difficult to give up on your beliefs, things that you own, your trust in another person, or your way of thinking in order to embrace new ideas, let go of resistance, and know that your way isn't always the right way. When you are willful, stubborn, and don't want to see anyone else's point of view, you're holding yourself back from possibilities that could be favorable to you. If you don't get your way, your reactions can turn bitter and negative because your personal desire isn't satisfied. This isn't beneficial and can cause you to embrace negativity instead of releasing it.

When you're open-minded—when you surrender your will and allow yourself to consider new ideas—you have the opportunity to grow on a spiritual level. One of these new ideas may be an important lesson on your spiritual path in this lifetime, but if you're blocking this information from coming to you by being stubborn, then you're stunting your own spiritual growth. As you work on raising your energy, consider that your will is not the be-all and end-all of learning about things in the metaphysical realm. If you have to surrender your desires at times, that's simply what you need to do. Don't resist it.

> * Let go of willful and
> stubborn behavior; it will
> only make you sour on
> the inside.

169. Release
Forced Spirituality

Have you ever met people who are so absorbed in New Age metaphysical spirituality that everything they do, say, discuss, or think about is all about spirituality, psychic, and paranormal topics? It's like an obsession. They don't look past the topic but try to live the topic in every way, shape, or form available to them. Yet, there's something that doesn't quite ring true; they're forcing their spirituality. Someone like this may come across as too warm, too fuzzy, or sickly sweet, so totally wrapped up in being "New Age" that they seem fake in their beliefs. We should all be spiritual, but when it's forced or faked just to fit into a certain crowd or trend, then that's not increasing your frequency or making you more spiritual. You're not connecting to your spiritual self because you're losing the truth in your spirituality. I'd much rather communicate with someone who is down-to-earth and knowledgeable about different spiritual topics but don't try to "be" the topic.

When you force your spirituality, you are defeating the purpose of spirituality; you're not truly connecting to Universal Energy. Only you know what your true spiritual beliefs are and how you feel about them. But here's a key thought: if people think you're faking it—that you're forcing your spirituality or that you're forcing your spirituality on them— then maybe you are. Sometimes it's just too much. If you come across as false, you need to take a good look at yourself to see if you're forcing your spirituality, if you're losing the grounded connection to Earth and this plane of existence. If you are, now is the time to make adjustments. You'll find that people will sense you're more truthful, honest, and straightforward in your beliefs instead of being someone who's living with their head in the clouds, coming across as if they can do no wrong or are wrapped up in the "goodness of positivity," which isn't a good thing at all. This is something that you can change. Your spirituality is *your* spirituality, and no one can change it, take it from you, or tell you what is right or wrong for you. The important thing here is to not get so wrapped up in "being" spiritual, psychic, or any other subarea of metaphysics that you miss the point of what you're trying to do. Your faith is not a fad.

> *Be down-to-earth and
> honest when it comes to
> metaphysics and spirituality;
> keep your head out of
> the clouds.*

170. Be and
Experience Energy

Energy is the source of everything; without it nothing would exist. Everything is made of energy, and energy constantly flows around us. It takes different shapes, forms, and manifestations, but it's there. Try going for an entire day thinking of the energy in everything that you encounter, including other people and yourself. Become one with these other energies to feel how each connection is different. For example, I'm sitting in a chair with a notebook computer on my lap as I type. As I tune into these objects, I feel that the chair has a different vibration than the computer. Its energy is calmer, slower, and more constant. The computer's energy is zinging away; it almost feels like it's on overdrive. My own energy is calm, steady, and strong. When you consider energy in this way, you're raising energy within your being.

Another example is if you're standing outside and a thunderstorm is approaching. The wind picks up, the sky darkens, and you can feel the energy of the storm surge through your body. Stay safe, don't get hit by lightning or anything like that, but experience the energy of the storm—be the energy of the storm—and you'll have a different outlook on how energy can raise your frequency even if it's as small as noticing how you're sitting in a chair or as big as a storm.

> *Feel the flow of energy*
> *through you in everything*
> *you encounter on a*
> *daily basis.*

171. Your Spiritual Truth

Spiritual truth is who you are at the essential core part of your being on a soul level. Consider it to be the genuineness of your soul. Each of us has our own truth to live by, and what is right for one may not be right for another; therefore, it's important not to judge others as you make this journey. You do not know what's right for them. You may not agree with their truth—and that's your right—but you do not have to judge them as wrong either. Living your spiritual truth means allowing others to live their own spiritual truth as well. When you understand what your spiritual truth is, then many aspects of your life will become clearer to you.

Are you a pessimist, an optimist, a caregiver, or an artisan? All of these help define who you are in this plane of existence, but do they accurately describe who you are at your core spiritual essence? If a description is negative, then it does not define the spiritual you.

If you're not sure what your spiritual truth is, or how to find out what it is, you need to ask yourself some key questions. You can think about these questions all day long in the back of your mind; you don't have to do any special meditation or creative visualization to achieve results. Some of the questions you want to consider are as follows: Am I a nice person, or am I cranky and mad all the time? Do I give of myself, or am I stingy with my time? The world ends for someone every day; if my world ended tomorrow, would I die happy? Do people respect me for my integrity and honesty? What are my beliefs about the soul, the Universe, and God? Am I comfortable with those beliefs, or do I feel there is something deeper going on that I haven't discovered yet? Do I feel whole in mind, body, and spirit? Am I being true to my beliefs? Is there more I can learn to understand my reason for being and my spiritual truth? Today, just ruminate over these questions and see what comes of it. Remember to record your thoughts in your frequency journal.

As you go through life, there will be times when you know that you have hit on a key Universal Truth. Someone will say something or you'll think something and suddenly you'll get goosebumps all over your body and feel icy cold. This is the sign from the Universe that you have hit upon a Universal Truth that is unique to you. The next time it happens to you, pay attention to what was said or done seconds before the wave of coldness came over you. These moments provide great insight into your spiritual truth.

You may have to dig
deeper to find your truth but
once you do, you will feel
more secure within
your spirituality.

172. Accept Reality,
Don't Hide From It

It's easy for us to take a negative slant on life and to complain about our reality by saying something isn't fair, such and such shouldn't have happened to me, I shouldn't have to go through this or that. Your reality is your reality because you decided before you were born that it was going to be part of your life lesson. And it's a simple truth: life lessons are difficult. You're going to run into situations you'd rather not be involved in. Some lifetimes we have an easier time of it than others. After experiencing a difficult lifetime, you may choose to learn important but not as difficult life lessons the next time around. Think of it as taking an easy elective in school after having a large class load of required courses the previous semester. The difficult life lessons are the ones that help us move further along our spiritual path. You achieve more growth with the difficult lessons than you do with the easier ones.

You have to accept whatever your reality is at this point in your life. Say you fell and broke your leg. Okay, you've got a broken leg. It's your reality at this point in time. What are you going to do about it? You're going to deal with the pain and wait for it to heal. If you try to blame someone else for your broken leg, then you're taking a negative position. If you take a positive position and think, "Okay I've got a broken leg. I'll take it easy, but I'm not going to let this stop me from doing the things I need to do," that's great! It's a good, positive attitude to have when faced with such a situation.

It's also important not to let someone else's opinion become your reality. In order to prevent this, you must be aware of your own spiritual essence, your spiritual truth; with this knowledge, you will be able to live your truth and not what someone else thinks about you.

When it comes to facing your reality, don't put the blame on anyone else. Accept responsibility for what you do in life. Accept your reality and work hard to improve it if it's negative or share it by helping others if it's positive. By doing so, you're raising your energy levels while staying in touch with your true spiritual self. Stop railing against your life and try to accept the bad with the good.

> * *Accept responsibility for*
> *your own spiritual reality—*
> *good and bad.*

173. BE SOBER, NOT DRUNK
ON NEGATIVE BEHAVIORS

Gluttony and greed are negative attributes that can lead you down a path of problems. It's easy to behave in a gluttonous manner or to be greedy no matter what it is that you want, so much so that you can become drunk on it. When you drink too much liquor, you're drunk on the alcohol. When you're too greedy, you're drunk on greed. Going to any extreme and being drunk on negative traits causes you to behave negatively, which brings down your overall spiritual energy. Try to have a more sober approach to life. This doesn't mean you'll no longer have fun; it means you'll no longer swim in negativity. You can imbibe without getting wasted. You can appreciate the things you get in your life without being greedy and always wanting more, more, more. You can eat in moderation and not stuff yourself to the point that you feel as if your stomach is going to blow up. These are all things that, if you are wise and do them in moderation, will keep you moving in positive ways. We all have negative behaviors and thoughts from time to time, but moderation is key to keeping these lapses from setting you back on your spiritual journey. Be sober, don't be drunk on negativity and you'll find that you're better able to keep your energy levels at an even keel instead of dropping it too low with excessive extremes.

*Anything in excess can
cause negative reactions
within your spirit.
Be moderate.*

174. Spiritual Realms

Your energy is always higher when you are connected to the spiritual realms. There's a true core in each of us where we know on a soul level that there's more than just this life. If you consider the spiritual realms—whether you call that heaven, the Other Side, or something else—and if you consider the entities on these realms (your spirit guides, master guides, and people who have passed from this life to the next), you'll feel a soul connection to your own spiritual truth. When you think of the spiritual, it's all about belief. There are many people who don't believe in spiritual realms and many who do; whatever a person believes, that is part of their lessons in this lifetime. It's all about what you're here to learn. Personally, I feel there is more out there, that there are spiritual realms, that our guides are with us, that our angels protect us, that there are deities who have our best interests at heart. There are so many things that have happened to me and to people I know that make me really consider and believe in the spiritual realms.

Today, ponder the existence and form of the spiritual realms. Do these ideas resonate with you? Examine why or why not. Even if you arrive at the conclusion that you do not believe in these realms, the thought you put into that belief will raise your frequency. Perhaps you have automatically believed in these realms and only now are thinking about what those places would look and feel like, and who or what might be there.

> * By considering the
> spiritual realms, you're
> tapping into your own soul
> energy and beliefs.

175. Synchronicities

Exactly what is synchronicity? Some people think of synchronicity as a coincidence that has meaning, but I feel it is deeper than that because I don't believe in coincidences; I believe that there is a reason for everything that happens, even if we don't know the reason at the time. Synchronicity is when you have an experience where two completely unrelated things happen at the same time, and this speaks to you and means something profound to you. These are usually two things that wouldn't have usually happened at the same time. It might seem to be a fluke. When synchronicity happens, look upon it as having special meaning from the Universe simply because it had to have been divinely guided to happen in the way it did. I believe synchronicity is a soul sign, an event planned to let us know that we're on the right pathway. If the synchronicity is profound, it's meant to let us learn through the event.

Here's an example of synchronicity. Let's say you're cleaning your closet and find your old high school yearbook. You flip through it, find a picture of a girl you used to know that you were pretty close friends with but you two drifted apart after high school and you haven't seen her in twenty years. Later that day, you run to the store for a gallon of milk and who reaches out to grab a gallon at the same time as you? Your old friend from high school! How is this synchronistic? What are the chances that first, you'd decide to clean today; second, you'd find your old yearbook; third, that you'll reminisce about your friend; fourth, that she'd show up in the same grocery store at the exact same time as you and that you'd both be getting milk? This frequently happens when I see or hear something that makes me think of a certain person, even if I haven't seen that person in a long time. Shortly thereafter, however, I will run into the person or someone they are close to, or I will hear news about the person in some way. This person might have a message for me, or they might teach me an important part of a life lesson I'm currently working on.

Here's another example. Say you go to the store with some cash, pick up one item, and the bill is $3.33. You open your purse (or wallet) and you only have $3.33 in cash because someone in your family borrowed the twenty you had and didn't tell you that they took it. What are the chances that, when you thought you had nearly $24.00, you would only have the exact amount of your purchase? This synchronicity might have to do with a current dilemma, a lesson you are working on, or another message that only you can make sense of.

When synchronicities happen, they have a positive effect on your energy if you notice them. Sometimes though, you may miss them if you're not paying attention. Be more aware of the little things so you'll notice the synchronicities in your life. I'm a firm believer that everything happens for a reason, so look for the reasons behind the synchronicities. You can use these "coincidences" to boost your frequency by noticing the divine design in your life or by being on alert for important messages that might be coming your way.

> *Pay attention to the
> synchronicities in your life
> because they are messages
> in disguise.

176. Utmost Honesty

When you tell lies, half-truths, or white lies, you lower your frequency. When you're completely honest with yourself and the people in your life, you increase your personal vibration. There's an old, old saying that honesty is the best policy, and I believe that's entirely true. When you lie, or don't tell "exactly" the truth, it will come back to bite you in the butt. It's always better to be upfront and honest, even in difficult situations. You may encounter times when the easy way out is to lie and not face the truth of the situation. Take the high road and say the truth. Can you imagine what a convoluted mess you'd have in your life if you told lie after lie after lie? If you were to be questioned about the things you've said, how in the world would you remember every lie you told and get out of the situation? It's sad to see someone who has put themselves in this kind of situation because they end up digging the hole deeper and deeper, trying to fix their initial lies. It's just best to always be honest and tell the truth in the first place. You'll find that utmost honesty alleviates the problems that you'll encounter in your life if you're lying.

Today, eschew all lies, even small white lies. See how you feel at the end of the day and be sure to record your thoughts about this experiment.

> *Honesty is a virtue that*
> *strengthens your core*
> *spiritual essence.*

177. Offer
Love Consistently

Nobody wants to get the hot/cold treatment when it comes to love. When you offer love, don't go back and forth on it. You either love someone or something or you don't. Love is a strong and powerful emotion, so it's important to be consistent in the way you offer love to others. Inconsistency will cause your energy to go haywire. Before you say those three little words and give your love away, make sure that you are completely certain of your feelings. If you can't make up your mind about what you love and what you don't love, by all means, keep your mouth shut until you know for sure. Inconsistent love or saying that you love someone when you're not really sure that you do can break that person's heart and cause them undue pain, especially if they already love you. Not only is inconsistent love confusing for the people in your life, it's confusing for you as well. Always be steady because love is such a strong emotion that you want to make sure you're being true in the love you give, which will bring truth in the love you receive.

Once you've committed yourself to love, give it freely and show it often instead of holding back. There's no joy in keeping your feelings under wraps. Even if you think the person you love already knows how you feel, they'll always appreciate hearing it again. Today, vocalize your love for the people closest to you.

Consistency in matters of
the heart is imperative.

178. Deep Soul Frequency

When I say "deep soul frequency" (DSF) I'm talking about your vibrational rate at the deepest part of your being within the soul. The higher your vibration on the earthly plane, the more enlightened you'll become and the higher your DSF will go. The more you learn about spirituality, psychic abilities, paranormal events, and anything of a metaphysical nature, the more you're positively affecting your DSF. This also applies to religion. If you're studying one particular religion or different religions from around the world, if that's part of your life lessons, then your DSF will increase.

The key to positively affecting your DSF is to be in spiritual alignment with Universal cosmic energy, moving within its flow, instead of countering the flow. As you do this, you will feel this cosmic energy within you. You will know when you are accessing and affecting your DSF because your life will suddenly seem clearer and more purposeful. Things will flow smoothly with little disruption and with a happy and joyful energy.

As you work to become more enlightened and as you learn more about yourself spiritually, always consider how the things you're learning are affecting your DSF. Are you raising your energy on the innermost, deepest levels of your core spirituality? As you accomplish this, you're going to feel lighter and more alive.

> *In the depths of your soul
> lies the greatness of you.

179. LIGHT
BODY FREQUENCY

Your light body is white light energy that flows from God—or whatever name you use for the source of Creation—which radiates from the Universe, infusing you with higher levels of consciousness. There are some theories that go into complex, detailed steps to activate the light body, which is also broken down into many different components. I believe the light body is our connection to the Divine, and that it can be compared to our physical bodies and our higher selves. The higher the elevation of your light body, the more brilliantly your soul light shines. You will find that as this happens and you become more enlightened, the more your light body grows and becomes spiritually elevated. People will be drawn to you, wanting you to share your inner light and knowledge with them. They'll want to know what you know that causes your light to shine so brightly. If you're connected to the Universe, if you're connected to God and to your spirituality, then your light is going to shine brighter than it will for someone who is disconnected from these things. To increase the power of your light body, you need to become one with yourself on a spiritual and emotional level. By doing this, you will be more enlightened overall so you can share your light with others.

> * You are a beacon; let your
> light shine for all to see.

180. Life is a Journey

Life truly is a journey. You can make it through anything the world tosses your way. We're born, we grow up, we die, and we go back home. Look at life as a continuous experience in obtaining knowledge and understanding our own spirituality. The life lessons that we decided to learn when we came here are what we take back with us when we pass over. Why put yourself in situations where you're going against the flow, doing things that cause you difficulties and hardships or that make your life harder? Be positive when trying times are presented to you. You can't change things that happen in life, it's going to happen the way it was planned before you were born; you can only change how you react to those things. If you consider life in this way, then you understand that everything happens for a reason and is part of a life lesson that you're learning.

Look for the lessons hidden in the situation when things are going badly. You can handle anything that life hands you if you always keep moving forward and remain accepting even though you may question the situation—those questions may actually be an important part of what you're learning. You can increase your energy levels on a daily basis just by handling occurrences that come up in a positive manner. Don't feel down or depressed if you can help it, and never give up. There are some things you can't change; make a list of ways you *can* make your life better. Start small and work up to the things that seem impossible to reach. As you accomplish each of the small goals, you'll find that you're one step closer to those big goals. Keep your motivation high and remember that with time, all things will pass.

Sometimes it's very difficult to concentrate on what you need to do in life and to stay focused on your spirituality when you have to deal with unexpected situations. What are you going to do if you're upset, having issues, or are struggling through life? It's hard but you'll make it through. You will not always feel the way you do now. As you move forward, you'll understand more about your own divine nature. Stay positive; keep increasing your vibration even if it's something small like humming a tune as you go about your day. It makes you feel good and attracts positivity to you.

*Keep your chin up and
your head held high and
focus on being positive
during times of trouble.*

181. You Are a Gift
to the Rest of the World

Has anyone ever told you that you are a gift and a blessing in their lives? Well, you are those things and more! Just as you can receive gifts in your life, you can also be a gift to others because there is no one else like you on this planet. Each and every one of us has individual qualities that make us special. We all have different ways of looking at things, unique ways of thinking, and diverse ways of expressing ourselves; each of these characteristics can be used to help enlighten other people. Your kindness, love, and generosity are all distinctive and special traits within your person, but they're also gifts when you share them with others. A big part of raising your frequency is doing things that will help others but will also help you on a spiritual level. When you give of yourself, you're going to grow spiritually and personally. Everyone needs a little help now and then. It may be as simple as opening the door for someone who has their hands full or as complex as moving in with someone temporarily to help them through a difficult time. Today, consider yourself as the gift that you are and share your uniqueness with others.

> *I shall be a light to others,
> a present wrapped in
> the shining paper
> of enlightenment.

182. Don't Put
Limits on Yourself

There are scores of ways you can raise your personal frequency. This book gives you 365 ways, but there are so many more than that. It's very important as you do energy work that you do not put limits on yourself. Every little thing you can do to make you feel better about yourself, that brings you happiness, that makes you look at a person or situation in a unique way, or that makes you look at something differently than you have in the past will be beneficial to you on this path. You're connecting to your spirituality, reaching a higher level of understanding. If you put limits on yourself, you'll just obstruct potential growth.

This entry marks the halfway point of this book. Today, consider how the energy changes you've been working on affect you at the molecular level within your body—the effect on your attitude, mood, and the way you think about life. This is a time of exponential growth; if you were to think negatively and limit yourself, you'd miss out on many opportunities to expand your horizons. During this time you may find yourself fighting for your moral values, flowing with a harmonious unity, and experiencing many eye-opening events. By keeping your core spiritual self free from any kinds of restraints or limits, you're allowing even more potential to flow to you from the Universe.

> *Believe that you can grow
> without limits and you
> will exceed your
> own expectations.*

183. Count Blessings, Not Troubles

When I was growing up, I always heard that you should count your blessings. This is excellent advice when it comes to your spiritual enlightenment. When you're counting your blessings, you're looking at the good things in your life in a positive manner. If you don't count your blessings, then you're probably counting your troubles. This can cause problems because you're no longer looking at the positives but at the negatives, and you're giving those negative things more attention and focus. Your focus gives troubles more power and can make them manifest into larger problems than they were originally. Instead of letting negativity get blown out of proportion, keep it in check with positivity.

You have many things that you can be grateful for in life even during times of trouble. If you can't think of any, just look around you at your family, friends, your job, neighbors, pets, and the things you've accomplished in your life. Can you be grateful for any of them? Are they a blessing in your life in some small way? Really think about this and you'll soon discover that your blessings outweigh your troubles. Make it a practice to write down the things you're grateful for every day. Start today by making a list of, say, five things. Tomorrow, write down five more, being sure not to reuse the same things you wrote down yesterday. Big or small, any little thing you are grateful for will count! Over time, you'll see how many blessings you have been given.

*Strive to count blessings
and not troubles to lead a
happy, carefree life.*

184. Do It Because You Choose It

Change is about choice. You can choose to continue living as you've been doing for years and let your energy levels stay where they are, or you can choose to change your life. You don't have to wait until something goes wrong to make the conscious choice of transformation through spiritual energy work. You can choose to do it right now, this very minute, this very second. If you want to feel at one within yourself, then make that decision and enact your choice. Don't guilt yourself into feeling that you should have made a better effort to change during turbulent times. Choose to acknowledge your spiritual path in this lifetime. Every decision that you make, whether positive or negative, either moves you further along your spiritual path, takes you a few steps backward, or holds you in a current pattern of thought and action. Using positive energy can make your progression and your transitions through transformation of the spiritual self feel smooth and filled with a natural grace. You may consciously make these choices for positive change, but sometimes they are made within you on a subconscious level. Regardless of how you make the choice, the forward momentum associated with change will propel you toward great accomplishments. Sometimes it's better to make choices quickly, while at other times you'll want to give them heavy consideration. What choices can you make today, and which ones are you building toward in the future?

*Don't put off a choice
that can bring you clarity of
mind, body, and soul.

185. Laugh at Yourself

Laughter is a light vibration. That means it can have a positive affect on heavier vibrations, such as fear, worry, or depression. Have you ever been nervous about something or afraid, and then just started laughing for no apparent reason? Laughter lightens up the lower vibrations, causing a rise in your frequency while increasing your ability to cope with a difficult situation. An example of this is when a woman is around a man she's romantically interested in—she giggles. It's nervous laughter that is increasing her energy so that she can more effectively deal with the situation. The same goes for guys too. They may not giggle, but you can definitely tell when laughter is born of nerves.

You can consciously use laughter to your advantage. The next time circumstances put you in a position where you're worried, nervous, or afraid, just laugh. Will other people think you're nuts? Maybe. Then again, they may be feeling the same heavy energy that you're feeling and your laughter could help them release some of their own anxiety. Laughter releases pent-up low vibrational energy, replacing it with higher levels of light energy. Don't take yourself too seriously. When you do, you may come across as stuffy and not a fun person to be around. Laughing can release overserious tendencies and bring happiness into your life.

> *Laughter can lighten
> the darkest of days.*

186. Live Life
without Regret

It's easy to fly off the handle and say or do things that you regret afterward, leaving you thinking, "What did I just do?" It's difficult to live life without regret because you're human and you're always going to have things that you look back on and wish you'd done differently or not at all. If you always believe that you will live your life to the fullest and without regret, you'll think before you say things or take action. You'll be aware of your actions, do your best, speak with tact and respect, and handle difficult situations to the best of your ability. I know that I try really hard to think before I act instead of just flying off the handle. That doesn't mean I never say things that I regret later, because I do; I'm only human, just like you, and no one is perfect. But when you do lose your temper and say things that you may not really mean or that you wish unsaid, then you have to look at the situation and decide what lesson you can learn from the incident. If you try to live your life without regretting anything you've done, you'll stay in a positive frame of mind. Then the times when you do things that you regret will be few and far between. Live your life filled with happiness and try to stay in control of your emotions so you don't have regrets.

Eliminating regret also applies to the things that you want to do in life. If there is something that you've always wished you could do, then do it. Don't wait. If you want to be a singer, then be a singer. Don't wait until you're seventy-five years old and then say to yourself, "I really wish I'd been a singer because I really wanted to do that and I would have been great at it." If you want it, do it. If you want to be a writer, write. If you want to be a dancer, dance. That's what is going to make you happy regardless of your age. You can start right now—even if you are seventy-five—because you don't want to regret missing out on the things you wanted to do in life.

Take today to eliminate both types of regret: think before you speak and examine your life to see if you have any regrets over things you have not done.

> *Regret can diminish your
> light, making you feel less
> than the wonderful person
> you are. Leave it behind so
> you can shine.

187. Let Go of the Past

When you hold on to the past, it holds on to you right back. Your past will always be your past; nothing will ever change that. To move forward in life, you have to relinquish the past's hold on you. Are there negative situations that are still affecting you? Did your past behaviors hurt those around you? You can choose to dwell on these events and have a huge pity party that never ends, or you can let it go. You don't have to feel sorry for yourself or put up impenetrable walls of protection. Just because one person treated you badly doesn't mean everyone in your future will do the same thing. Just because you behaved poorly or made bad decisions doesn't mean you'll always do those sorts of things. By acknowledging and accepting your past, you can analyze it, learn from it, and move on. Holding on to a lack of trust means you're not giving people the opportunity to prove that the past doesn't have to repeat itself. When you hold on to negative past emotions and experiences, you can sabotage your own happiness today. You can't change your past, and the future is yet to unfold—live in the now.

> *Past hurts can hold you
> back from reaching your
> fullest potential.

188. Go beyond Being Content to Find Happiness

Being content with your life may be an indication that you are stuck in a rut. Your life may be going well—you're successful and feel as if everything is right in your world. But when you are just "content," you may no longer be striving toward new goals or seeking to bring new moments of happiness into your life. Don't become complacent. That will make you lose sight of the little details that help you move forward in life. Leave contentment behind to strive for a new awareness and deeper knowledge in your daily life. Even if you only choose to learn one new idea or do one fun thing that you've never tried before, achieving that goal takes you out of the contentment rut. If you feel stuck in content complacency, do something different to get you out of it today.

Complacency can make you become less aware of the world around you. You may no longer feel the need to venture into new directions, to take chances that enable growth. It can make you unaware of obstacles, dangers, or treacherous people in your life, and it might make you not want to be an active participant in your life. You could be thinking, "What I have is fine, why change anything?" It's much better to be less content and more aware because through awareness you will strive to achieve more than you will if you're just contentedly watching life pass you by.

Always go for the gusto.

189. Open the Windows to Your Soul

The eyes are the windows to the soul, but those aren't the windows I'm talking about here. We're going to go deeper than the eyes. Let's travel all the way down to the core essence that is your true spiritual being. Sit quietly for this exercise and breathe deeply. Now use creative visualization to look deep inside yourself, not physically, but into your being. How does it feel in here? Is it stuffy? How long as it been since you opened the windows of your soul to allow fresh air to flow through you, cleansing and rejuvenating you while revitalizing your energy? Think of it like opening the windows in your home during the springtime to clear out the stuffiness of winter. Imagine that you're standing in the center of your soul and it looks like a house full of windows. Open the windows and feel the drafts moving over you, cleansing and revitalizing your soul energy.

Have you ever heard the expression that when a door closes, a window opens? If you find that you're facing a lot of closed doors in your life, then do this creative visualization exercise and open up the windows of your soul. One of those windows could bring new opportunities your way. Every now and then, it's a good idea to open up the windows of your soul to refresh you and bring new things into your life on many levels. It will get rid of lethargy and the doldrums and liven up your energy.

Refresh, cleanse,
and rejoice in your
spiritual essence.

190. Self-Worth

The way you perceive and project your own self-worth can reflect the level of your frequency to others. If you feel you are worthy of the good things that will come your way, then you will project an image of self-assurance, confidence, and poise. If you feel unworthy, then you may seem uncertain, doubtful, and indecisive. Not only will you appear this way to others, but you'll feel this way about yourself. Feeling worthy is a positive attribute, while feelings of unworthiness are negative. When you feel unworthy, you may be blocking your own path. Do you say that you feel you are worthy when in reality you feel that you're not? If this is the case, you need to analyze why you're feeling this way. Make it a point every day to acknowledge to yourself that you deserve to receive good things in life. Unworthy feelings can appear at any time and sabotage your best efforts, so this is something you'll need to revisit periodically throughout your life. If you want more joy in your life and have been working hard to achieve joy, but unworthy feelings overcome you, they can prevent you from obtaining joy. If you are open to receiving joy, it will come to you in abundance. Make sure you're not pushing away good things because you feel unworthy of having joy in your life.

> * Accept what you
> deserve and deserve
> what you accept.

191. Connect With the Frequency of Colors

It's easy to take color for granted because it's such an ingrained part of our lives. You see different shades of colors every day, but what if our world wasn't colorful? How bland would life be then? When days are gray and overcast or stormy, you can often be in a worse mood then if it's a bright, sunny day filled with vibrant color. This indicates that color affects mood. When you are lacking color in your life, or you're stuck on gray color tones, basically living your life in black and white color schemes, then your energy will be lower unless you purposefully make an effort to increase it. To do this, add more vibrant colors to your surroundings and clothing, which also allows you to feel more joy and happiness. Colors can energize all aspects of your life. Try adding vibrant colors to the decor in your home and workspace. If you don't have yellow, add some. If you already tend to go with bright, vivid colors, add a calming color for balance.

As you experiment with color, you'll find the ones that you connect with and feel as though they resonate with you. This might be the color you've always thought was your "favorite," or it might be an entirely different shade—keep an open mind! The colors you resonate with might also change over time as you grow and have different experiences. You can energize your life simply by using your resonating colors more and consuming food and drink of that color.

*Add an explosion of
color into your life.*

192. Blue

Blue is a cool, calming color. People who use a lot of blue are loving, peaceful, affectionate, analytical, creative, and intelligent. Blue inspires loyalty in those around you. Because blue is the color of the sky and is a natural part of our physical world, it helps you to connect to the spiritual realms and the higher self. It is useful when linking to your intuitive nature, in increasing energy, and in understanding yourself and the situations in your life. Blue is a color of peace, harmony, and trust. It is associated with the throat chakra and communication. If you tend to be anxious, nervous, or on edge, add more blue to your life. Wear it more often, eat blue tortilla chips, or add a blue screen saver on your computer. Creative, sensitive, and inspirational people often wear blue, so add blue if you want to add these qualities to yourself.

When there is too much blue in your surroundings or if you wear too much blue, it indicates that you're afraid of failure or loss. This could be loss of position, career, status, money, or friends. To rid yourself of this fear, you'll need to address the situation. Start by removing some of the blue in your surrounding and replacing it with vibrant colors. Instead of wearing blue, try yellow or orange.

* Wear a blue ring
or pendant to help keep
anxiety at bay.

193. RED

Red is often associated with power, authority, great wealth, or prestige because red is a hot, high-energy color that draws attention. People who are fond of red are ambitious achievers, but they can sometimes be controlling. If you're a calm, down-to-earth person, adding red to your life will energize you. Your next car could be red (just be careful because drivers of red cars tend to get more tickets than any other color car), or you may choose to color your hair red or buy a red toaster. Any way that you can bring red to you will act as a stimulant. Red can make you more enthusiastic, confident, and motivated to take action. Red is associated with the root chakra and feelings of safety and power.

You want to be careful that you don't add too much red to your life, however. Too much red can be overstimulating and can have the exact opposite effect than you're trying to achieve. You could ratchet your energy into overdrive with red without raising it one bit on a spiritual level, which is not the goal. Too much red can cause feelings of anger and resentment; it can get tempers running high for no apparent reason. This happens simply because your senses are overwhelmed with the abundance of red color and energy.

Enjoy a big slice of
watermelon to add a touch
of red to your life.

194. PINK

Pink is a variation of red that is more soothing. It's a more romantic color of love and protection, whereas red is a color of high energy. It is a light-hearted color of happiness and fun. Pink can make you feel safe. It's why you see a lot of pink around Valentine's Day. You see a lot of red too, but pink indicates safety in love. Pink is a relaxing color that makes you feel at ease with yourself and those around you. This is why it is often used in prison holding cells; it calms erratic or violent behavior for the short term. People who are drawn to pink are often affectionate, with a loving nature. It is a good color to add to your home and work environment or to your person because it releases and prevents depression. If you have issues with coworkers, try adding pink to your desk. Pink flowers work well and will also make you feel safe and at ease in your work environment. If an annoying coworker shows up and starts bothering you, chances are that they will feel the effect of the pink you've put in your work space and back off.

You have to be careful with pink because, as with red, too much can make you angry and upset.

*Show your unconditional
love with pink gifts.*

195. Orange

Orange always reminds me of Halloween—the pumpkins, the orange and black decorations, a cool chill in the air. It reminds me of autumn and of an orange moon. All of these are positive, happy thoughts that increase your energy. Orange is a warm, happy color that increases your level of physical activity, helps you stay motivated, and will make you want to get up and do more. Orange can increase your creativity, bringing ideas that seem to flow with ease. It's a productive color that will help you get a lot done in a shorter amount of time. If you want to increase your activity, creativity, and desire to succeed, use orange to accomplish these goals. Fans of orange tend to be outgoing, have a lot of friends, and can be very competitive. These folks will give you the shirt off their back if you need it and then they'll race you to the finish line. Orange is connected to the sacral chakra and the enjoyment of pleasure.

Orange is also known to be related to people who are easily frustrated or who are suffering from exhaustion. If you fit that description, then you'll want to bring in a neutral color to eliminate frustration or remove some orange from your person and environment if you have too much around you. Orange people may often seem edgy and hyper. Orange tones can cause controversy, so use it sparingly in your surroundings.

> *If you're sick, avoid orange
> because it can make you
> feel worse.*

196. Yellow

Yellow is a cleansing, empowering, and stimulating color that can bring balance into your life. Yellow aids in concentration, and it raises your mood and energy levels because it is reminiscent of the sun. It can make you more optimistic about life. You can add yellow to your food by eating a banana or some squash. Find interesting ways to add yellow to food, clothing, and living spaces. For instance, you may add splashes of yellow to your interior decor through fixtures or accessories. When you enjoy yellow and use it in your clothing or home, it shows that you're full of spontaneity; active and happy. It shows that you're a bit of a risk taker, an idealist with unique thoughts who tends to make friends easily; you set goals and stick with them. If you're not functioning at your best, put on a yellow shirt to help you increase your energy throughout the day and make it easier for you to focus. You'll no longer feel lethargic but will enjoy all the activity going on around you. Yellow makes it easier for you to deal with the challenges and stress that life throws at you.

Yellow is tied to the solar plexus chakra, the seat of the will. If you dislike yellow, it's indicative of low self-esteem and low personal power.

> *Let your light shine by
> associating yourself with the
> color of the sun.*

197. Gold

The law of attraction and Feng Shui often go hand in hand. If you'd like to attract more wealth into your life, add gold to your home, especially in the kitchen. One of the principles of Feng Shui is that the kitchen is connected to wealth. Gold is the color of enlightenment and divine protection. It can increase your personal power and success. In the kitchen, you can use gold as the primary or secondary color. When using it as a primary color, choose gold-colored tiles, paint the walls a bright gold color, or choose appliances in shades of gold. Another option is to use gold as a secondary color. Use it as a trim in your painting scheme or choose smaller appliances in a golden color. Add hand towels, salt and pepper shakers, or canister sets in gold tones as accents. This will attract wealth in an aesthetic and pleasing manner. To increase your personal power, wear gold jewelry or gold clothing and accessories.

Be careful when decorating with or wearing gold, as too much can become very tacky. There is also negativity associated with using too much gold because it can bring feelings of conceit or imagined privilege and superiority to you. Use it sparingly to reap the most benefits.

Glittery golden tones
awaken Universal attraction
magnets for you.

198. Green

Green is the color of health, fertility, and new growth. It is symbolic of nature. Green connects you with feelings of unconditional love, hope, peace, and harmony. Green is a refreshing, cool color that can revitalize you. It is the color of health and vitality. When you're healthy, it's easier to elevate your core energy. People who wear a lot of green or like to have green around them are very good at making decisions. They are calm, like to observe life, make decisions easily, and have an abundance of self-control. When you add green to a room, it creates feelings of peacefulness, tranquility, and quietness. The study or library in your home is a good place to have green, as is the dining room or wherever you're eating your meals. Green helps you focus on the tasks at hand instead of being easily distracted. The porch and balcony are also good places to fill with green plant life and enhance your communication with nature. Green is a healing color that brings balance and harmony. When life is in disarray, green will bring you back to normalcy. Green is associated with the heart chakra and feelings of love and affection.

Be careful that you don't use too much green because it can make you lazy and cause you to lose your motivation.

** Use green to become
more emotionally open and
receptive to new ideas.*

199. TURQUOISE

Turquoise is known to be used for spiritual protection and healing. People often think of the ocean when they think of turquoise. This color is excellent to use when you're feeling lonely because it will stimulate you to act and increase communication with the people in your life. It will help you raise your energy and find balance when you feel as if you're at the end of your rope. Turquoise is a thinking and creative color that will make you more confident and calm. If you're stuck in your creative pursuits, adding turquoise to your surroundings will get those creative juices flowing again. Many people, especially in the New Age community, love turquoise—both the color and the stone. Metaphysically minded people often think about other alternatives and things outside of the realm of possibility when using turquoise.

It also comes with a warning, especially when it comes to your energy: If you use too much turquoise, it can make you shut down or close yourself off from people, and your energy can plummet. If you see someone who is wearing a lot of turquoise, notice their actions. Do they seem afraid of change? Are they stuck in patterns of negative emotional behavior? Sometimes people wear turquoise when they're feeling this way and it's almost as if they use the color as a barrier to hide their true feelings.

*Wear turquoise jewelry
if you're feeling especially
mentally drained.*

200. Violet

Violet is one of the colors associated with metaphysics, energy levels within the body, psychic abilities, and high ideals. It is a spiritual color that allows you to connect to the beauty, inspiration, and creativity within yourself. Violet will enable you to see possibilities when you thought there were none. This is likely because violet is the color associated with both the third eye chakra and the crown chakra, linking it to intuition, inspiration, and spirituality. People who tend to use a lot of violet are often thought of as mystical or mysterious. They are generous and selfless. Violet is a color that can make you think in a more open-minded way. You will look at the bigger picture as well as tiny details and consider ideas and theories that you may never have considered before. In addition to being a spiritual color, violet is also a power color. Use it to make you feel more positive about yourself and sure of your own abilities. Violet is also a very soothing color. If you're having difficulties sleeping, use violet sheets, wear violet pajamas, or add a violet night light in your room to get a good night's rest.

An overabundance of violet can have a negative effect, resulting in low self-esteem, depression, suppressed emotions of anger and rage, and insecurity. If you're wearing violet to mask your emotions from others, don't overdo it; this could have an undesired effect on your energy and your soul essence.

*Use violet flowers as the
centerpiece at your next
party to inspire your guests.*

201. Purple

Purple is a spiritual color often associated with royalty, religion, and psychics. It is a calm, serene color of understanding. When you're surrounded by confusion and don't know which way to turn, use purple to enlighten and guide you. A purple pendant hidden beneath your shirt will keep you calm and focused. It is the color of stillness; when things are hectic and busy, purple will help to bring balance. It will increase energy because it is a protective color that soothes with calming peacefulness.

Purple is a protection color, and you'll often find it used in jewelry. When you want to gain more insight into topics that you're researching, wear purple; it will draw the information to you, making it easier for you to find, absorb, and understand new concepts. If you use a lot of purple, you have high standards. You look above and beyond the norm to find people who, like you, stand out in a crowd. Purple can be used to attune yourself to a greater awareness and more accurate perception of both your life and spirituality.

If you don't like purple, then you may feel confined, as if you're being held back from reaching your fullest potential. Too much purple and you'll feel alone, separated from those around you, as if you don't belong.

Add purple to your diet
by eating beets, grapes,
and eggplant.

202. Silver

Silver balances, harmonizes, and is mentally cleansing. Silver helps you to change things about yourself that you want to improve. It's a catalyst color that aids in public speaking, enhances your spiritual balance, and lends patience and perseverance. Silver is an important color when it comes to learning about new things and moving along your spiritual path. Silver is often worn as jewelry because it is a conductor and communicator, which increases with contact with your body. It is often used in the home and office as an accessory color, in dishes, and in cutlery.

Silver reminds us of the moon and is often used under a full moon to energize crystals and stones. It can eliminate negative energy that is stored in your body or convert it to positive energy, which helps to keep you in balance. It is the color of spirituality and means you're on the right spiritual path. It's also indicative of physical abundance in all areas of your life. Silver has a calming effect; it soothes you on a soul level, which is why you'll often find it in holiday decorations. Silver can be used to manifest money since it is used in coins. It is symbolic of your spiritual awakening and the enlightenment of your spiritual being. Silver is a dignified color that is symbolic of wisdom, insight, and self-control.

> *If you normally wear gold
> jewelry, try wearing silver
> for a change of pace.*

203. Gray

Gray is a cool color that is somewhat bland because it doesn't cause strong emotions. It's considered a balanced, neutral color. Using gray can add calmness to the atmosphere of a room, which is good in places where people occupying the space may be stressed or on edge. Gray is often worn as business or school uniform attire, at weddings, and (depending on the shade) it can be a color that adds mystery and intrigue to a room or to the person wearing it.

People who like gray are independent types who are in control of their lives. They may work too much instead of taking time for themselves. Gray is also a color of loneliness or anxiety. If you find yourself feeling this way, then you need to replace the gray in your life with more vibrant colors that reflect high energy and positivity. Using too much gray is a sign that you have unresolved fears. If your fears aren't faced, you could become distant and depressed. It's also an indication that you're purposefully blocking others, are on guard around people, and are putting up walls to keep good things from coming to you. Too much gray makes you passive about life, and you may give up on goals and plans.

Check out your closet.
If you see a lot of gray
clothing, it's time to add
some color to your life.

204. Black

Black is indicative of self-sufficiency. It's an authoritative color of control. People who wear a lot of black like being in control and do not easily give up their personal power; alternatively, some people who wear black are trying to blend in and not be noticed. Black is often used for protection because it keeps negative emotions such as hatred and jealousy away. It can ground you and, in some situations, make you feel invisible. People who are sensitive, such as highly emotional people or people with psychic abilities, find comfort in black because it calms you and can make you feel more at home in your skin. When black is used sparingly in decorating, it can be very uplifting and classic.

When you're using black to increase your energy, you have to view it from a point of inspiration. Add black in small amounts; if you begin to feel isolated and separated from others, or as though you're becoming withdrawn, then you know you're using too much black. To rectify this situation, simply remove some of the black in your color schemes or in your wardrobe. You can also accessorize with vibrant colors to offset any negative emotions you're having due to too much black. Too much black in decor or wardrobe can cause depression, increase fears, spark unrealistic or imagined fears, or cause you to be more paranoid and suspicious.

> *Black with bright red is an excellent color combination.*

205. WHITE

White is the color of purity. It is the color of pure light used for protection, cleansing, and empowerment. White is a balanced color that is reflective of new beginnings, one of the reasons that it's used for weddings, christenings, and other religious ceremonies. It will make you feel as if you're starting over; fresh and inspired with no negativity around you. Wearing white can help alleviate feelings of sadness and disappointment. White is often used in hospitals because it is a clean, neutral color. It is also a reflective color. Not only can it reflect the sun, but it can also reflect other energies that may try to attach to you, sending them back to where they came from. It is a color of truth and honesty, pure light, and spiritual well-being. People who like white are drawn to it for these qualities. You can energize yourself spiritually with white by imagining your core essential self as a beacon of pure light energy: pure white, so brilliant that it hurts your eyes to look at it.

If you don't like white, you may be in a situation that you need to get out of or your energy could be at a low point, requiring rejuvenation. Too much white in your decor or clothing can cause feelings of isolation and aloneness.

> * Use white to cleanse and
> protect, to infuse your being
> with purity.

206. Rainbow Colors

Rainbow patterns indicate a person who lives very much in the moment and is on an enlightened level of existence. They are often very intuitive, carefree, and spiritual in nature. When someone uses rainbow patterns in their color schemes—whether it's in their home, at work, or as part of their personal wardrobe—they are open-minded and are often light workers or energy workers. These people tend to have deep interests in spirituality and metaphysics, are open to new ideas and thought processes, and are often leaders in their chosen field.

To increase your vibration with rainbow patterns, consider how you feel when you see a real rainbow. What types of emotions flow through you as you gaze at that multicolored arch? Are you happy? Melancholy? Maybe you're filled with a feeling of delight. By connecting to the feelings associated with finding a rainbow, you can apply those feelings to your spiritual essence. Once you feel balanced within yourself, you can use these same rainbow patterns in your home or office space. Too many rainbow patterns can look tacky and cheap, so limit how much you use this beautiful combination of color. As your frequency increases, you may see more rainbow patterns around you in places that you never expected to see them.

> *Have you ever searched
> for the end of a rainbow?
> It's impossible to find but
> fun to try.*

207. Brown

Brown is an earth tone that gives you a sense of stability in life. It can neutralize negative energy and offer a sense of stability when you feel that your life has gone topsy-turvy. Brown is a nurturing color that increases your common sense. People who prefer it are supportive but can tend to be narrow-minded, especially if they're overusing brown. Brown indicates a thirst for knowledge, and people who enjoy it are often seeking answers, trying to further their education of the world, and they are frequently teachers who share the knowledge they've obtained. When you see someone who has decorated their home with a lot of brown tones, that indicates the person is honest and protective but they hide their secrets well. Always keep this in mind because appearances can be deceiving and it's good to know this about brown so that you can understand the people who like it better. It is the color of soil and can connect you to Earth's energy, which you can use to ground you when doing energy work. Brown is also the color of structure. When you need to present information in a structured way, wear brown or use brown in your presentations to increase impact. Eating brown foods is generally healthy for you and this color is often used in healing.

> *Brown indicates a need to
> be accepted by others when
> used in excess.*

208. Sparkles

Have you ever been sitting in dim light and noticed sparkles in the upper corners of the room that look like little blips of light? I'm not talking about dust particles in streams of light but about brilliant sparkles of white light that seem to move past you at a fast speed. This happened to me when I went to see a medium for the first time. It was a group session and I didn't know what the sparkles were, but I kept seeing them flit and flutter around the room. After the session, someone asked me if I'd seen all the spirits in attendance. I asked her to explain and that's how I found out the sparkles were the manifestation of spirits in the room during the medium's channeling session. I wasn't really convinced at first. After all, it was my first time in a group medium session and I hadn't decided how I felt about it yet. After several more sightings in groups on my own, I realized that what I'd been told was true.

You may see sparkles in the corner of the room, fluttering around your head, or somewhere off to the side in your peripheral vision. These are an indication that a spirit is close by. When you recognize them, you connect with the energy of that spiritual entity, which enlightens you.

Though small glimmers and sparkles of light can indicate a spirit is nearby, remember to rule out logical answers first. If a streetlight is shining through your vertical blinds and reflecting on the wall, that's not a spirit. It's important to rule out nonmetaphysical reasons before you chalk up every flicker of light that you see to a spirit or spirits.

Try sitting in a dimly lit room and notice if there are sparkles in the upper corners near the ceiling. These may be someone you know paying you a visit, or it could be your angels and spirit guides.

* The world shimmers with
visitors from beyond.

209. Agate

Agate is often formed by bands of tiny quartz crystals, which makes its energy stable. It comes in many colors including gray, white, brown, red, orange, black, yellow, blue, and purple, each of which has its own metaphysical meanings specific to the color. Still, there are many properties that apply to agate regardless of the color. When you need to calm down, the crystal to use is agate. Its soothing properties will bring you back to center. Because it is formed in layers, agate is a slow-working crystal that makes you strong, raises consciousness, enables you overcome negativity, and gives you a feeling of security. Agate is beneficial in aiding memory problems, helping you sleep better, and eliminating bad dreams. It's a grounding stone that will allow you to face and speak your own truth. It strengthens your aura, aids in channeling information, and brings balance to relationships. Agate also allows you to release your inner anger as well as any bitterness you may be holding against someone else. When you're working on your spirituality, frequency, and getting in touch with your core essence, keep agate in your pocket, wear it as jewelry, or carry it somehow on your person. Don't stick it in your purse or briefcase because the distance between you and the crystal will be too great.

Use blue agate to bring peacefulness, happiness, and less stress into your life.

210. Amber

Amber isn't really a crystal but I include it with crystals because of its strong connection to Earth and its metaphysical properties. Amber is actually tree resin that has fossilized, and it may include insects or pieces of plants. It's a transparent golden or yellow color. Amber is often used for healing because it can draw pain from the body, relieve stress, and ease stomach ailments. Amber is used for spiritual grounding; it stimulates the mind and clears depression. When you're faced with opposition, wear amber to dissolve the opposing energy. It can neutralize negativity and aid in increasing positive energy in your life. Amber assists with decision making and is good for self-expression. It's beneficial for balance on both spiritual and emotional levels. Amber will give you a happy disposition, offers peace and understanding in difficult situations, and brings success in reaching your goals. If you're interested in your past lives, use amber because its high frequency will help you connect to and remember your past lives and balance any emotions, fears, or situations that have carried over from a past life into your current lifetime. Because it is used in healing work, it should be gently cleansed often.

> * The more you wear amber,
> the more you will benefit
> from its energy.

211. Amethyst

Are you searching for inspiration? Does your creativity feel like it's taken a nosedive? When normal levels of creativity and inspiration feel off and you can't put your finger on what's out of sync, try using an amethyst quartz crystal to bring your energy levels back into balance or take them to new heights. Amethyst is a mass of several large quartz crystals that are purple in color due to iron and manganese. It's often used to bring balance and is considered a very spiritual stone.

Hold the amethyst against your forehead at your third eye. Allow white light to wash over you and clear out any blockages that are holding you back from embracing your fullest potential. The purple color of the amethyst will connect to the purple associated with the third eye, bringing your vibration to a higher, more inspired level. Amethyst is used for protection, clarity, and enhancing the comprehension of new ideas. When you're doing energy work, amethyst is an essential stone to have in your collection. Amethyst will move you forward on your spiritual path, allow you to deal with the stresses of life, and alleviate health problems. It has a calming effect when you're angry, nervous, or are dealing with sadness and grief. It builds up self-esteem, increases psychic abilities, and protects against psychic attack.

> * When using creative
> visualization, wear amethyst
> to increase the strength of
> your visions.

212. Aquamarine

If you have fears that you're having a difficult time eliminating from your life, an aquamarine crystal will benefit you because it reduces fear and increases bravery. It is a clearish crystal that will also make you more sensitive and creative. Aquamarine is useful when you're trying to increase your spiritual awareness and connect to your core spiritual essence. If you're working on enhancing your intuitive nature, psychic abilities, or your relationship with the Divine, you can use aquamarine as an energy conduit. It will also enable you to have more courage in life, and it will protect you during your travels—especially if you're traveling by boat or ship on the ocean. It will make you be more tolerant; if you tend to be too judgmental, aquamarine will lessen that quality within you. When using aquamarine, you will be able to increase your energy because it connects to your spirituality and enhances spiritual growth. It's an important crystal to use if you're developing clairvoyant and mediumistic abilities. It protects against negative influences and gossip and will keep negative energy from attaching to you. Aquamarine helps you to express yourself truly and freely by giving your words more power. In life, things will go more smoothly for you if you're wearing an aquamarine crystal because it brings harmony to you. Aquamarine is the name used for blue or turquoise shades of beryl.

> *Aquamarine brings
> harmony, honesty, and
> relaxation into your life.

213. AVENTURINE

Aventurine is the crystal to use if you're not sure what is making you unhappy in life. It brings insights and knowledge to you that will reveal things about yourself on many levels. Once you can see yourself clearly, you'll know what areas you need to work on first. Aventurine will bring new ideas and then give you the patience to act on those ideas and follow through until you're successful. It can enhance motivation. It's a crystal of protection, relaxation, and calm emotions. Sleeping problems are often resolved with aventurine. When you want to contact your spirit guides, it can clear the way for communication. It dispels anxiety, negativity and stress. This is also a crystal of prosperity. It protects against negative energy attacks and promotes an overall feeling of well-being. When you feel like you can't go on, that what you're attempting is too difficult, then keep aventurine close. Its properties and energy will help you stay the path and persevere until you meet your goals. It is also a good crystal to use when you're working on enhancing your empathic abilities. Aventurine is usually green in color, and it brings wealth to the person wearing it; it is often used as a good luck charm by people who like to gamble or play games of chance.

*Use aventurine to lessen
out-of-control emotions.*

214. Celestite

Celestite is a mostly clear crystal that you can wear to attract your guardian angels. It has an extremely high vibration and is considered to be the stone of the New Age movement. Wearing celestite allows you to absorb its high frequency. It brings peace and understanding of the spiritual dimensions. If you're trying to communicate with your angels, this is the best crystal to use because it has such strong connections to the angelic realms. If you're at a plateau in your spiritual development or if you're having problems with a theory associated with metaphysics, celestite can help. It will also aid with spiritual problems. It is considered to be a divine crystal, one that can assist you with astral travel, aura healing, and even remembering your dreams. It will stimulate your clairvoyant, mediumistic, and psychic abilities. This crystal encourages you to move forward in your spiritual enlightenment, increase your intuition, and improve your connection with your guides. Celestite can increase your energy patterns at a rapid rate, help you understand metaphysical topics and ideals with ease, and bring about clear vision. It is an essential crystal to have in your collection, especially when you're trying to enhance your connection to your guides, angels, and develop your psychic abilities. Celestite is a soft stone that chips easily, so handle it with care.

*Celestite connects
you to the flow of
Universal Energy.*

215. Chrysocolla

Chrysocolla is a sustaining stone, one that will enable to you to persist when the going gets tough. It will give you energy when you're exhausted. It draws off negative energy of all kinds, invokes great strength, and is beneficial in rocky relationships. It is a tranquil crystal that lessens guilty feelings and negative emotions such as regret, loathing, and resentment. When you have these types of feelings under control, you're better able to move on with life in a positive manner. Chrysocolla promotes harmony in your life and increases your ability to love unconditionally. When your heart is broken, it will help it heal faster. It gives more self-awareness, brings inner balance and strength, is a healing stone, and opens you to psychic visions. It's good for confidence and creativity, and it enables you to overcome phobias. This blue-green copper silicate has many purposes: it enhances personal power, increases self-awareness, helps you during times of drastic change, gives you more drive if you're lazy, reduces nervousness, erases irritability, and is good for staying calm in stressful situations. It's a stone that can make you feel better overall. It's also effective at enhancing the power of other crystals. By wearing chrysocolla close, you can eliminate many negative tendencies or at least keep them at bay.

*Heal your heart with
chrysocolla so that you
may love again.*

216. DIAMOND

A diamond is a symbol of purity. Diamonds are often used in engagement rings because they represent love and clarity of relationships. It bonds relationships together to make them invincible so they'll last through all time. Diamonds increase fidelity and enhance your ability to trust. Diamonds give you clear insight into your own situations in life and spirituality. They bring order when things are completely disheveled, keep you from having to compromise, having to tolerate rules or situations that do not fit your energy or restrict you in some way. A diamond can aid your inner judgment and make you more ethical and honest. It can also assist in overcoming fear and depression. It will make you more aware of physical problems and give you more control over your feelings and moods. It increases logical thinking, makes it easier to learn, and helps you through times of change. Diamonds also boost the power of other crystals. It is protective and stimulates your imagination and creativity. It brings spiritual energy to you, which increases your personal vibration while clearing any obstacles that may be blocking you. It is useful in spiritual awareness and in overcoming anger and negativity. Wearing diamonds can make your creativity and inventiveness increase while reflecting your true spiritual essence.

> *Diamonds are symbolic
> of new beginnings, whether
> it's in a love relationship, a
> work project, or a move.

217. Emerald

Emerald is a deep-green power stone that is used for spiritual growth. It enhances your clairvoyance, gives patience, and is a stone of inspiration. This stone can assist you on both physical and emotional levels to bring balance and higher vibrations. It motivates you to raise consciousness and take positive actions in your life. It opens you up to your clairvoyance and intuition as well as psychic and mediumistic abilities. Emerald is also a stone of prophecy. If you tend to be clairvoyant, keeping an emerald stone with you can enhance your ability to see future events or experience them in prophetic dreams. It allows you to connect to Universal Energy and obtain information from the Universal Flow of ideas, which will help you in life. It's a stone of regeneration, and its healing properties are greatest during the full moon. It helps you make friends, find love, and stay alert and mentally young. An emerald gives you the ability to overcome the bad things that happen to you in life and brings balance when you're off-kilter, enabling you to understand things that you may have misunderstood. Emerald is also considered important when it comes to love and bringing two people closer together. If you've had an argument with your significant other, giving emerald as a gift will help clear any lingering negativity and make the relationship stronger.

*Emerald will help you
overcome a bad temper.*

218. Fire Agate

Fire agate is a rare, grounding gemstone that can give you support during times of hardship. It's a protective stone, especially when you're dealing with people who wish you harm. It protects you against psychic attack and works like white light with mirrors to send that energy back to the person wishing you harm while giving them the insight to understand that what they were doing was negative and harmful. It's linked to fire and alleviating fear. It has a deep connection to Earth, so you can use it during grounding exercises. Fire agate aids in relaxation, increases vitality, and makes you more secure. It eliminates cravings, assists in overcoming addictions, and reduces heat within the body. Fire agate will make you courageous and stronger. This doesn't mean you'll get physically stronger, but you'll be stronger in character and in purpose. It is often used to enhance spirituality and to bring the person using it closer to his or her true self. It gives a sense of mystery and intrigue to the wearer, which will draw people to them. Because gemstone-quality fire agates are fairly rare, they also hold a certain amount of prestige. This beautiful stone has red and orange tones and gives the optical illusion of depth when cut properly. Looking at a true fire agate can be like looking into the smoldering coals of a fire.

> * When you need to take
> action but fear is holding
> you back, use fire agate.

219. Jade

Jade is a cleansing and healing stone. It clears you of negativity and allows you to become who you really are on a soul level. Jade awakens hidden knowledge that you hold within yourself as a spiritual entity, in order for you to access this knowledge and progress down your path of enlightenment. Jade is often used to increase the clarity of your dreams, making them more insightful and meaningful on a spiritual plane. It can integrate mind, body, and spirit to connect you to your core spiritual truth. It's a stabilizing stone that releases retained negativity. You can wear this beautiful stone as a necklace, pendant, or earrings, but many people like to wear jade bracelets and wouldn't be caught without them on their arms. Wearing jade infuses your body with a steady influx of powerful, positive energy, which allows you to heal from past emotional pain.

Jade encourages you to understand yourself, to realize your potential, and to act on that potential. Wearing or using jade allows you to see yourself as a spiritual entity and aids in the progression along your spiritual path. It is often considered to be a stone of good luck, good fortune, and protection. It is a stone of purity, serenity, and harmony. It gives shamanic access to the spirit world.

> *Jade comes in a variety of
> green hues, with each one
> having specific attributes.*

220. Kunzite

Kunzite is considered to be a spiritual stone. It is good for the heart, blood pressure, and skin and will give you a sense of overall well-being. It removes obstacles from your path, is protective, and removes negativity. This is a calming stone that is used for centering, which makes it an optimum choice to wear or use during meditation. It is often employed by those who have a lot of tension in their lives because it eliminates stress. Kunzite is frequently used when trying to reach higher levels of consciousness. This pink or lilac gemstone will help you give and receive unconditional love. It aids in the expression of creativity, keeps panic attacks at bay, and helps boost the immune system. Wearing kunzite can also enable you to have more freedom of expression.

Kunzite can detach energies that have attached to you and also protect you from those energies reattaching to you. It is a stone of peace and love. It connects to Universal Energy and thus elevates your core energy when you wear it. When you're having emotional problems, kunzite can bring you balance and alleviate those unwanted emotions, or it can help you understand why you're feeling the way you do. It brings together the intuitive and logical parts of our nature and inspires us to greater heights.

> * Kunzite is often worn
> as a pendant to increase
> its effectiveness.

221. Magnesite

Magnesite is a pale or colorless crystal that allows you to learn to love yourself and others. It is regularly used in situations where giving unconditional love is difficult due to the behavior of the person you love. Often used in cases of addictions, it enables you to stay grounded while dealing with the addicted person's problems. It has calming properties that increases your tolerance of people and situations. In its natural state, magnesite roughly resembles the human brain, therefore it enhances everything associated with your mind and thoughts. It boosts your brain power, brings new ideas, and can make you more creative. It promotes originality, inventive ideas, and dynamic thoughts. When studying, keeping magnesite nearby or on your person will help you to retain more information.

If you place magnesite over your third eye, it will enhance your clairvoyant ability. It lets you look at life in a positive manner, enhances your listening ability and gives you the capacity to hide in the shadows. It's often used as a healing crystal for people who have a magnesium deficiency. It decreases headaches, relieves stomach cramps, and increases the metabolism of fat in the body. If you're irritable, magnesite can help rid you of this negative attribute and enable you to regain a sense of focus.

> *Magnesite can help you
> remain calm and tolerant.*

222. Moonstone

Moonstone is connected to the moon because it looks a lot like the moon—pearly and a bit reflective. It is used by people interested in metaphysics because it increases all types of psychic abilities, especially clairvoyance, mediumistic abilities, lucid dreaming, and intuition. It's more powerful during the full moon. It makes us remember our dreams and increases how deeply we feel things. It's considered to be a lucky crystal, a stone of new beginnings. Moonstone assists in keeping emotions under control, decreases overreaction to situations, and cools aggressive tendencies. It opens your mind to serendipity and synchronicities.

There is a warning associated with moonstone: It can sometimes cause difficulties with getting caught up in illusion. If you're already prone to that type of thinking, you need to be careful when using this crystal. Otherwise you could end up lost in a fantastical metaphysical world. You'll be so caught up in the "woo-woo" of psychic abilities, the cosmos, the Universe and its laws that you'll forget to stay grounded in reality. If you're finding that you're beginning to think that you're the be-all and end-all in the New Age movement, then don't acquire moonstone and get rid of any you have. It's better to be grounded in reality and the truth of metaphysics than to be in lost in the clouds of your greatness.

* Wear moonstone as a symbol of acceptance of your psychic abilities.

223. Onyx

Onyx is a stone that is often used to increase self-realization; however, it also has a bad reputation as being used by egotists. It is also believed to cool down lust when worn as a pendant. Onyx allows us to pursue our goals and is often used by people who are followers as opposed to those inclined to be leaders. Conversely, it gives more self-confidence and the ability to be assertive and makes you feel at ease in unfamiliar places. It promotes the making of wise decisions instead of foolish ones. Onyx stimulates the quest for knowledge, thought processes, and improved concentration. It's thought to be a stone of secrets that can hold your energy inside itself. Through psychometry, psychics can touch an onyx stone that holds your energy and read this information. Onyx is also useful in accessing past-life information and in healing past-life traumas that could still be affecting you in your current lifetime. In addition, it can also help you see into the future and will give you the strength needed in order to master your destiny. Onyx is useful in making you more productive in the world, helping you break bad habits, and multitasking easily and efficiently. Because of its black color, onyx can absorb the sun's energy and bring it into the body, energizing and rejuvenating you.

> *Onyx is also helpful when
> you need to make decisions;
> it brings the wearer luck
> and happiness.*

224. Pyrolusite

Pyrolusite lets you get to the truth of matters, especially problems, so you can see the solution. It repels negative energy from the aura, promotes confidence, and boosts determination. If you're having a problem with a friend or loved one, wearing pyrolusite will help to resolve the situation quickly by making you more optimistic and more confident. True to its black color, pyrolusite can provide strong protection. If you have mediumistic tendencies, it keeps interference from the spiritual world at bay and is often used to prevent psychic attack. It can restructure energy. Pyrolusite can be used with specific intention to bring about significant changes in your life. If you're debating whether or not to make a change in your life, you can use this stone to aid you in making your decision by wearing it while meditating about how you should proceed. It allows you to stay true to your core spiritual nature and the beliefs that you hold as your truth. It prevents others from manipulating your emotions. Pyrolusite can protect you from toxins and danger if worn or kept on your person. This crystal also gives you material comfort when it comes to your possessions.

> *Pyrolusite can block
> entities from the lower astral
> planes from interfering
> in your life and attaching
> themselves to you.*

225. Rose Quartz

Quartz is one of the most powerful crystals on Earth. Regardless of the color used, quartz amplifies energy and is often used in spiritual work because it can take your spiritual energy to the highest level attainable. It enhances psychic abilities, tunes you in to your soul's purpose, and increases your connection to your core spiritual being.

Rose quartz, specifically, is the crystal of unconditional love, infinite peace, and serenity. It promotes loving yourself, loving others, and inner healing. It's often used to bring healing to relationships, whether those relationships are between loved ones or coworkers. It's useful in bringing calmness to traumatic situations. During stressful times in your life—the birth of a child, the death of a loved one, a midlife crisis, or a change in your employment status—keeping rose quartz on you at all times will mediate the high stress levels and shorten their duration.

Rose quartz can be used to bring love to you or to drain negativity and replace it with positive, loving energy. It can be used to elevate your frequency because it specifically works with you internally, increasing not only frequency but feelings of self-esteem, self-worth, self-trust, self-forgiveness, and an overall acceptance of your true spiritual nature.

Place rose quartz around
your home or wear it on
your person to connect to
and enhance your true
spiritual being.

226. Ruby

Ruby promotes positive dreams and aids against psychic attack. It allows you to keep wealth, aids in survival issues, and guides you to follow your desires. This brilliant red stone can be used to energize you and give you more vigor in your life, but you have to be careful because it tends to overstimulate and can cause negative traits like anger to arise. It is good to use when you're making changes in your life, especially new beginnings. Ruby is often used in distance healing and gives you the will to live during illness. It is a rejuvenating stone that will fill you with enthusiasm for life and can bring you up when you're feeling down. It's an excellent stone to use because it gives passion and drive. Ruby wakes you up, increases awareness, and attracts sexual energy to you. It's a stone of abundance, balance, health, and protection. It increases your ability to learn.

When you want to increase your psychic abilities, ruby should be part of your gemstone/crystal collection. Ruby crystals are used during astral travel to give focus and intention to the work. It will allow you to acknowledge psychic gifts that you may not have even realized you possessed. It's also been used to help earthbound spirits leave places where they're not wanted by humans or cross over to the Other Side.

> *Leaders often wear
> ruby for its ability to
> increase motivation.*

227. Sapphire

The only crystal that is harder than sapphire is a diamond. Sapphire is known as the "wisdom stone" and comes in a variety of colors. For example, black sapphire gives confidence in your own intuition, blue sapphire brings you spiritual truth, green improves your psychic visions, pink aids in manifestation, purple awakens you spiritually, royal rids you of negativity, star opens your intuition, white greatly increases frequency and spiritual awareness, and yellow attracts wealth. It is also known as a stone of prosperity and gives the wearer the ability to attract both material and nonmaterial gifts and to easily fulfill their hopes, dreams, and desires.

Sapphire brings serenity, motivates you to reach your true nature, helps you to know and accept yourself, and neutralizes depression. It encourages you to be straightforward and honest. Sapphire also increases your belief and motivates you to seek out truths and gain knowledge. It assists in the elimination of the things in your life that no longer serve your greater good. Sapphire can help you break ties with people in your life who tend to pull you down more than they lift you up. It also aids in the connection to your spirit guides, spiritual wisdom, accessing the Akashic Records, and in astral traveling. Sapphire has healing properties that can help you overcome physical, mental, and spiritual problems.

*Wear sapphire to ease the
path to your dreams.*

228. Smoky Quartz

Smoky quartz raises your personal vibration, especially when used during meditation, as it is a grounding and protecting stone. It releases negativity and fills the empty space with positive energy. It releases fear of failure and depression and aids in detoxification. This stone can promote positive thought, healing, stress reduction, focused concentration, and communication. It allows you to relax, deal with sorrow, and makes you more resilient during times of difficulty.

Wearing smoky quartz will give you a realistic approach to life instead of living with your head in the clouds. If you're having bad luck and financial problems, you need to have smoky quartz on you at all times. Not only does this crystal help to keep bad luck away from you, it can also help you regain control of your finances and greatly improve them. If you're having body image issues, don't get plastic surgery; instead, try using a smoky quartz crystal to become more accepting of your body. If you need to exercise, work out with smoky quartz in your pocket to get faster results. Smoky quartz will keep your spiritual energy grounded. Lots of the smoky quartz you find in stores is manmade, but natural smoky quartz will give you faster and longer-lasting results than the synthetic variety.

> *Place smoky quartz under
> your pillow at night to rid
> yourself of nightmares and
> increase positive,
> happy dreams.

229. Sunstone

Sunstone is a very positive crystal that will give you strength, energy, and vitality. Like the bright sun, this brilliant stone brings abundance to all areas of your life and increases longevity and health. It eliminates fear and stress and protects you from negative energy and entities. Sunstone is related to the sun and gives us a more "sunny" nature and even-tempered attitude. It improves overall mood, makes you more optimistic, and can help you heal yourself. It has an antidepressant effect on the body overall. If you're going through hormonal changes in your life (puberty, midlife crisis, menopause), carrying sunstone with you can help to bring emotional balance until your hormones are stabilized.

Spiritually sunstone allows you to connect to the truth of yourself on a soul level and lets you live life according to that truth. Its connection to the sun will allow you to raise your frequency by tuning in to the intense frequency of the sun. It increases confidence and feelings of self-worth. Sunstone gives us the feeling that we need to take action, to move forward in life and live life to the fullest. If you can't say no to others, always carry sunstone with you so that you have the willpower to say no; by doing so, you indirectly help the person asking you for help to stand on their own.

*Sunstone will give you
new perspectives on life.*

230. Tiger's Eye

Tiger's eye has a high vibrational rate, is grounded, and has the capability to draw spiritual energy to you. When you're weak or sick, wearing tiger's eye will help to increase your strength and get you well faster. It has properties that encourage the flow of energy throughout your body, which aids in healing.

Tiger's eye also increases your intuition and gut instincts. It's often carried to ward off negative energy from those wishing you harm. It brings out your integrity and honesty. It will motivate you to accomplish goals that you've set for yourself and aids in manifesting desires. It allows you to be clear in your intention when working with spirituality, whether in your career or your home life. You will be more committed to all that you undertake. It can clarify wishful thinking by showing you the reality of a situation. Tiger's eye is in direct connection to how a person feels about themselves. It can assist when you have blocks in your path or if you're being overly critical of yourself. This luminous golden or red-brown gem makes you pay attention to details and gives you more energy. It makes you more courageous in the face of danger or controversy, strengthens your morals and convictions, and gives you more overall confidence in all that you do.

Use tiger's eye when you feel the need to "go for" something in your life or when you need to achieve immediate results.

231. Topaz

Topaz is an important crystal to use when you need to direct energy to a specific area within your body or soul, as you would do when undertaking energy work. It is a stone that stimulates and recharges you physically, emotionally, and especially spiritually. It promotes truth, not only in your words but in the way you feel about your own spirituality. It also allows you to more readily forgive yourself and others, which is important when it comes to releasing negativity within your core spiritual essence. The positive energy of topaz brings joy and abundance to you. It's useful when you're manifesting. It will stimulate your discovery of the riches residing inside of you on a soul level and will encourage you to share those parts of yourself. It allows you to develop and listen to your own inner wisdom and soul truths, to grow spiritually, and aids you when you share that wisdom and knowledge with others by giving you the ability to speak clearly and with authority. Known as a stone of good fortune, topaz is often associated with success in business as well as personal success and growth. In its pure state, topaz is clear, but it is often tinted with impurities that lend it other colors. It is often used to cleanse the aura, to increase your ability to speak clearly, to become more aware on all levels, and to recharge your vitality.

> * Topaz is often used to
> increase faith in yourself,
> others, and spirituality.

232. Tourmaline

All tourmalines will increase your self-confidence and increase your psychic abilities while helping you grow to a greater understanding within yourself. Many are used when communicating with the higher realms, specifically spirit guides. There are a variety of colors of tourmaline available and each of them has specific purposes. Black tourmaline is often used to repel psychic attacks and negative energy. It is a highly protective, grounding stone that's also used in scrying and to clear the aura. It relieves stress and encourages positivity of mind, body, and spirit. Blue tourmaline is useful in increasing psychic visions and is often used by healers so that the negative energy they release from the person they're helping doesn't attach to their own energy. It's also worn to destress. Pink tourmaline attracts love, while green tourmaline aids in visualization and dispelling fears. Yellow tourmaline enhances personal power.

There are many more colors of tourmaline than I've mentioned here. Regardless of the color of tourmaline you use, this crystal will allow you to increase your frequency since it works with your energy and emotions. Stick a few under your pillow to recharge yourself overnight. During the day you could wear a tourmaline bracelet to recharge—just make sure the tourmaline touches your skin for the best connection.

> *Use a variety of
> tourmaline colors to benefit
> you on many levels of
> spiritual growth.*

233. Unakite

Unakite is called a "stone of vision" because it balances your spiritual self with your emotional self, combining green and pink colors in mottled patterns. It can guide you when connecting to your higher self and the spiritual planes. It is often used to aid access to past lives, to bring the memory forward so you can readily recall details of that past lifetime. It's also useful in your current lifetime to become more accepting on a soul level of your past-life experiences, especially when they are negative. It aids in understanding and learning from these experiences. Oftentimes when you are able to understand the root cause of a past-life problem, you can rid yourself of any physical connection in this lifetime.

When you're having blocks in your life, unakite can alleviate them or move them out of your way so you can make forward progress on your life path. When used in expanding your spirituality, it enhances your ability to have clairvoyant impressions and gives more strength to creative visualization, especially if placed on your third eye during these activities. It radiates a calm energy, which makes it useful in removing negativity. Unakite is often used for scrying and in emotional and spiritual growth activities. It helps you recover more quickly from illness by bringing the cause of the illness to the forefront.

*Use unakite to clear
electromagnetic pollution
from your home by placing
it near the source.*

234. ZOISITE

Whenever you need to convert negativity to positivity in your life, zoisite is the crystal to use. Its primary property is the conversion of energy from bad to good. It aids in the connection to the spiritual realms. This is a creative crystal often used in manifesting because of these properties. It's a hard, slow-acting stone, so it's important to wear it in contact with your skin for long periods of time. Wearing it as a pendant or bracelet works well as long as the actual stone touches your flesh. As a protective stone, zoisite keeps undue influences away from you, especially those people who want to bend you to their will or who try to get you to act in ways that are out of character for you. It keeps your own negativity at bay. It will help you realize your dreams while following your own path instead of the norm. Zoisite will keep you active and in the moments of your life. If you have destructive habits, wearing zoisite can turn those negative tendencies into positive, constructive behavior, and it works really well for laziness. This is also a good crystal to use when you've been sick, as it quickens your recovery time. This angular crystal is usually pale in color and has a beautiful luster.

*Zoisite can help you
mentally return to your task
if you are interrupted.*

235. Crystal Ring/ Necklace

Wearing a crystal ring or necklace raises your energy, centers you, aids in protection, and keeps negative energy away. There are thousands of different kinds of crystals, only a few of which I've discussed in this book. Depending on what you want the crystal for and what you've programmed it to do, if you wear it on your body, you have a constant connection to that crystal's energy. You can wear a crystal as a ring or pendant, make a bunch of them into a necklace or bracelet, adorn your watch with them, or wear them in many other ways. Wearing crystals can attune your body and your energy to the energy of the crystal. If you don't have a crystal you wear on a regular basis, go to a store and use your instinct and intuition to find a crystal that you feel a connection with and wear it to see how it works for you. You may even want to put a crystal on your key chain. Men can put a small crystal in their wallets and carry it in their back pocket all of the time. It's still connected to you because you're carrying it on your person. The constant connection to the crystal and what that crystal means to you will motivate you to increase your energy on a daily basis.

*Keep a crystal close for
empowerment and focus.*

236. Crystal Cleaning

I found several large quartz crystals on our farm when I was a kid. One of them I cleaned and kept in my pocket or purse for years. The other two I left dirty because I like that they hold soil from our farm; I always have a piece of home with me. Usually you want to cleanse your crystals as soon as you obtain them. You can do this with a damp washcloth or a little soapy water, depending on how dirty the crystals are. Just be careful that you don't chip or crack the stone.

Getting the dirt off is only part of the cleansing process; you also want to clear it of any residual energy. Unless you dug it out of the ground, other people probably handled your crystal before you owned it, leaving behind an imprint of their energy. You want the crystal to be attuned to your energy alone so you can use it to elevate your personal vibration. You need to remove all energy that isn't a natural part of the crystal, even if it's someone else's positive energy.

My favorite clearing method is to use creative visualization to "white light" the crystal. I imagine white light flowing through the crystal, illuminating every facet of it, leaving its natural energy intact but removing any other imprints. Another easy method is to hold it and gently blow your breath over all its surfaces. In your mind, intend that all negative energy be released from the crystal and flow off of it and away from you. If other people handle your crystal, you'll want to repeat this process. Don't do it in front of the person—you wouldn't want to hurt their feelings. You can also cleanse your crystals with ocean or salt water, but be careful, as some crystals will disintegrate in water.

> *Cleanse crystals so they
> remain pure and best
> able to serve you.*

237. Crystal
Programming

In any kind of metaphysical work, you should always work with the purest of intention, to bring the greater good of the Universe to yourself and those around you. This especially applies to crystals because they have higher frequencies and will attract negative energy if you're not using them properly. While you may work with the best intention, your mind could wander or negativity could slip into your thoughts. It's always a good idea to cleanse all previously absorbed energy from crystals and program them prior to first use so they'll always work for the greater good.

To do this, you first cleanse and clear the crystal by holding it between the palms of your hands. Focus on the clear, radiant energy of the crystal as you say out loud that the crystal will only be used for good and that it will never be used for harm. Then give the crystal a specific purpose relevant to your needs. It may be that it will protect you from malicious people or it will calm you down when you're stressed out. Focus on this intent while you hold the crystal, looking deeply into the stone. If your goals change over time, you can cleanse and reprogram your crystal for a new purpose.

> *Program crystals to aid
> you in achieving specific
> goals in your life.*

Part Seven

Manifestation

238. Risk and Trust

Trust is a big issue in today's society. Many times there isn't a reason to trust others or to take any risks at all. It's better to play it safe, stay out of everyone else's way, and only trust in yourself, right? Not necessarily. There are times when you must take a risk and dare to trust. If you've been hurt in the past, this can be a difficult feat to accomplish. Still, you have to try. Not every person you trust will betray you, and not every risk you take will put you in danger. It is the *fear* of risking and trusting that keeps your energy at a lower level. It takes positive energy to take a risk and trust in the outcome or to trust in another, especially when you've been hurt because you gave your heart and soul to another only to have that precious gift betrayed. In order to trust others, you have to be sure of your trust in yourself and then step out of your comfort zone. You have to accept yourself as you are, know your strengths and weaknesses, and be okay with those qualities about yourself. Then you must let your guard down, step outside of any boundaries that you've put up to protect yourself, and give part of yourself to another.

> *＊Belief in your soul*
> *essence is essential in*
> *trusting others.*

239. Close Your Eyes and Look Beyond

There's an old saying that sometimes you can't see the forest for the trees when you're in a tough situation. Everyone else around you might see the forest, the truth of what is happening, but you're just lost, looking at one tree and then another, unable to see the overall picture of what you're going through. How can you raise your energy in times like these?

First, see yourself involved in the situation; be cognizant of the way you interact with the other people involved. Look at the situation, let the scenes of what you're going through unfold in your mind as if it's on a movie screen. Now imagine trees growing up from the ground, filling in the area until you can't see anything but the trees. The people you were with are lost somewhere within the trees. You can no longer see rooms, buildings, or roads that may have been part of the scene playing out in your mind. There's nothing in front of you but the trunks of trees, the bark rough against your hands, their leaves high above you in a canopy that keeps you in the shade or dark. You feel the coolness of the forest and the dirt beneath your feet. Close your eyes. Imagine that you are standing still and the trees are moving away from you at a great speed. The trees somehow rush away from you, leaving you in the open. When you feel that the trees are no longer surrounding you, open your eyes. The forest is now in the distance and the situation you are involved in is being played out, your part included, in a clearing just outside of the forest. It's far away but you can hear and see everything that is going on as if you're right there. Watch the situation from the outside looking in. Now you see the forest, the whole situation, and not just the trees, those individual events you're involved in. Listen closely to what the people are saying and the actions they're taking as you watch the situation unfold before you.

Look at how you act and respond to them. Now that you've stepped back, do you see something different? Do you notice emotions you couldn't see before? Are you at fault in any way, or is someone acting without your best interest at heart? Do you see something in yourself that you don't like? Now is the time to face the truth of the situation and make changes in your life to improve it.

*See the forest of your
personal circumstances for
greater understanding
and clarity.*

240. Thoughts and Words Have Power

I'm a firm believer that your words have power, that what you say goes out into the Universe and will come back to you in abundance. Because of this, it's important that you make sure your thoughts and words are filled with positive intent so you can bring positivity back to you. When you think in a negative way, it is often reflected in your actions and words. It's necessary to keep your thoughts just as positive as your words so that there aren't any ill effects on your actions. People don't like to be around Mr. or Ms. Negativity, so keep pure intent and positive focus through your thoughts, words, and actions.

Since I believe this, I try very hard to not say negative things that might come back to bite me in the butt later. That doesn't mean I never complain or snap. I can lose my temper just like everyone else, but when I do, I try to find my focus and bring my soul energy back to center and then infuse it with positivity by saying something to balance the negative thing. Negative thoughts hold the same power as negative words. I try to stay positive in my thought processes as well. I'm also grounded, so I understand there will be days when I'm overwhelmed with negativity from other people or frustrated with situations that bring out the worst in me. When these times come along and I fall into the flow of negativity and lower my frequency, I try to recognize this right away and take steps to counteract it by doing or saying something positive.

As a young adult, my group of friends had a running joke. Whenever something happened that was negative or that we wished hadn't happened, we'd pretend to hold a television remote control and we'd say "delete, delete, delete" to erase whatever just happened. Sure it was corny, but when we talk about energy work, deleting whatever you just did that is

negative and then replacing it with something positive raises your awareness and energy. Because words have magnetic power, whatever you say
will come back to you. For example, if you said to someone, "I hope you
fall and break your leg!" you just may be the one to fall and break a leg.
Or if you tell someone that you hope they get the promotion at work, you
may also get a promotion. See how it works?

*Put positive thoughts
and words into the Universe
to reap rewards.*

241. Try One New Thing

When was the last time you tried something new? When you try new things, your energy will automatically increase because the effort taken to do something new raises your energy's rate of motion. What could you do new today? Have you ever been bungee jumping? If you have, good for you! If you're like me, you may want to keep your feet firmly planted on the ground instead of diving headfirst off a bridge attached to a big rubber band. I'm not that much of a daredevil. Instead of plummeting to the ground at ninety miles an hour, maybe you'd like to try the new frozen drink the local restaurant has concocted for the season. If it's a flavor you've never tasted before, give it a try. Trying something new doesn't have to be as scary as jumping off a bridge. It doesn't matter if the something new you're trying is simple or difficult, safe or dangerous. You have to try new things that appeal to you and that you think you'll enjoy. Staying stuck in your safety zone and never trying anything new will eventually put you into a boring rut. You'll have the same routine, the same experiences over and over again, just because you're unwilling or afraid to take a chance on change.

> *Challenge yourself to have
> a new experience today.*

242. WRITE AN
ABUNDANCE CHECK

Sometimes you just need more abundance in your life. Not just an abundance of money, although that would be nice, but an abundance of blessings, work, friends, etc. An abundance check is a way to manifest more riches in your life, regardless of the type of riches you want to attract. Don't be surprised if your abundance shows up in an area that you didn't intend. The Universe will give you what you need even if you don't realize you need it at the time. It's a connection between the Universal Energy and your subconscious mind that manifests the abundance you seek.

First, find out when the new moon is each month. An abundance check should always be written in the twenty-four hours after the new moon. On this date, take a check out of your checkbook and fill it out. If you don't have a checking account, be creative and make a drawing of a check. This is all about intention and your energy behind creating the abundance check for yourself. Put your name on the "pay to" line, the words "paid in full" in the dollar amount box and on the line under "pay to" where you write out the amount in words. Then sign the check with "The Law of Abundance." Don't date the check and don't fill in anything in the memo section because you don't want to limit what the Universe may give you. Put the check somewhere for safekeeping, imagining that it's sending its energy out to the Universe. Now forget about the check. This is important; if you're continually worrying about whether or not it's working, you're defeating the purpose. Allow the abundance check to do its job.

*You deserve abundance in
your life; draw it to you and
embrace it as the gift it is.*

243. Letter to God

A good exercise to do is to write a letter to God, or whoever heads your religion or system of faith. Write down all the things that you'd like to say to God should you meet face-to-face. Ask questions and explain your troubles. Feel free to write anything and everything that you want to say in your letter. Doing this will raise your core essence because you are clearing your soul and unburdening yourself in the letter, while getting things off your chest. If you're having a particular problem, tell God all about it in detail showing the pros, cons, and possibilities. You may find that you even come up with answers to your questions or solutions to your problems as you're writing the letter. That's God helping you find answers as you write to him. You're working out your situation both in your mind and on paper. This exercise releases frustration, annoyance, hurts, and confusions. It can make you less stressed once you've finished writing. It doesn't matter if you believe in a Father God, Mother God, or both, or if you believe in goddesses or in any other name for the greater source of energy from which we came. Write the letter to the being that you believe in. If you don't believe in any religion, write the letter to yourself.

> *Using pen and paper,*
> *write from the heart with*
> *emotions pouring forth*
> *like rain.*

244. Make a
Manifestation Board

Sometimes called a vision board, this tool is used to bring things into your life that you desire. It's basically putting your positive thoughts and affirmations in visual form to represent your strongest desires. It is also important because you're making a positive forward motion to do something for your own spiritual energy. When you create a manifestation board, you can make it on a poster board, a cork board with push pins, or any type of material that feels right to you. Once you select the material for your board, the next thing that you'll do is make a list of the things you'd like to manifest in your life. It may be a better job, a more reliable car, or a deeper understanding of spirituality. The things you choose to manifest can be material or spiritual. If you're having difficulties coming up with what to manifest, try thinking of the things you don't want in your life and then write down the opposite of it.

The next thing you'll do is find images from magazines or other print sources that show what you will achieve once you have manifested your desires. You may have a picture of a car you'd like or a person in a yoga position to indicate a deeper spiritual understanding. Choosing the pictures helps you to decide what the most important things are to you at this point in time. As you choose pictures of the things you desire, think about why they are so important to you. If you're putting a picture on your board and something just feels off about it, maybe it doesn't belong there. Evaluate that item more closely to uncover the reason it feels odd. Does something else seem to fit better than that item? If so, use that instead. Now place the pictures on the board in any random order. As time passes, you'll update the pictures as things manifest in your life. Once you have the better job or nicer home, you can remove that picture and put something else in its place.

The final part of this exercise is the most important. You need to put the manifestation board somewhere you'll see it throughout the day, every day. You don't have to sit and stare at it for a half hour in the morning and evening, but you do want it close by so you can see it easily. Whenever you look at your board, visualize what you want in your life. Take a minute every time you notice the board and imagine one of the items on it coming to you. As you do this throughout the day, the positive thoughts and creative visualization will bring a heightened sense of attraction to your energy, which will bring the items on your board into your life.

Place desires before you
to bring them to you.

245. Invent Something

Have you ever had a fantastic idea for a new product or method of doing something? Maybe it was a really great idea, but you didn't pursue it, either because you didn't believe in yourself or you thought actually "inventing" something would be too hard. I'm a firm believer that there are a gazillion ideas flowing in the Universal Energy and that at any given time, you could be either given the idea for a product or new method of doing something or you could tap into this energy and snag an idea for yourself. What you do with one of these ideas is up to you. If you don't act on it, then someone else may snag that same idea and do something with it before you can. You're utilizing your creative nature in conjunction with a unique idea, so connect with the energy of the Universe and then stick your hand in and see what you pull out. It may be the next fantastic idea on the marketplace if you pursue it. Even if you don't come up with the next amazing piece of technology, you'll be exercising your creativity in a new way, which will raise your frequency while you're having fun.

> *You can invent anything*
> *if you'll only try!*

246. Active
Creative Visualization

Creative visualization is a fantastic tool that you can use every day to manifest the things you want in life, make changes, and project your needs and desires into the Universe so the law of attraction can bring them back to you. It's easy and only takes seconds to do. Try this exercise. If there is something you want to change in your life, imagine the change you want to happen, then send your desired change and outcome into the Universe. This is positive action that will help manifest what you want and need in your life. Let's look at some examples. Maybe you want a promotion at work with a corner office. Each morning when you walk into work, imagine you're turning into that office instead of going down the hall to your own. Imagine your name on the door plaque. Maybe you need a new car; when you're driving, imagine you're driving the car of your dreams. Maybe you'd like a new watch; every time you look at your watch, visualize the one you want on your wrist. By seeing yourself doing, wearing, and being what you are striving to realize in your life, you actively use creative visualization while you're participating in the activity of drawing what you truly want to you.

Today, pick one thing—large or small—to begin manifesting with simple daily creative visualization.

*See yourself being who you
want to be, obtaining what
you want in life.

247. Connect with
the Frequency of Air

When you connect to the frequency of air, it's different from connecting to the wind. Yes, wind is air in motion, but for this exercise I want you to think of air instead of wind. To connect to the air, imagine it as being completely still around you. It's unmoving, so still that you can almost touch it. Take a deep breath, feel the air as you inhale and exhale. Move your arms and feel the air around you. Does it have a positive or negative charge? Sometimes the air around us is positively charged and there may be a calm stillness to it. There's nothing happening, nothing going on, the wind's not blowing, the air is just still. Now breathe in that positively charged air. How does it feel? Is it increasing your energy as it fills your lungs? It should. Now what if the air is negatively charged? How can you tell? If you're sitting in a room and the air is negatively charged, you're not going to feel so great. You're going to feel anxious or nervous or something will feel off. There is a way you can correct a negatively charged air feeling. When you breathe out, use creative visualization to positively charge the carbon dioxide that you're breathing out. When that breath is released, imagine all of those positive particles converting all the negative particles in the room to positive as they touch them.

Through creative visualization, you've changed the way you feel about the charge in the air. You've changed it from a negative to a positive and have increased your frequency. You have to breathe to live, right? Start to become more aware of each breath that you take. Feel the air invigorate and energize you. Every time that you're aware of your breathing, think about increasing your energy by converting any negativity around you to positivity. Every time you move through the air, even if the air is still, use creative visualization to imagine something positive. You may imagine that you're swimming through the air. The air may feel thick and you have to force your way through it—not in a negative way, but as if you're feeling the resistance of the air around you. All of these things increase your frequency because you're making yourself utilize and influence something that you can't even see.

> * Feel the stillness; in it you
> will connect to your soul.

248. Make an Effort, Meet a Deadline

Being organized and striving to meet deadlines revs up the energy within you because you're working diligently to meet your goals. Even self-imposed deadlines will achieve the same results and have a positive effect on your energy. Just making an effort works because your energy is moving at a faster rate, thus raising itself to a higher point. Set goals for yourself and make a valiant effort to reach those goals by a self-imposed deadline. If you don't have any goals set for yourself, now is the time to make some in all areas of your life: career, personal life, spirituality, home life, or any other goals that fit your lifestyle needs. The act of putting something into action through its creation and striving to meet a goal associated with what you want will help you achieve it.

When you put deadlines on yourself, you can also avoid falling into that pesky negative action called procrastination—putting off until tomorrow what you could do today by choosing to do less important tasks that can stand to wait. As you put forth the effort to meet your deadline, self-imposed or otherwise, you can avoid procrastinating by looking at the whole project in small sections. This will give you feelings of accomplishment prior to completing the entire project. Today, take steps to meet an important deadline.

*Organization lends
itself to stronger focus and
personal success.*

249. Create a Group and Meet Together

Oftentimes you will have greater success doing energy work if you come together as a group instead of trying to achieve your goals alone. In a group setting, each person acts as a support system for the others, providing encouragement and different points of view. If four or five of your friends are all doing energy work, get together and do the work together. Name your group, set a meeting place and time, and then stick with it. Have a different person plan the meeting each session so that everyone has a turn to be the group leader. While each person will add positive suggestions and thoughts at the meeting, giving one person the opportunity to take the lead and have the group do exercises they find personally helpful gives a feeling of positivity to the overall energy of the group. Meet once a week or once a month, talk about your progress, and tell people about your group so that it grows. At your meetings you can do your own exercises or use exercises I've shared within these pages. After you've finished the exercise for the meeting, discuss how you felt during the exercise, suggestions for improvement, or other ideas. Keep notes in a planner so you'll know what topics you've covered in the past and have a place to jot down ideas for upcoming meetings.

> *Group efforts are a fun
> way to obtain a connection
> to Universal Energy.

250. Surround Yourself
with Like-Minded People

It's hard to work on your energy when you're surrounded by people who don't share the same beliefs or who are so negative that their main goal in life is to make you as miserable as they are. It's easier to be successful when you're surrounded by people who are of a like mind and who are striving to achieve the same or similar goals. This applies to all areas of your life: exercise, studies, career, or business. Look in your area for people who specifically work with energy to see if they offer classes. If you find any, this could be a great way to meet people who share your interest in energy work. As you get to know them better, you'll find those who are interested in specific subareas of energy work. You'll make new friends, find people who share your goals, and interact with others who think like you do.

Surrounding yourself with successful people who aren't necessarily interested in energy work is also a smart decision. They are motivated, have a plan of action to reach their goals, and are usually optimistic with a bright outlook on their future. People who are successful can influence you to be more successful. You'll aim high and strive to reach your goals just as they do. They're a positive influence on you.

> *Plant yourself in the
> middle of a successful,
> positive group to achieve
> your goals.

251. Daydream about Goals

Daydreaming is letting your mind relax and roam freely in any direction it wants to go in. When you daydream about your goals, you put yourself in a semitrance and imagine yourself in a situation you'd like to happen. You're projecting a final outcome in your mind that is positive and happy. By doing this, you're giving equal and like energy to what you want to occur. You're removing clutter from your mind while fantasizing about something you'd like to manifest or reliving some random event, changing the actual outcome to what you wished had taken place instead of the way it actually transpired. If you're daydreaming about upcoming plans, add some intention to the daydream to give your thoughts even more powerful energy. As you daydream, your personal vibration rises, connecting with the energy of your goal so you strive harder to reach it. It's similar to affirmations. The more you say something over and over, the more you believe it and strive to reach that goal, the easier it becomes to attain it. You're actually bringing it into your life by saying what you want in a positive manner. You're manifesting your goals and increasing your frequency in regards to that goal as you daydream about it.

> * *Walk in the day of your*
> *dreams to find the secret of*
> *your success.*

252. Affirmation Stickers

Saying positive affirmations during the day is a great way to stay on track when doing any kind of spiritual work or to help you stay upbeat and positive when faced with drama in your daily life. Put a fun twist on affirmations by writing them on stickers and then placing them in random places where you will see them throughout the day. For instance, you may put one on the bathroom mirror, one inside the fridge, one in your car, or several around your workplace. When you see these affirmation stickers, read them out loud. Put the positive words on the sticker out into the Universe so they can come back to you in abundance. Be solid in your belief in the affirmations. When you feel doubt creeping in, especially when life gets stressful, seek out one of your affirmation stickers and say it out loud until you feel better. You can make your own creative stickers by cutting them out of colorful cardboard, decorating them, and then taping them to whatever surface you'd like. Or you can buy precut designs in various shapes and colors that already have the sticky backing on them. This is quicker and easier, but if you're a creative person, designing the notes yourself will also help raise your spiritual core energy.

> * Play hide-and-seek with
> affirmations by having a
> friend place the stickers
> for you.

253. Visualize Obstacles

We all have obstacles in our path. Sometimes those obstacles feel like huge boulders blocking us from what we truly seek. How can you get rid of the obstacles in front of you and raise your frequency at the same time? One way is to imagine that each obstacle is a stone or a boulder, depending on the size of the obstacle. Use creative visualization to imagine that you're standing at the beginning of a path and your way is littered with stones and boulders blocking your way—little ones, big ones, medium-sized ones. As you walk the path and encounter each stone or boulder, give it a name. Pick up each stone up and address the issue (e.g., "I'm not going to let this difficult coworker affect my day tomorrow"), then place the stone off the path and out of your way. Go to the next obstacle. For large problems that are boulders, push them to the side and out of your path. Use creative visualization to imagine solutions to your various obstacles. It may take some pushing and grunting, but by doing this exercise in your mind, you've figured out how you're going to fix the problem. Moving the boulder/stone out of your way releases its hold over you. Do this for each obstacle in your path. Now you have come to a resolution in your mind that you're going to resolve the dilemma and have laid the foundation for a solution. By addressing the issue in a positive manner, you're opening your mind and looking at the issue in a positive light instead of looking at it in the darkness of negativity.

> *Don't hide in the dark*
> *what you can resolve*
> *in the light.*

254. Coincidence
and Frequency

I don't believe in coincidence. I think that everything happens for a reason, even if I don't know the reason at the time or don't understand the why behind the reason. There's always a spiritual purpose behind all of our experiences. It's something that we planned out before we began this life, some lesson we need to learn or that we've agreed to help someone else learn. You might realize this reason two months down the road, a week later, or a minute after it happens; sometimes you'll never discover it in this lifetime. If you believe in coincidence, that means the Universe isn't really functioning properly or things aren't happening as they should on the earthly plane. If you don't believe in coincidence, then you're looking for spiritual purpose behind all of the things that happen in your day-to-day life. You're looking for your motivation and the lesson that you're supposed to learn from every event. By searching for this motivation, you raise your energy patterns at a soul level. Don't chalk something up to coincidence; instead, look for deeper meanings, even when it comes to the little things in your life. Thinking that everything happening to you is a coincidence that doesn't matter is taking the easy way out. Look for deeper meanings to events in your life.

*There is purpose in the
moments surrounding you.*

255. CHANGE YOUR HABITS

Do you do the same old thing in the same old way, day in and day out, over and over again? Isn't that boring? Your frequency thinks so. If you find that you've become a creature of habit, now is the time to kick it up a notch. Instead of doing the same thing each day, make changes. If you have a tuna sandwich every day for lunch, have ham and cheese tomorrow. If you always wear sneakers, put on a pair of dress shoes. If you always go to bed at midnight, try hitting the hay at ten instead. See how much of a difference two more hours of sleep will make in the way you feel the next day. If you have a habit of saying negative things about yourself, turn those negatives into positives by giving yourself a compliment. Turn on your charm with others. When you change your daily habits, you make life more interesting. Make a promise to yourself that today you will do at least one thing differently than you usually do, even if it's as simple as changing your route to work or selecting a different type of food at the grocery store. This adds spice to your life and keeps you out of a boring rut. Before you know it, your habits will have transformed into fun-filled adventures.

> * Add zing and zest to
> your life to uncover glorious
> unexpected moments.

256. Attention, Interest, and Materialization

When you're interested in something and giving it your attention, you're also giving it positive energy. When you give that interest focus, it's easier to manifest it in your life. For instance, if you're interested in the paranormal and you want to bring that into your life, your interest draws it to you. If you decide to go on a ghost hunt, you may not expect anything unusual to happen but when it does, how are you going to react? You may have heard the old saying "Be careful what you wish for," and this idea certainly applies here. If you're not sure the things you're giving focus to are truly wanted in your life, don't seek them out. If you want to learn more about spirituality, then you're putting more energy into bringing positive energy to your core spiritual essence. Don't be surprised when what you're focusing on and learning about manifests in your life. The more attention and positive energy you put out, the more likely it will come back to you in the form of the thing you seek. Most people call this the law of attraction. Many people use this to bring more money to them, career success, or more joy. It doesn't matter what it is you need, want, or desire—by giving it positive energy and asking that it comes to you, it will.

*Be sure that your
desires fit your reality.*

257. Don't Give Up, Have Faith

It's easy to give up when things aren't going well. When you try and try but you can't get ahead, you may feel like just throwing in the towel. Perhaps you've been trying exercise after exercise to raise your frequency and aren't feeling any real results. Never give up in life; never quit. When you persist, the more likely it is that the thing you're pursing will happen. When you give up, maybe you don't really want what you're trying to achieve, you don't have the stamina to accomplish it, or you want it for the wrong reasons. Consider why you're going to give up before you do it. Is it too hard? Is it taking too much time? Once you determine the reason, you can look at the situation in a different manner and use the solution you find to make a positive change to get past the point of giving up. Giving up lowers your energy because you stop trying or think you don't deserve what you're after. Have faith. When you believe in yourself and have faith that you can accomplish your goals, then you'll keep moving forward. If you also have faith in God and the protection of your guides, you will feel safe and secure on your path. This will enable you to push further than you would if you didn't have faith and belief in yourself. Believe that you can do it and you will. Keep trying and experimenting with frequency-raising exercises and you're sure to find some that resonate with you. Never, ever, ever give up!

*Believe and strive
forward to attain your
ultimate goals.*

258. Make a Wish List

When was the last time you wished upon a star? Can you remember when you had a desire so strong that you could feel the emotion leaving you as you wished for something different in your life? This isn't like wishing that annoying coworker would go away. That is negative. What I'm talking about is when you're in a dire situation and are looking for a different result—wishing for something very badly as you say in your mind what you're wishing for. You're making your wish with true feelings behind it, putting it out into the Universe in the hope that it will manifest in your life, so don't wish for something that you don't really want or need. Remember that your wishes are words with power and will come back around to you. Make wishes from the heart. Also make wishes for other people, not just for yourself.

Today, make a wish list and then wish for those things with intention to raise your energy. Wishes should be kept to yourself, not said out loud. Don't just wish for material things but for intangible things like an increase in your spirituality, more love in your life, or that someone who is ill recovers quickly. Don't be selfish when you make your wish list.

*Fill your wishes
with positivity.*

Part Eight

Intention

259. Turn Unplanned
Events into
Opportunities

I believe that everything we experience is planned prior to our birth, but because we are on the human level of existence, you may not always recognize these planned events. On this plane of existence, these experiences may feel like random or unplanned events. You can take advantage of these things by turning them into opportunities. Awareness is an important factor in recognizing opportunity. Let's say you attend a ball game at the local stadium and while you're there you run into the head of programming at a local television station. He's a friend of your father's and you've known him for a long time. Maybe you also have a new project going on at work that would be well suited for a television feature interview. You have two choices: you could say nothing to your father's friend about the project, or you could tell him that you have a new project he may be interested in. He may ask about it and decide that yes, the station would be interested in featuring your new project. You may not have planned to run into this man at the stadium, but you turned a seemingly random event into an opportunity because you took action. Perhaps your soul planned for this opportunity while mapping out your life lessons. Be aware of your world to take advantage of these random opportunities that arise in your life.

> * When you least expect it,
> you'll find an open door
> of opportunity.

260. Don't Respond To Criticism

People are often critical of things they don't understand, ideas that are different than what they know, and people who make them feel uncomfortable. People will criticize you to feel better about themselves, to make you feel small, or to make you appear like an idiot in front of others. When it comes to your spiritual path and getting your energy in line with higher levels of spirituality, you simply cannot listen to criticism. You may find yourself faced with someone who wants to argue every aspect of your beliefs with you. They may tell you that what you believe is wrong. This may be because what you've experienced isn't part of their path. Trying to force someone into your beliefs never works. Just as you came to believe what you do because of your life experiences, they are the same way. When you encounter a skeptic who only wants to criticize you, just don't respond. Let them rant and rave all they want but don't let their tantrum affect you or draw you into their negativity. I've encountered this kind of behavior from people throughout my life. I've been told that there's no way I could possibly believe in the things that I write about and discuss. However, this is my truth based on my experiences. Other people don't have to agree with me and I'm fine with that; I simply ignore their criticisms and continue on my own path.

*Believe in your own truth
and don't let negative people
change those beliefs.*

261. Find Your
Animal Totem

Just as we all have spirit guides, each of us has animal spirits that guide us, also known as animal totems. Animal guides come into your life to deliver messages, and they may be a life guide or short-term guide to help during times of trouble. All animal guides are positive in nature, but some could invoke fear in you because they are trying to get you to change something negative in your life. This is probably something that you need to act upon but feel attached to, such as a self-destructive belief or behavior. This frightening animal totem will keep reappearing to "scare you straight," until you make that change. The animal may be a bear, tiger, or other ferocious beast. They are warning guides; if you see an animal guide that scares you, search your life for what needs changing.

You can't just pick your favorite animal to be your totem. Nor can someone else assign an animal totem to you. The animal spirit picks you. There are two ways to discover what your animal totem is: The first is when an animal appears to you out of nowhere repeatedly. For me a dragonfly is my animal totem right now. Every time I turn around there's a dragonfly in front of my face, just staring at me. Just yesterday I was stopped at a stoplight, looked out of the driver's side window and there was a baby dragonfly hovering right there. The animal totem makes itself known by appearing to you on a regular basis until you notice it.

The second way to discover your animal totem is to seek it out. To do this, lie down, close your eyes, and clear yourself of all negativity. Soon you'll see an animal in your mind's eye. Regardless of the animal, it is your totem even if it's an animal that you dislike, like a snake. The animal totem doesn't care if you like it or not. It has a job to do in your life, and it will do it. Connect to your animal totem, embrace it, and communicate with it as much as you can. After you finish the exercise, honor your animal totem by wearing its image on your clothing or as a necklace, by supporting it in the wild, or by donating to rescues for the animal. If your totem is an animal that is used for food or clothing, however, do not eat or wear the animal's products. That's just not cool. You could protect your totem animal through various organizations and shelters. Throughout your life you'll find that you may have more than one animal totem. Some come and go, and some stay with you forever.

Your animal totem
is by your side, guiding,
protecting, and
enabling you.

262. Put Feelings
Behind Your Words

Have you ever talked with someone and felt they weren't really listening to what you were saying? Their response to you might have been vague, consisting of noises or short things like *okay*, *yes*, *sure*, or *I guess*. After the conversation, you felt like you'd been talking to yourself or to the wall. You probably were. Do you do this same thing to other people when they're talking to you? If you are, this is negative behavior. Make sure that you actively participate in conversations with others instead of having your mind on other things and paying little attention to what the other person is saying. Put your feelings into your words. Give the person you're talking to your full attention and complete focus. Let the person know that you're really listening to them and understand what they're trying to convey to you. There's nothing worse than feeling like you've been politely ignored. When you thank someone, really mean it and let them know that you mean it by the depth of your feeling. When you're actively listening to another person, you're not controlling the conversation by only talking about yourself. Instead, you show you care about the other person by asking about their life and then actively listening to what they have to say. Try to actively listen to someone today and see if it changes your perception of the conversation. Remember to record your impressions in your frequency journal.

> *Pay focused attention to*
> *the people in your life.*

263. Repetition
Becomes Belief

What would you do if you were sitting at home and your cat crawled up into your lap and you heard the words, "I'm hungry"? The cat is staring at you pitifully and you're sure you just imagined the cat saying it was hungry. The next night at around the same time, the exact same thing happens again. This time, you hear the cat's tummy growl in addition to hearing the words telepathically. Is it still your imagination? What if it happened every day for a month? Would you begin to think that maybe you were somehow able to communicate with your cat and that the cat needed feeding at that time of day? And what if you started feeding the cat at this same time and then you no longer had this experience?

I've had similar things happen with animals for as long as I can remember. I felt that one of my horses was always so hungry that I fed her extra hay. Later, I found out when I wasn't around to feed her that the person I'd hired to care for her wasn't feeding her correctly and she was indeed hungry. Another time, I was clipping a foal and heard a shouted, "It's hot!" and he moved quickly away from the clippers. When I clip a horse, it's the type of electric clippers that a hairstylist would use to trim neck hair or give a buzz cut, except horse clippers have a more powerful motor and rounded edges on the blades. They can get hot after long use, so I changed the clipper head and he was fine for a while, until it warmed up again. I had to laugh because the reaction was so in tune with the words I heard. When this first started happening to me, I thought I was imagining it, but now I listen.

It's the same with anything you do in life. The more times something happens, the more it becomes belief. Let's look at an everyday example. What if your Internet connection slowed down to a crawl every time it rained? After it happened numerous times you'd believe that the rain had something to do with the slow connection. You'd begin to expect a slow connection along with the rain, right? With repetition comes belief. When you are in connection with your beliefs, your personal vibration naturally increases.

> *Notice the things that
> happen repeatedly in your
> life because they will
> become belief.

264. It's Okay To Say No

The world is a busy place. Everyone has full schedules and a million things to do, and it's often hard to tell someone no when they ask for help. To raise your energy, sometimes you have to say no. There's nothing wrong with telling someone that you just can't accommodate what they want from you. For people who are natural caregivers, saying no can be difficult. You may feel guilty if you say no. Guilt is a negative emotion that will lower your vibration. Accept that you are only one person and allow the word no to become part of your vocabulary. You'll encounter some who may not like it, especially if you're always doing things for them, but if you say yes to everything asked of you, your energy will start to dwindle down until you're completely worn out. You can't be everything to everybody and still have time left over for yourself, which each of us needs to function properly in our daily lives. Don't overthink your response. If you feel uncomfortable or simply don't want to do something asked of you, then just say so. When you don't say no although you should, your emotions may run high. You may become forgetful or be ruled by strong emotions that can turn negative because you're overwhelmed or resentful.

> *Don't "yes" people to
> death. Let them stand on
> their own sometimes.

265. Turn up the Heat

Have you ever been really, really cold? Imagine being stuck outside in the winter until your fingers feel numb and frozen. This is similar to how your vibration can get stuck at a particular level. If you think of your energy as cold at lower levels and hot at higher ones, then just as you'd rub your hands together to warm up in the winter, you can do the same thing to heat up your frequency. Here's a fun exercise. Focus on your energy. Slowly rub your palms together back and forth. Each direction counts as one—back, one; forward, two; back, three; forward, four; and so on. I rub my palms together ten times per set and do ten sets to rev up my energy to a higher plane. Feel the friction created as you make the back-and-forth motions. With the second set, move your hands a little faster, increasing the speed with each set. Your palms will be really energized and warm, and they may even feel hot. When you finish the last set, immediately place the palm of your left hand on top of your head and the palm of your right hand over your heart. Feel the energy you've created in your palms flowing into your body, surging and vibrating all through you. As it does, imagine it filling your soul energy with love and light.

*Heat up your energy
through movement.*

266. Babysit

Working with kids raises your energy on a number of levels. Your actions during this time are either going to positively or negatively affect a new soul to the earthly plane. If you're patient, kind, and loving, it will be a positive experience for the child and you; if you're frustrated, quick-tempered, and irritable, it will be a negative experience for both of you. The first way you're increasing energy is by practicing patience, which children can try at times. The second way is by being in a position where you can see the world though the eyes of a child, something you may have forgotten how to do. The third way that you're raising your energy is by being around the child or children who can teach you a lot about the Universe because of the way they think (provided they are old enough to speak). While you don't want to drill them about things they might or might not remember about the Other Side, you can notice little kernels of truth when you're talking to them. Sometimes they reveal information about past lives, angels they see in the room, or people walking by that you can't see. Babysit with an open mind and enjoy being with the children in your care.

*Children aren't clouded
with negativity due to
years of life.*

267. Fill Your Cup
to Overflowing

Sit down, stay a spell, let me pour you some tea. Is your life's cup empty, half full, or overflowing? Look over the rim, what do you see? If it's empty, fill it up. If it needs topping off, do it. Fill your cup of life so full it is spilling over the edges, dripping down into a saucer of increased energy awareness. When you fill your life with love, caring, and happiness, it's overflowing. If doubt, sadness, and anger rule your life, then you're going to see an empty cup and feel empty inside. When you have people in your life who love you and you love in return, people you can joke around with and enjoy, they keep your vibration in upward motion. If you have a job that you enjoy, groups and like-minded clubs that you're a member of, if you socialize regularly, if you consistently strive to become enlightened, then your cup is overflowing. When you separate yourself from other people, have a job that you hate, and wallow in your negativity rather than take steps for change, then that cup is bone-dry, my friend. Now is the time to turn on the tap, hold the cup underneath, and let the water wash out the dust and grime. Now fill your cup of life with sparkling energy.

> * Living a full life means
> living life to the fullest.

268. Lucid Dreaming

Lucid dreaming is a technique in which you are aware that you're dreaming. If you are aware of your dream state while you're having a horrifying nightmare, you can say to yourself, "This is not real, this is not happening. I know I'm dreaming therefore I'm not afraid of these things because it's only a nightmare and I can wake up now." By doing this you're counteracting any negativity from your subconscious, overriding it with positivity from your conscious mind.

When you're having a lucid dream, you can also include information that you're trying to attain in life. By putting this information in your dream and having it acted out in the dream, you're giving it positive energy that will help to raise your frequency both during the dream and when you're awake. This gives the goal the energy it needs to manifest into your life. Let's say you're dreaming about buying a new car. In the dream you're having difficulties with the salesperson giving you a fair price. If you are lucidly dreaming, you can say to him that he must give you a lower price because that is what you want. By experiencing this in the dream, you may have fewer difficulties when you're actually purchasing a new vehicle because you've put your desires into Universal Energy while dreaming.

*Slip into dreamland with
full awareness.*

269. Prophetic Dreaming

Prophetic dreams, also called precognitive dreams, are dreams that have a striking feature that stands out in some way so that you know it is different from a regular dream, and the events will probably happen in the future. While you can't control whether or not your dream is prophetic, the way to practice prophetic dreaming is to ask your guides to give you signs that a dream is prophetic and to remember these signs upon awakening. Each person has their own unique way of prophetic dreaming. Ask your guides to help you notice the difference. When I have a prophetic dream, it feels different to me than a regular dream because the colors are so vibrant and intense that they feel as if they are alive. I also view prophetic dreams differently. In a regular dream, I just watch everything happening in a sequential manner. In a prophetic dream, I watch everything that is happening from above and I can see what everyone is doing at the same time. Prophetic dreams are often of things that happen in other places in the world and not directly to you. This might happen because there is so much energy involved in the event that your subconscious can't help but pick up on it. For instance, you may dream of trains crashing and then turn on the television the next morning to discover the tragedy of a derailment in some part of the world.

*Prophecy often reveals
itself through slumber.*

270. Physical
Grounding Techniques

When we talk about grounding, we're talking about getting ourselves connected to Earth so we can discharge any excess energy instead of holding it within our body. We bring energy into ourselves from many different places. We can bring it in from the sun, from the air around us, from other people, from the food that we eat … anything that can increase your frequency can also create lots of energy inside you, and that's a great thing. But sometimes we need to get rid of some of the excess energy, otherwise you may start to feel anxious or nervous or you may not feel that you're comfortable in your body when you should be relaxed and at one with your core spiritual being. When you have too much energy inside, it's got to come out somehow and you'll either get frustrated or lose your temper if it doesn't.

You can purposely ground yourself to Earth by doing this exercise. You want to make sure you're grounded and that any excess energy doesn't come out in an explosive manner, but that you control the way it exits your body. Use creative visualization to seek out any negativity or excess energy that may be within you. Start at the top of your head and move down, gathering and pushing the excess energy down your body, through your head, neck, shoulders, your arms, chest, stomach, hips, pushing all the excesses down into your legs and finally into your feet. Now imagine that these excesses are flowing out of the soles of your feet and into the ground, absorbing into Earth and dispersing like water all through the ground and away from you.

When it comes to grounding, one of the main ways you'll increase your frequency is to ensure that the amount of energy flowing in is equivalent to the energy that is flowing out. By keeping yourself in balance in the way that you ground yourself, you're increasing your vibrational energy. If you have too much energy coming in and not enough going out, you're going to short-circuit. If there is too little coming in and too much going out, you're going to be tired, you will not be able to communicate well, and may have additional problems. Find a good balance within your energy levels to stay grounded without causing any negative effects.

*Release excessive energy to
ground yourself spiritually.*

271. Handcraft Jewelry

Handmade jewelry in today's world is an art form. You can come up with innovative, creative designs for unique, one-of-a-kind pieces of artwork that people will treasure and that will be worth more than manufactured pieces of jewelry. One way to raise your personal energy is to create jewelry for yourself or for resale. The physical act of making the jewelry is what raises frequency. You can raise it even higher by programming the jewelry with intention. Create individual pieces for each thing you want to accomplish in life or for each type of metaphysical quality or lesson that you're working on. You may have one piece that is programmed to keep you grounded, another programmed to help you meet your fullest potential, one for discharging negativity, one for loving unconditionally, and one for energy work. You don't have to wear a piece constantly to obtain its effects (unless you just want to). Wearing it regularly while switching between several different programmed pieces works just as well. When you are making handmade jewelry, you are working with intricate small materials and tools, which causes you to focus and use care while putting everything together in a beautiful manner. Handcrafting jewelry with focus and intention is a creative way to get in touch with your soul energy.

*Create a handcrafted
piece of jewelry for yourself
and give it the intention of
strengthening your
soul essence.*

272. Write It Down, Keep a Journal

Working with frequency can get confusing if you don't write down what you're doing and your accomplishments to date. We forget around eighty percent of the ideas we have, our "wow" moments, insights we have when working on our spirituality, epiphanies, and other revelations we have when we're in the midst of doing energy work. It's important to always write things down so you don't forget them, even if it's a note on a napkin until you can access your journal. Keep up with what you're doing: the day, the time, how your attempts worked, and how you felt afterward. Were you frustrated because an exercise didn't work the way you wanted it to, or were you flowing with so much energy you could feel your frequency increasing? Always write down how you feel about everything because that's very important when you look back on your progress. You'll be able to see what's working for you and what's not working.

If you've fallen out of practice with your frequency journal, rededicate yourself to it today. Get a fresh notebook, binder, or folder. The presentation doesn't matter as much as the fact that you have something to write in to log your exercises. Keep the journal with you so you can write things down as they happen and keep working forward to achieve your goals.

* Write down even small and insignificant items— they may speak volumes to you later.

273. Try by not Trying

When you want to succeed through your accomplishments in life, some-times you can try too hard, putting yourself in a negative position. In-stead of a trusting and positive form of manifestation, you're putting too much focus and energy on what you're trying to accomplish. You can end up frustrated and tired, and you may even give up. This is when you need to try by not trying. Sometimes you have to say, "Okay, I'm going to do this," use creative visualization to see it in your mind's eye, imagine what you want to happen as the desired result, and then forget it. You have to release the energy associated with trying so it can move freely. Con-stricting that energy with too much effort will backfire. It's like telling someone that they can't do something. Their reaction may be, "Oh, yes I can! You can't tell me what to do!" Trying too hard creates conflict within yourself because you want to achieve your goal but you're trying so hard that you're creating a block within yourself. When trying to accomplish a task, put effort and energy into it and then release it. Let it move out into the Universe and do whatever it is that it's going to do. This way you're putting purpose behind your actions and releasing the energy associated with it instead of holding that energy to you with your desire and focus.

> *Too much effort can create
> blocks in your path.*

274. Watch a Slow-Moving Fan

Have you ever put your ceiling or rotating fan on low, stretched out across the bed or sat in a chair, and watched it slowly moving around and around? Have you ever thought about how your energy is like that fan? Sometimes it's moving slowly and gently. Other times it's moving at a medium pace, and other times it's spinning so quickly you may feel like you're bouncing off the ceiling. Look at the fan and feel yourself relax and connect with the internal movements of your own energy. Now, imagine that your frequency is speeding up until it's moving faster than the fan. Keep doing this until you feel a solid increase in vibration within you. After watching the motion of the fan, you're relaxed and able to focus more intently on your own energy. The motion can hypnotize you, freeing your mind from worries or hidden stress, which allows you to pay more attention to what you're feeling in your body. You may notice a surge of energy moving through you as your frequency elevates. Your hands and feet may tingle, and you may experience a feeling of lightness or weightlessness. This means negativity is leaving your body and positive energy is increasing. This is a big step along your spiritual path because you're taking mindful steps to do energy work on a soul level.

*Slow down to speed up
your vibrational energy
patterns.*

275. How Do You Feel?

While intention is one of the keys to reaching a higher degree of vibration, the most important key is to notice how you feel inside as this increase happens. You can do all the exercises in the world, but if you're not tuning into your feelings, noticing the subtle changes in your body as you do energy work, then you will not recognize the subtle rise and fall of your vibration. It's particularly important to pay attention and notice these differences—to be really aware of yourself—because sometimes the changes are so subtle that you could miss them if you're not specifically trying to detect them. Does your breathing change? Is it slower or faster than normal? Do you feel a tingling sensation anywhere inside your body as your energy moves into higher levels? Maybe you feel a sense of peace and calmness wash over you that's so strong you could fall asleep. Does everything around you look more vibrant, filled with life and color? Are scents more distinct? Each person will react differently to an increase in their vibration and it will affect all the senses differently, including the sixth sense. When your frequency elevates, you may begin to notice that you're more in tune with your spiritual self and your psychic abilities.

> *Pay special attention to
> changes in your body so you
> will know when you've
> been successful.*

276. Take the Stairs

When you take the stairs instead of an elevator, not only do you get physical exercise, but you can dramatically affect your personal vibration. Consciously choose to take the stairs. As you go up each flight of steps, concentrate on ways you can raise your energy. Maybe today you'll decide to help someone with a project, focus on being positive, or decide to read a book on spirituality, psychic, or paranormal topics to help you become more enlightened. As you climb the steps, consider all of the different options before you. When you reach your floor, begin putting the things you thought about into action. For example, if you decided to be more outgoing today, say hello to the first person you meet. Taking the stairs is a useful tool that can get you into an "increasing frequency" mindset at any point in the day.

You can also take the stairs down to accomplish a slightly different type of energy increase. As you walk downstairs, release any negativity that you have accumulated, reground yourself with each step, and imagine that all stress and excess energy is being released from the soles of your feet into the staircase. By the time you reach the bottom of the steps, you've brought balance to your energy by releasing negativity. If you do this at the end of your workday, you'll release the stress and negativity from your job and not take your work home with you. Instead, you're looking forward to the rest of your evening with a happy attitude and are leaving any issues with work to be addressed on the following workday. Give this exercise a try the next time you have the option to use an elevator or the stairs.

> *Take the stairs to get a*
> *workout for the mind,*
> *body, and spirit.*

277. Commit to Your Decisions, Choices, and Spirituality

As you learn about your energy on a soul level, you will encounter topics and information that feel right to you as a core spiritual truth and some ideas that don't make any sense at all. I always tell the people I mentor that if you read or hear something that strikes a chord in your soul and it feels like a Universal Truth to you, take that information and make it your own. Incorporate it as part of your belief system. If you learn something that doesn't feel right or make sense to you, then the time isn't right or this information isn't part of your life lessons in this lifetime. It doesn't mean that it's wrong; it's just not right for you and should be discarded for the time being. If you encounter this information again in the future, and at that time it does feel right, that means you have grown spiritually and are at a place where you can make it your own. You have choices that come up in life and once you make that choice, you should commit to it and see it through to the end. By doing so, you're being true to yourself. The same thing applies to your spirituality: commit to your new beliefs so that you are fully engaged in these new ideas.

> * *The truth of your soul*
> *essence will become*
> *known in time.*

278. LOOK AT
THE NIGHT SKY

When you look at the night sky, you see darkness surrounding millions of stars (and the few planets you can see with your eyes). When you look at the night sky, you're connecting to the energy of those stars and planets and the darkness surrounding them. Think of the potential life on these planets and the relationship of the size of the Universe as compared to you as a single entity on Earth. Makes you feel pretty small, doesn't it? We're only a minute portion of a grand scale and we're still learning much about ourselves, the world we live in, and our own spirituality. Looking at the night sky can help you see things from a different perspective, which increases vibration. You can also count shooting stars just for fun. When you're lying on the ground, relaxing, staring into the night sky sprinkled with stars, looking for the streak of a shooting star as it passes by, you raise your energy by taking a new perspective and looking into different dimensions in a unique manner. You'll get a definite frequency boost from this activity. This also works when you're sick. When your frequency is low—like during times of illness—you can feel better by relaxing and simply looking into the night sky. Look up at the stars and space and imagine the infinite possibilities held within its depths.

> *Sprinkles of light in the
> night sky are peepholes to
> the Other Side.*

279. Remove the Phrase "I Can't" from Your Vocabulary

I've always heard that "*can't* never could do anything," which is very true on so many levels. If you don't try, then you aren't going to be able to do anything. Saying "I can't" is negative and prevents you from moving forward in life and along your soul's path. Instead of saying "I can't," say "I can" just like the little train that said, "I think I can, I think I can" as it struggled up the hill. The same applies to you. You've got goals to reach and things that you want to do in life. Even if it's a struggle, tell yourself that you can accomplish anything you set your mind to until you reach your pinnacle of success. It doesn't matter what that success is about— your spirituality, your job, your career, or your ability to make friends. Whatever it is, you have to take "I can't" out of your vocabulary and use "I can" more often. Every time you say "I can" and you succeed in what you set out to do, that's increasing your frequency even more. When you find "I can't" sneaking into your mind, ask yourself "Why not?" Then you can uncover the reasons why you think you can't do something and replace them with reasons why you can succeed. Apply this idea even to small matters today to see how the positive phrasing affects your mood. Instead of saying, "I can't meet you at that time," say, "I have an appointment then, but how about an hour later?"

> * *The words you use affect*
> *you in many ways. Make*
> *wise choices.*

280. Amuse Yourself
and Others

When you amuse yourself, you have fun, right? It alleviates boredom and gives you something interesting to do. You're connecting to the happy part of yourself when you're keeping yourself amused. When you can make other people laugh, you have fun and so do they. When you're amusing other people, you're connecting to the happiness within them, whether they're laughing at your jokes or if they think the things you're doing and saying are funny. You're increasing your vibration because you're sharing your positive energy with other people. Life would be very boring if you didn't amuse yourself or laugh with others, even if it's at your own expense. If you find that you're not getting enough laughter in your life, do something to amuse yourself. Get together with your friends and do something fun that will make you happier and more joyful. Amusing yourself could be something as simple as repeatedly tossing a ball against a wall, drawing random shapes until you have a bigger picture, or cooking something new for fun. Try visiting interesting blog sites or looking at videos online to pass some time while amusing yourself. Pick funny ones that will make you laugh or ones that deal with a topic you enjoy. Just don't get your amusement at the expense of other people. That's negative and not very nice.

* Visit an amusement park.
The name says it all.

281. Control Reactions, become Stable

To start this frequency-lifting exercise, ask yourself some questions: Are you the kind of person who flies off the handle at every little thing, someone who loses it, falls apart, or has an emotional breakdown over the smallest incident? Or are you the type of person who controls their emotions and reactions? Do you hold it together in times of stress or emergencies? If an injury occurs, can you handle the situation while it's happening and do whatever needs to be done to help the injured person? Or do you fall apart with no clue what to do except cry or retreat from the situation? Do you blow up and make situations worse because of a hot temper, or are you able to calmly look at the situation from a logical, rational point of view considering both sides before making a decision?

If you're able to control your reactions and maintain stability in the way you react to other people and the situations you encounter, you're raising your energy. You'll be less stressed because losing your grip all the time means your energy is out of balance due to the way you're handling things. Maintain control and preserve stability to move through your day with happiness and you'll maintain high energy levels. Being stable in your approach to life will enable you to achieve all that you desire.

> *Resolve to fall apart later;
> by then, you may not need
> to fall apart at all.*

282. Make a Routine to Stay Focused On Your Path

A lot of people work well with routines. You may be very organized, plan your day out with schedules and appointments, and keep the routine functioning day in and day out. When you're able to create this kind of routine in your life, you're better able to stay on course. Routine keeps you in the now, keeps you focused on your forward movement and your spiritual and personal growth. It helps you stay organized so you don't run into snags throughout your day or forget an event. A routine also lets you know when you'll have free time to do something fun in your day. With as many obligations as we have in life, it's good to stick to a schedule and have a routine. When you're feeling scatterbrained and it seems like everything is falling apart, get out a pen and paper, make a list of what you have to do and the times you can do them, and you'll find that it will be easier to stay on track. By doing this you'll increase not only your energy but your focus too. Just don't become so stuck in your routine that you'll never venture away from it; that is negative and will have the opposite effect of what you're trying to achieve. As with everything in life, balance and moderation are key. Start new routines with small steps.

> *Strike a balance between routine and spontaneity.*

283. Reconnect
with Old Friends

As we move through life, we encounter hundreds of people. Some become really good friends while others are only acquaintances. If there are people in your past whom you considered good friends, who meant something to you, and who you haven't seen in a long time, look them up. Reconnect with them and see how they're doing now. The feeling of getting back in touch with someone from your past will increase your frequency because of shared, joyful experiences. Through those shared experiences, you also share an energy bond. If you look up someone from your past, don't expect them to be the same as they were when you knew them "back then." They've changed, you've changed, and you can never really go back to the way things were between you, but that doesn't mean you can't create new memories when you reconnect. Get to know the person as they are now. You may even like them better then you did in the past. When you reconnect with old friends, you'll share memories and laugh about old times, which will also increase your vibration. You can right a wrong or maybe even rekindle an old flame as long as you're not disrupting a current relationship to do so.

*Find an old friend online.
There are many social
networking sites where you
can reconnect with people
from your past.*

284. MAKE EYE CONTACT

When you make eye contact with someone, it shows them that you're unafraid, confident, and sure of yourself, which means you have a high level of positive energy within you. When you really connect with someone, you look them directly in the eye. Think of romantic couples and how they're connected and stare into one another's eyes. Most people will make eye contact with you. People who won't look directly at you when they're talking either have something to hide, have self-esteem issues, or don't want you to see their true self. They say the eyes are the window to the soul and it's true. Have you ever looked into someone's eyes and seen pain and suffering? Trust what you feel when you look someone in the eye.

Making eye contact shows that you aren't afraid to connect with people, which will also increase your energy. It lets people know that you're upfront and honest. You're saying "Hey, look at me, this is who I am." If someone can't hold eye contact or quickly looks away, you should be wary of this person—they may have self-esteem issues that could drain you. If you have trouble making eye contact with people, start practicing. Don't try to go too fast; start small and gradually increase until you're more comfortable in this new eye-to-eye role. If you're making another person uncomfortable because you're gawking at them, that doesn't count and you should stop annoying them. In normal circumstances, make eye contact to let people know that you're self-confident and sure of yourself.

Make eye contact often
but don't stare people down.

285. STAY POSITIVE IN STRESSFUL TIMES

It's difficult to stay positive in stressful times. I've been in situations where I've been so stressed out that I didn't know if I was coming or going. I have a lot of responsibilities in life, and sometimes it's difficult to handle everything that is on my plate and remain calm and focused when doing so. If you're sleep-deprived, it will make this worse and you'll be crankier, which makes it even harder to stay positive. If you notice that you're behaving negatively when you're under stress, you need to take time out to sit down and bring yourself back to center. This will decrease the stress. Do grounding exercises to remove negativity from your body and do positive affirmations to bring your vibration up. The main thing is to try to stay positive. When stress is pushing down on you, it's easy for negativity to join the bandwagon and press down on you too. Then you absorb the negativity as well as the stress, and your life is even more difficult. Don't do that. Instead, when stress and negativity are pushing down on you, push back, which could be as simple as changing one little thing. Imagine stepping to the side, out from under the stress and negativity, and letting it hit the floor beside you. Release unrealistic expectations and refuse to let stress rule you.

> *Even when the world looks
> bleak, positivity can light
> the way.

286. Be Grateful

When you're appreciative of the people in your life, you often show them how much they mean to you through your gestures. You may give them flowers on a special occasion or buy them cards that let them know how much they mean to you. Quite often we take the people and things in our lives for granted. Sometimes, we feel so unappreciated by another person that we check out of the relationship, leave the other person behind, and forge a new life without them in it. It's important to remember to be grateful for what we have, regardless of the form it takes. We have to remember that people are with us for a reason: either to help us learn life lessons or to learn something from us. When we forget to appreciate the things we have in life, the people that touch our lives, and the things others do for us, we move away from our true spiritual essence and lower our energy into slow-moving patterns. Take a minute to stop and really analyze your life, the people in it, and the things you've obtained and accomplished. Appreciate the accomplishments of the past and then make a conscious decision about what's important in your life right now in this very moment.

** Your life is filled to the
brim; be grateful for it.*

287. Do Something
without Expectations

In today's society, everyone seems to be out for themselves. More often than not, people expect something in return for the things that they do, even if they weren't asked to do them. When was the last time you did something just out of the goodness of your heart, without expecting—or secretly hoping—that your actions would result in something you wanted in return? When you're able to give unconditionally, not only are you increasing your vibration, you're making great strides along your spiritual path. If you haven't given of yourself, your time, or your abilities for a worthy cause, choose what you will do and act upon it. Do something for someone just because you want to and for no other reason. Maybe a coworker is having a difficult time at home and you know about it. Her workload is piling up because she's behind. Why don't you complete some of her work as a surprise? She may appreciate it more than you know but even if she doesn't, you've raised your frequency by giving without expecting anything in return. This doesn't mean you have to always give physical or monetary items—sometimes the best gift is simply a helping hand, your time, or listening to someone who needs to talk.

> * Give unconditionally; you
> will reap spiritual rewards,
> which is better than any
> earthly reward out there.

288. Intention

If I had to name the most powerful tool you could use to raise your energy, it would have to be intention. The purpose you put behind your thoughts and actions as you focus on increasing the vibrational rate within your soul's energy is what will allow you to achieve your goals. Intention is a powerful tool that you can use throughout your day. You can begin your day with a specific intention and add more as your day unfolds. Perhaps today's intention is for inner calm despite tense situations, or for confidence in all that you do. The stronger your intention, the more focused your actions. You'll tap into your own energy as well as Universal Energy without even realizing what you're doing when your intention is strong enough. Intention will bring fast results. Having powerful intention behind you doesn't mean that you're trying to control people and situations; it's exactly the opposite. You're only focusing on yourself, your own intention and will, which should not affect anyone else. Intention enables you to have greater control over your life. Without it, you may meander along on your spiritual path, never really achieving success because you're not focused. Intention makes it easier to deal with obstacles. Be clear in your intentions; be specific instead of thinking of your intention in a broad, generalized way. This gives your intentions purpose so that you are better able to realize what it is you're intending for your life. Today, pick a specific intention for the day and hold it in your heart until you go to sleep tonight.

*Intend for it to
happen and it will.*

289. Practice Patience

I've always heard that patience is a virtue. But that doesn't mean it's an easy attribute to have in your life. I consider myself to be a patient person but there are days when I feel like I'm at my wits' end and impatience seems to be the leader of my emotions. Getting through times like these is challenging because once you're out of patience, you're out of sync in your energy and your frequency has taken a nosedive. To bring your energy back up and elevate it higher, you have to practice patience even in the worst of times. When I'm out of patience, I feel a tingling sensation throughout my body because I'm usually pushed way beyond being frazzled. I focus on that tingling sensation and slow it down using creative visualization. During this process, I take deep, calming breaths to allow oxygen to flow through me, bringing me from that frazzled place of being on edge to deep inside the cave of calmness. Once I'm calm, the tingling sensation is replaced by a feeling of peace. That lets me know that I've passed over the breaking point without losing my temper and have come back to center. It can be difficult to accomplish, depending on your level of impatience, but it can be done. Today create your own visualization to use the next time you reach the end of your patience rope. Use images that are deeply calming for you, and remember to incorporate what you've learned about frequency into the scene.

*Patience is a virtue that
requires practice.*

290. Connect
To Darkness

Connecting to darkness is to feel darkness. A lot of people are afraid of the dark. You'll find that this happens frequently in people who have psychic abilities or who are really connected to the energies of the Universe. You may be able to better sense paranormal or spiritual entities like angels and guides in the dark. Connecting to the darkness is the same as connecting to yourself. There's darkness in all of us, even if we're mostly light. By connecting to that darkness, you can alleviate it and become more enlightened.

To connect to darkness, simply stand in the dark. Make sure there is no light coming into the room for this exercise. Find a room that doesn't have a window and put a towel at the base of the door so no light can seep in that way. Now, stand there in the dark. Soon you'll be able to see in the darkness as your eyes and other senses adjust. You're illuminating your soul and increasing frequency by feeling the energy of the darkness. Maybe it's your own inner light that is illuminating the room around you enough that you can see. This exercise helps you look at darkness in a whole new way. Don't be afraid of the dark—embrace it. You're only afraid because you can't see. Let your own light illuminate your way.

> *Darkness within, darkness
> without, let your inner light
> shine to cast it all out.

291. White-Light
Cleansing, Protection

To cleanse your mind, body, spirit—or your home, office, and any place where you spend a lot of time—use white light to remove any negative energy that is sticking around and affecting you. Use creative visualization to imagine white light washing over your body as if you stepped underneath a waterfall. Feel the power of it flooding over you from head to toe, cleansing you of problems and adverse energy that is attached to you, raising your vibration to a higher level at the same time. Once you feel you're pulsating with positivity, imagine the flow of white light going underneath your feet and forming a protective bubble around you until it completely surrounds you and closes at the top of your head. Now imagine mirrors attached to this bubble of protection. The purpose of these mirrors is to reflect any negative energy that tries to attach to you back to its source.

You can also use white light cleansing and protection on your home, in your car, or for any location you wish to purify. This exercise will outline how to do white-light cleansing and protection on your home, then you can apply this method to any place you like. Start at the front door and move through the house, flooding each room with a powerful burst of white light. Make the light so strong that it fills every nook and cranny, even places you can't see, until there isn't any space left in the room that's not illuminated with white light. Move through every room in the house doing the exact same thing. Imagine that the white light is a fast-moving foam filling each room to overflowing until the entire house is full. Send the white light through the house until you reach the back door and imagine it going outside through that door and then turning into a protective egg-shaped dome or bubble that covers your entire house. You can even imagine that it goes underneath the foundation of your home so that the protective enclosure is complete. Put shielding mirrors around the bubble and use intention to give the white light purpose. The goal is to remove negative influences during cleansing and to keep them away with the protective bubble and mirrors. You can do this exercise in a matter of seconds after you've gone through the visualization a few times. It's fast, efficient, and will cleanse and protect you immediately. Most of all, it works. You can do white-light protection for yourself, for others (with their permission), and at any time or in any place.

> * *White light is a very*
> *strong energy source that*
> *you can tap into at any time.*

292. Your Life Is Your Choice, Make It Shine

If you do your best in life, that's all anyone can ask or expect of you. But only you really know if you're giving your best or if you're doing just enough to get by. It's up to you to determine your fullest potential, to have the stamina and the get-up-and-go to do what's required. If you're not able to do that, you'll have issues throughout life. You may not be living to your fullest potential if you're not making your life shine. If you choose to be less than you can be, you're missing out on a big part of potential life lessons in this lifetime. Make a point to really live a full life. Do the things you want to do and don't give up until you achieve your goals. Always have a positive outlook instead of a negative outlook—just that change will cause you to excel. The higher your vibration, the more your light shines into the world, drawing people to you. It's all about making the most you can of the life you have. Life is short, so don't let it pass you by because you were afraid to take opportunities or let fear keep you from being your true core spiritual self.

*Shine your light into
the world and make it a
better place.*

293. Make Better Choices

Choices can be difficult at times. You don't know exactly what choice you should make in some situations, so you weigh the pros and the cons before making a decision—but even then you may be unsure that the choice you're making is the right one. Such is life. It isn't supposed to be easy. Some choices are very hard to make while other choices are fairly easy. Sometimes we make the wrong choice simply because we aren't thinking things through or looking at the possible repercussions of our decisions. As you move through life, you'll find some difficulties and problems could have been avoided if you'd made a better choice at some earlier point.

If you have a decision to make or a choice in front of you, even if it's something as simple as what time you're going to go to bed tonight, you have to look at how each of your decisions will affect you. How will it affect your day tomorrow if you stay up really late? Do you have an early appointment in the morning? Or maybe you're really tired and need the extra sleep. If you go to bed earlier, you'll be refreshed and ready for that morning meeting instead of feeling tired. On the other hand, perhaps you have important chores yet to do today and going to bed early is just a way to avoid those tasks. They'll still be there tomorrow, however, and you'll be a day behind. Even little choices like this have big effects. If you have a big decision to make, look at the consequences of each choice prior to making it.

Choose wisely.

294. BELIEVE IN YOUR PATH

No one has the same path as you do, but if you don't believe in your path in this lifetime, you're not going to make forward movement on that path. Believe in yourself and in what you do on a daily basis; as you strive to reach your goals, you'll find that life will be easier for you. The path of spirituality and personal growth is the backbone of your life. You're making memories and living life to the fullest when you believe in your path. You're a spiritual being who created your life map before birth, and by following it and believing in yourself, you're accomplishing what you set out to do and learning the lessons you set out to learn. As your energy increases, you'll find you will believe more and more in your own personal truth, your spiritual core self, and in the reasons that you are on the earthly plane of existence. Doubt can be a big deterrent to belief. Doubt is a little devil snapping at your heels, making you think that you're less than you are, that your light isn't shining brightly. Usually you'll feel doubt when you're on the verge of making a breakthrough in your enlightenment or when you're about to discover a new spiritual truth. You can make your truth stronger when you send doubt packing.

*When you believe,
anything is possible.*

295. Frequency Transformations

As you transform your personal vibration from a lower level to a higher one, you'll find that you often have to use your willpower to ensure that you're staying true to your course. Changing negative behaviors to positive ones isn't done overnight, especially if you're trying to change a long-time habit. When you've done something one way for years, breaking that habit requires conscious awareness on a daily basis to transform it from a negative habit to a positive one. As you make changes in your life, you'll quickly notice that while you may have to rely on your willpower a lot more in the beginning, it soon becomes less necessary. You'll discover that you're more in tune with and connected to everyone and everything in your life on a soul level. As your energy continues to increase, your life is flowing in a positive way, things come to you more easily, and you're able to manifest what you need in life. You see the connections on a spiritual level simply because you've made a conscious effort to recognize these associations. By taking a positive, hands-on approach to your spirituality, you can make transformations that will move you along your spiritual path with ease. Changing your negative thoughts, actions, and behavior to positive ones is beneficial to you, so don't block yourself from this change. These transformations can build momentum and start to increase your frequency exponentially if you allow them to.

* Transform your thoughts
and you'll transform
your life.

296. Smile

You've probably heard that it takes more muscles to frown than to smile, yet many of us walk around with the corners of our mouths pointed at the floor and a worried look etched on our faces. The stress of everyday life can pull you down, lower your energy, and cause all kinds of problems … *if you let it.* Not letting the day-to-day grind affect you in a negative way is a major step along your life path. To avoid falling into negative thoughts or actions, whenever you notice that you're frowning, make a conscious effort to smile. You'll decrease the tension in your muscles and will feel lighter all over. Smiling not only lightens and raises your energy, it tells those around you that you're actively participating in your life. They see the light in your eyes and the smile on your face and will probably smile in response. Smiling is contagious in a very good way. You don't even have to be face-to-face. Have you ever been talking to someone on the phone and heard their smile? Smiling puts people at ease. When you're happy, you'll smile a lot, so it only stands to reason that if you're unhappy you can make yourself happy again by smiling. It's not always easy, especially when you're sad, but it works. Give a grin and enjoy the day!

** Make time every
day to smile.*

297. Skip, Jump, and Play

When you were a child, life was full of fun, games, and playfulness. Playing is fun. It takes you away from the stress of the world, gets you out of a rut, and makes you happier. Have you lost that sense of fun as an adult? Well, now's the time to get it back! Playfulness is an excellent way to elevate your core essence because it adds lightness to your being and gets those energy waves moving at a faster rate. When you feel your energy is low, find a way to play. Maybe you pick up some crayons, modeling clay, building blocks, or finger paints. Smile as you play. Feel how carefree your soul is right at this moment because you took a few minutes for yourself just to play. Adults play differently than kids, so whatever you consider fun can count as playing. Is it riding a motorcycle or going out on a boat? Maybe you actually prefer the kind of activities that you enjoyed as a child, like coloring, bike riding, or games like football and soccer. Maybe you can talk your friends into playing a game of hide-and-seek. Your idea of play could be building a sandcastle or just taking a long, ambling walk. Play to increase your energy, alleviate stress, and remove negativity from your life. Play is a great pick-me-up for times when you feel down.

Make a play date
with yourself.

298. Baby Steps

Your frequency will not change from a low vibration to a high vibration overnight. Although there may be times of great frequency jumps, this work is mostly done in small doses. It is accomplished by taking baby steps, gradually raising your vibration by choosing to deliberately think and act in positive ways. Choosing to think differently than the way you thought in the past will produce new feelings within you, and sometimes you have to deal with those emotions before you can take another step forward. If you're feeling sad or depressed and want to change, start by changing your thoughts. Instead of thinking that your situation will never improve, think that your situation is getting better even if it may still seem to be in the same place. The only thing you're changing is your thought, but by doing so you're energizing your life and adding positivity within yourself.

When trying to make a change, don't try to jump right to the end instead of progressing steadily toward the final result. Break down what you're trying to accomplish into easy baby steps and celebrate as you succeed. Think of each baby step you're taking while making the change as a mini goal. By the time you have completed all of the baby steps, you've manifested the change you were trying to achieve. It may take some time—changing a habit usually does—but you will eventually reach your goal.

*Achieve more through
doing less but progressing
steadily forward.*

299. Run for Your Life or Stay to Fight Fear

Are you a runner? I'm not talking about exercise here. Do you flee situations that make you uncomfortable? Are you afraid of what people may think of you, say about you, or do in regard to you? The next time your inborn fight-or-flight instinct rears its head, stay and fight instead of running away. That doesn't mean to physically fight the people around you or the situation; it means you will fight the tendency to run and will face your problem instead of avoiding it. If you analyze your feelings about the situation, you can understand why you feel the urge to flee. If you take the fear you're feeling out of the equation, there isn't a need to run. Eliminating fear is a hard thing to do, but it can be done if you'll only address what the fear is, give it a name, and own it. Ignoring your fears doesn't make them disappear. A fear will sit there in the back of your mind, festering, just waiting for an opportunity to rear its ugly head and breathe its hot breath on the back of your neck. When this happens, you can either cringe in fear or turn around and say, "Stop doing that!" Discussing your fears with a close friend can help you see them in a new light and allow you to release them.

> * Running never solves
> anything, it only prolongs
> the inevitable.

Part Nine

✳

Conscious
Living

300. Clean Your House

There's an old saying that cleanliness is next to godliness. You feel much better when you're clean instead of stinky, grimy, and sweaty, right? And when you are in clean surroundings, there is a positive energy flow around you. If the house is clean, it's much easier to maintain a high level of positivity because the negative energy of clutter, dust bunnies, and grit on the floor is gone. Whether you clean daily or weekly, any time you feel that your vibration is low, get out the broom, mop, and cleaning supplies and get to work. It's also true that when you're doing routine tasks like cleaning your home, your mind calms and opens up to positive thoughts. I've discovered I get most of my best ideas when cleaning the house or mucking out a horse's stall. Thoughts just seem to flit in when I'm doing mundane tasks, so cleaning can also be a source of inspiration. I find I'm able to do my work quickly and more efficiently when the house is clean. When it's not, the energy feels blocked. I'll clean and then go back to the tasks at hand, and it always seems to flow more smoothly. When you release negativity and clutter, you'll find that you're able to function with more clarity of purpose.

> *Spit-shine your home until
> it sparkles to keep the energy
> stream flowing.*

301. Stand in the Rain

Water is cleansing. While it's no fun getting caught in the rain when you don't want to get soaked, you can choose to get caught in a rain shower to raise your energy. The next time you're at home when a spring shower or summer rain starts, throw on some old clothes and then stand in the rainfall, letting the water cleanse you. Hold your hands up, spin around slowly, and feel the power of the heavens as the life-giving rain cleanses you. Let the feeling of being one with the power of the storm flow through you. Now, you do not want to go out in the middle of a thunderstorm. There's no need to get struck by lightning for this exercise. But a light drizzle, shower, or even a downpour that isn't accompanied by thunder and lightning will make your energy soar. Lightning storms can also raise your energy, but you have to connect to the storm from the safety of your home or other structure. Then after the rain has passed, embrace the unique fragrance it leaves behind. It doesn't matter if you're on a farm or in the middle of a city; there is always a fresh, clean scent after a rain.

> *The cool chill of rain*
> *invigorates and revitalizes*
> *the soul, for through*
> *cleansing comes clarity.*

302. Feel the Energizing Heat of a Fire

Power outages, especially in the dead of winter, can really be an inconvenience. Here in Florida, we often have outages due to storms, hurricanes, or everyone running their air conditioners at once during times of extreme heat. I grew up on a farm in Virginia and snow storms often caused us to lose power, so we had to heat the house with the fireplace. During those times, there wasn't anything to do but sit around the fire to keep warm. These remain some of my fondest memories. Looking into the fire and watching the flames flicker and roar as the wood burned was soothing and comforting. It allowed me time to think about anything I wanted and gave me a feeling that all was right in the world, even if the power was out. I didn't know it then, but during these times I was able to raise my frequency.

You can accomplish the same thing without a power outage. While you may not want to build a roaring fire just to do energy work, you can light candles and watch the flicker and glow of the flame. You can even watch a fire in a fireplace in an online video. If you don't have candles, watch the flame of a lighter (be careful not to let it get too hot as you hold it). It's the act of watching the flame and your connection to it that is important.

*Connect to the
flickering light of a fire.*

303. Become an Animal

I majored in theatre arts in college. One of the required classes was Movement, where you learned about characterization through motion. In one of the exercises, we were assigned an animal and a situation. Then, as that animal, we had to act out the situation and it had to be believable. I practiced my scene many times before I got it right. You have to dig deep and connect with what you feel is the animal's essence before you can move as that animal. This is an excellent exercise because you truly have to connect to the energy of the animal you're portraying. As you become the animal, you position your body and move as the animal moves, and you would then be faced with a situation called out by the instructor. You would tune in to how that animal would react. In my case, the situation was that I, as a deer, became caught in the headlights of an oncoming car. As I stared at the imaginary headlights, I felt a feeling of confusion, then fear, then full-blown panic. This was not because I thought the car would hit me, but because I, as the doe, didn't understand what I saw. This exercise is a combination of creative imagery and acting that can enlighten you. Today pick a random animal and tune into the animal's essence, then try to move and behave as that animal would. Really tune in to your instinctual nature.

> *Become an animal in
> a unique situation to
> experience the essence
> of that animal.

304. Get a Mud
Facial or Mud Bath

Have you ever seen a pig wallow in mud? Go online and search for a video if you haven't, you won't be sorry. It sure brings the pig a lot of joy, doesn't it? Mud can bring you joy too. I had a mud facial recently and when it hardened and cracked on my face, it was pretty scary looking. What is it about hardening mud on your face that makes your energy increase? Maybe it's because you look funny and you're able to laugh at yourself, which makes the mask crack and then you look even funnier. In addition to the way it makes you look, a mud mask or bath feels thick, heavy, and dull when you're in it, but you can feel its effects as your pores tighten. Mud baths and facials are used to improve your complexion, detoxify your skin, and aid joint and muscle health, and they leave you feeling rejuvenated. It can also promote your circulation and stimulate the immune system. Total immersion mud baths normally last about twenty to thirty minutes. You're connecting yourself to the soil of Earth and its restorative properties. It makes you feel relaxed and complete and at one with nature. Start with a facial, which will make your skin feel tight and refreshed, and then move to a full mud bath for a totally unique experience. You can even start with an at-home mud mask, if you prefer.

** Wallowing in mud
isn't just for pigs!*

305. Talk It Out With Yourself

Anytime you have an issue and you don't have anyone you can discuss the situation with, you can always talk it out with yourself. Some people think that talking to yourself means that you're crazy, but I believe speaking things out loud enables you to look at the pros and cons of the situation and decide which way you want to move forward. This is more concrete than just thinking things through in your head, since hearing your words makes them more real to you. Whatever it is that you're trying to get a good feel for, speaking it out loud will allow you to make points that you may not have thought about otherwise. Record yourself and then listen to what you had to say. Maybe there's a gem there that you didn't even realize because you were talking freely and not putting preconceived notions on what you said. Even if you have people to provide input on your situations, always remember to carefully consider your own feelings. If you don't listen to yourself, you're not really making a decision based upon what you want. You might be making a decision based upon someone else's ideas and what they think you should do, which may not be in tune with your life lessons. Listen to yourself and do what feels right at the core of your being.

*Consider the input of
others but ultimately stay
true to your core
spiritual essence.*

306. Make a Joy List

In life, you have things that are very joyful for you, but you might not realize what those things are. If you make a list of the things in your life that bring you joy, you'll be more apt to notice them in your life. You may also be surprised to discover that some of the items that show up on your joy list are things you never really considered until you made the list. These may or may not be the same types of things you thought of when making a gratitude list. Think of things that make you smile, then see how you can experience them more often. The smell of fresh-cut grass, a nap on a Sunday afternoon, or the sound of the ocean might be on your joy list.

Maybe one of the things on your joy list is to hold a newborn baby even though you don't have children of your own. Maybe you could volunteer at the nursery in the hospital or just ask a mother if you could hold her child for a few minutes. There are many ways to do the things that bring us joy in life even if they're not conventional. By making a list of the things that give you the most joy in life, not only do you become more aware of them and more appreciative of them, but you will also discover new things to do that will bring you joy. Joy is one of the primary ways we increase our energy. Happiness and joy will allow you to live a fulfilled and meaningful life and allow you to feel your energy at a higher vibrational rate.

*Find your joy and you'll
find empowerment.*

307. Sinking and Melting Away Exercises

A good way to connect with your energy is to practice sinking exercises. You can do sinking exercises with creative visualization. Lie on your bed and then imagine your body sinking into the mattress. As you sink, you'll feel the softness of the mattress surrounding your body as you descend down into it. You can also do sinking exercises while sitting on a chair. Imagine your body is sinking down through the chair until you are on the floor. Now lie down on the floor. Imagine yourself sinking into the hardness of the floor. How does the flooring material feel as it wraps around you? Does it hold you firmly in place? As you do these exercises, you're connecting to the vibrational rates of the materials that you're sinking into.

Melting away is when you imagine your skin melting away from your body, shedding off of you like a snake skin. This sounds gross but bear with me. Imagine it piling up around your feet and as it does, it releases all negativity. Now imagine that it reattaches to you, bringing positive energy back to you as you become whole again. If you can get past the ick factor, this exercise will take you to much higher levels. An alternative is to pretend your bones are collapsing, leaving you in a puddle on the floor; you then rise up to be the complete person that you are inside. Try both of these exercises today and record your impressions.

*Sink and melt for
complete rejuvenation.*

308. See others as Spirit

We are all spirit. At our deepest core self, we are spiritual entities made of energy—we only temporarily inhabit these flesh-and-bone bodies. Why is it then that we don't look upon one another as spiritual beings? Sometimes it's just too easy to get stuck in seeing only the physical, in understanding only with mental capabilities, that we forget about the energy essences of the people we come into contact with every day. When you consciously try to see deeper into a person's essence, to see who they truly are on a spiritual level, then you're raising your own energy as you gain a better understanding of them.

The next time you look at someone, see them as energy. How do they look? Do you feel a difference in the way you perceive them when you look past the physical body to the spiritual being underneath? By thinking of people as spiritual entities, you're making forward motion on your own spiritual path. You're looking deeper and considering the person on a soul level instead of only seeing them in the role they play in your daily life. When you consider that we are all the same on the inside—that we're all learning lessons and growing on our spiritual path to get back to our spiritual home—prejudices will fall away.

> *Spirit to spirit, soul to*
> *soul, we are all one.*

309. WATCH AN
UPLIFTING MOVIE

Take time to watch an uplifting movie, one that makes you feel better about yourself, has positive information, is funny, and makes you laugh. The time spent immersing yourself into something different and positive has a wonderful effect on your core energy. Many books are made into movies because they suspend belief and take you away from the troubles of daily life. A horror movie or scary movie would lower your energy if you tend to get scared during these kinds of films. If that's the case, don't choose a horror theme but instead choose a feel-good movie, one that will be fun and entertaining, that makes you laugh out loud and connect to the happy part of yourself.

Escaping into a world that is different from your reality will reduce your stress, give you a break from your worries, and provide a chance to restore your energy into upward motion, all of which will bring you joy. The next time you're feeling blue, rent a movie, catch a matinee or evening show, or just give yourself a short solo break and some downtime from your day. Whether you're watching science fiction, a romantic comedy, or a popular animated film, just make sure it's not a movie that is depressing and sad—that would have the opposite effect.

*Grab some hot, buttered
popcorn to enhance your
movie experience.*

310. Lend a Helping Hand

It doesn't matter if you volunteer at a hospital, school, or library or if you simply hold the door for someone, help carry groceries, or go out of your way to do something for someone who needs help but refuses to ask for it—you are giving of yourself to help someone else in need, whether the need is small or large. This makes you feel better about yourself and increases your natural giving nature.

Everybody needs help at some point. If you give help readily, maybe others will help you when you need it. This is often called paying it forward. It's not a guarantee, by any means, but it is the law of attraction. There will likely be times when you pay it forward through good actions, time, money, and sacrifice only to have others turn their backs on you when you need help. It's definitely happened to me in the past and can often be one-sided. Yet I keep helping others when I can. I still believe that what you put out into the Universe comes back around and that I will receive good energy back in the long run, regardless of the actions of others.

> *Acts of kindness are like
> a boomerang—they come
> right back to you.

311. Cook a Special Meal

Standing over a stove cooking a large meal can be tiring, time-consuming, hot, and frustrating if you're cooking for a lot of people. It's hard work that may or may not be appreciated. The people you cook for might wolf down the meal, and sometimes you don't even get a thank you. But if you look at the people who've eaten the meal you took the time to create—especially if it's a holiday meal for a large number of people—you can see the satisfied looks on their faces. You may feel an inner gratification because you can tell by their actions how much they enjoyed the meal you cooked. It's much better that they wolf it down as opposed than picking at the dishes and not eating, right? Then you'd wonder if it tasted bad and didn't turn out the way you planned. You can put extra time and energy from yourself into the meal. It's cooking with love. You're sharing part of yourself with that meal because you were being creative in making that special dish. If you don't have anyone to cook for, cook a special meal for yourself. It doesn't matter who you're cooking for—it's the act of cooking and partaking of the food that raises your energy, even if you're eating alone.

*Pull out the cookbook and
try a new recipe today.*

312. Feng Shui at Home

Feng Shui means "wind (and) water" and is a 3,500-year-old Chinese method of aesthetic arrangement that begins outside the home and moves to the interior. It is the arrangement of furniture and accessories within a space to increase the energy flow for optimum health, wealth, success, happiness, love, and peace of mind.

Feng Shui uses the concepts of polarity (ying and yang), trigrams, and *qi* (CHEE) within its procedures and methods. Feng Shui combines heavenly concepts with earthly ideals and uses Universal laws to make the outer and interior environments beautiful and balanced. It creates harmony and flow through the use of five primary elements—water, metal, wood, fire, and earth—all of which are used in the creation of most of the objects in our homes, work spaces, and recreational areas.

There are also four celestial animals that are an important part of Feng Shui. These mark direction, time of the year, and the megaconstellations. To the north is the Dark Turtle, representative of the Winter Solstice; to the south is the Red Phoenix, representative of the Summer Solstice; to the east is the Green Dragon, which represents the Spring Equinox; and to the west is the White Tiger, which represents the Autumnal Equinox.

It's important when using Feng Shui that you always have fresh moving air. Fans placed in front of windows accomplish this, as does opening the windows on both sides of your home to create a natural flow of air through the space. Cleanliness and neatness are also important; when your space is dirty, it obstructs the energy flow.

Did Fido chew up the leg on your favorite table? Maybe your uncle broke the lounge chair you keep on your porch when he sat on it. Sometimes furniture can wear out or break. When it does, it's time for a replacement. Feng Shui teaches that damaged, broken, and worn-out furnishings can cause negativity in the home.

According to the principles of Feng Shui, furniture that is in ill repair can even cause you to have health problems. To prevent yourself from getting sick and to maintain your energy levels, replace broken items as soon as possible. If you can't replace them, at least give the damaged articles away. If possible, have them repaired. When you use Feng Shui in your personal living, working, and play areas, the energy flow in the space increases. Learn more about Feng Shui today if this idea resonates with you and see what small changes you can make in your home right now to increase your *qi*.

** Rearrange your interiors
for maximum energy flow.*

313. Herbs

Herbs utilize the inner and outer parts of plants, including the leaves, seeds, roots, flowers, and bark. Herbs are used in cooking to add flavor to food, as medicines, and in spiritual practice. You could add oregano, bay leaves, dill, or rosemary to your spaghetti sauce, or you can use sage to cleanse your home. They can even be used as pesticides. Did you know that bay leaves will keep ants away? Peppermint can be used to open up the sinuses. Herbs are important because of their scent, flavors, and healing abilities. Herbs are useful because you're using part of nature to enhance your life, to make it more enjoyable and stress-free. If you currently don't use many herbs, try a few new ones and you may find a new staple for your spice rack or a new way to incorporate herbs into your daily life.

Herbs are also used to help you connect to your psychic abilities. For example, cinnamon tea is specifically used to raise your frequency, while celery tea helps you focus more so you notice your psychic experiences. Herbal incense is also used as an aid in connecting to your psychic abilities and the spirit world. Always check with your doctor prior to using herbs, especially if you have a medical condition that requires you to take daily medication.

* Try herb-scented
shampoo to experience
benefits through fragrance
all day long.

314. Painting
and Coloring

As kids in elementary school, we learned to color within the lines, to draw a little bit, and to finger paint. Our creativity was nourished and encouraged. As adults some of us continue to paint as a hobby or as a profession. When was the last time you colored or painted something? Painting—even if it's a "paint-by-the-numbers" picture—elevates your energy through creativity and focus. The next time you're at the store, pick up a box of crayons and a coloring book. Stay in the lines and feel your energy increase as you use color to fill in the image. Make it pleasing and aesthetic, or mix up the colors to make it fun and crazy. If you want to try your hand at painting, get some finger paints (or brushes if you don't want to get your hands really dirty) and a small canvas. Use your imagination to create a plethora of colors in an abstract painting, or try your hand at painting a specific object. You'll feel the warmth of your energy fill you as you create your masterpiece. Painting and coloring helps you to release pent-up feelings, whether they're happy, sad, or frustrated. These activities also enhance hand-eye coordination and stimulate your creativity.

> *Be proud of your work.
> Hang your creation on the
> wall where you can see it.

315. Make People Connections

When you meet and interact with a lot of people on a daily basis, those interactions give you a feeling of community and well-being. If you don't have many people in your life and you're very much a loner, then you may find that you are operating on lower levels. It's because we, as humans, need interaction with others. We need people to talk to, to laugh with, and to be a part of our lives. If that's lacking, you can run into situations and problems where you feel like you don't fit in, that others don't like you, or you can feel isolated and alone. Purposefully make people connections by talking to others and making new friends and acquaintances so that you avoid negative feelings. Make an effort to go out and do things with people, even if you're a loner. Interaction with others will raise your energy and it's fun to socialize. It's good to have people in your life to share things with while enjoying their company. While you can achieve social interaction online through various social media websites, nothing can take the place of real people in your local community. You don't have to be part of a group every night, just make the effort at least once a week.

* Interaction with other
people is a necessary part
of living a full life.

316. Clover

Where I grew up, there were clover patches all over our backyard. I would spend hours looking for four-leaf clovers because they are considered lucky, especially if you find them when you're not actively looking for them. The act of searching through the clover, moving the leaves aside without damaging the plant while looking for that one special clover, gives your mind time to clear, your body time to relax, and your stress levels a chance to drop. It's a wonderfully exciting thing when you find a four-leaf clover. If you don't have patches of clover where you live, start looking around for them in other places that you visit. When I lived in North Carolina, I walked a six-mile trail that was lined with clover patches. Because I was power-walking while pushing a double stroller, I didn't have time to dig around in the clover, so I made a game with myself. I watched the patches as I walked to see if I could spot any four-leaf clovers. I kept count of how many I saw in my head just for fun. You could try something similar as you walk; or if you find a patch of clover, you could also plop yourself down in the grass and start searching. That's the most fun of all.

*Four-leaf clovers are hard
to find but even just looking
can give you a feeling of joy.*

317. Ice Cream
and Special Foods

If you're feeling down, why not pick yourself up with a special treat? Go ahead and pull out your favorite flavor of ice cream or other comfort food. If you enjoy a big steak dinner, go have a big steak dinner. Food is an essential part of life and we can derive so much more than just nutrition from it. Enjoying foods that you like or that you crave will make you feel better, especially if you've gone through something negative. It doesn't matter if you cook the food, if someone else cooks the food, or if you have a special restaurant you like to visit. As you enjoy your favorite meal or special food, connect to the energy of that food. Does it make you feel happy, full of joy, content, peaceful, or safe? Food can cause all kinds of reactions within us and it's up to you to understand those reactions. One of my favorite snacks is regular Doritos dipped in chocolate ice cream. Mmmm, talk about yummy! The next time your energy feels off-kilter, enjoy your favorite foods or dip a Dorito in chocolate ice cream and see how you like it. Taking comfort in food doesn't mean you have to turn into a bottomless pit and eat the whole gallon of ice cream and the whole bag of chips. Eat in moderation, or the benefits will be lost and you'll end up with an upset stomach. Be sensible instead of being gluttonous.

> *Food creates a plethora of
> sensations and emotions.*

318. Be Creative

It doesn't matter what your creative outlet is, the act of creating something—of making it with your own two hands—will elevate your spiritual energy. Oftentimes we can get blocked in our creative effort. Writers may experience writer's block and artists may see a blank canvas in their mind's eye. To keep your creative ideas flowing, change up what you do or try working with a different medium. Mix it up, do something different to enhance your creative flow. If you're an artist who draws in pen and ink, try painting with watercolors instead. Maybe you're a writer for a local sports column. How about trying your hand at a short story? There are a million ways to be creative. You just have to tap into the channel you enjoy the most.

Even if you feel that you don't have a creative bone in your body, you can find something creative that you enjoy doing. You may discover that by enjoying and appreciating artwork, stories, or the creativity behind a spectacular event that someone else created, you will find inspiration for your own project. Maybe you enjoyed the flower arrangements at a wedding and decided to make one for a friend's ceremony and discovered you were really good at it. Don't close yourself off to creative ventures just because you don't consider yourself a "creative" person.

> *Release your inner creator*
> *to make your own kind*
> *of masterpiece.*

319. White Noise

White noise can be the sound of rain, the ocean, the hum of a machine, waterfalls, crickets, birds singing, a fire burning, or a fan running, to name a few. White noise helps you focus, keeps you from becoming distracted, lowers stress, and drowns out other noise. People who suffer from ringing in their ears often use white noise to alleviate the tinnitus. White noise is technically a combination of all the different frequencies of sound. You can use white noise or your own simulation of white noise to increase your internal vibration by specifically noticing it from time to time as it's going in the background. When you notice it, does it make you feel at ease and peaceful? Or is the noise grating and bothersome? If it is, you need to pick a different pitch or type of white noise. It should be soothing to you, help you focus better, and be more in tune with your core spiritual self. If it's not accomplishing that, then it's the wrong type of white noise for you.

The steady monotonous sound of white noise easily masks other noise. For instance, if you work in an area where everyone is typing, having white noise in the background will drown out the sound of the other typists touching the keyboard. It can also minimize sounds that come from outside, like traffic or people talking loudly.

> *Add white noise to your*
> *bedroom to help you fall*
> *asleep easily.*

320. Work in the Yard

Yard work is labor intensive. You have to mow the lawn, pull weeds, rake up leaves in the fall, landscape, mulch, and tend to the plants, flowers, trees, and shrubs. But after a long day of sweating and getting dirty, when you look out across the beautiful yard at your handiwork, don't you feel proud of a job well done? As you were working, did you notice that your mind drifted to consider things that had nothing to do with yard work? When the body is occupied with physical labor, especially something as boring as pulling weeds, the mind wanders and can come up with innovative ideas, solutions to problems that have been evading you, and a plethora of other useful information. You may get messages from your guides or feel connected to Universal Energy, all of which raise frequency. When you have a hard day or just have physical tasks on your to-do list, use the time to connect to your spirituality, come up with a new idea, or solve a problem. Yard work also has physical benefits because you're exercising your muscles and breaking a sweat. It gives you a sense of accomplishment when you look at the results you've achieved; your self-esteem will rise, especially if your neighbors compliment your work.

Plant flower seeds with the intention that by the time they bloom, you will have realized at least one goal on your spiritual path.

321. Plant a Garden

When I was growing up, we planted a garden every year on my grandparents' land in the big field across from the ponds. And every year, I worked in the garden, pulling ears of corn, digging up potatoes, and gathering all of the fruits from the orchard and vegetables from the garden so they could be canned or frozen for the winter. I didn't realize it at the time, but working with nature and bringing in the harvest increased my vibration. It was a lot of fun, and we ended up eating as many strawberries and apples as we took back to the house to be "put up." Planting a garden, tending it, and enjoying the results brings you in contact with Earth and nature's cycles. As an adult, I no longer have the opportunity to work in a garden but I still occasionally find a strawberry farm where they let you pick your own. I still think its fun to get down there and search for the reddest, juiciest berries.

If you'd like to try gardening but have limited space, you can buy herbal garden kits for the kitchen or an inverted mechanism to grow tomatoes on your patio. The key element when using gardening to increase your frequency is that you care for the plants, watch them grow, and reap the rewards of your labor by eating the food the plants produce. Of course, if you have the room, you can create an extensive garden in your backyard.

*Grow your own
food and enjoy!*

322. Shop at a
Farmers' Market

Eating foods directly from the garden or a farmers' market invigorates your life force and increases your vitality because you're consuming the food when its energy is still elevated from being connected to Earth. The longer fruits and vegetables are disconnected from their source of life, the lower their energy-raising ability. Sometimes you can obtain really fresh fruit and vegetables from the grocery store if they buy directly from local farmers. It's the produce that has been imported or shipped from great distances that will have the lowest vitality because it has been removed from its life source for so very long. It may not have even been ripe when it was harvested. That doesn't mean these foods can't be delicious, just that their energy isn't as potent as produce that has been harvested recently. You can tell the difference when you eat them because they just don't seem as fresh. Try shopping at a farmers' market or go to a farm and pick your own apples or strawberries when they're in season. It connects you with nature, and the taste of the produce is excellent. There is one warning when shopping at farmers' markets: Make sure that they are reputable and have regulations for sellers, especially regarding fertilization of the foods, chemicals for insects, and other regulatory issues. You may have to pay a bit extra for fresh, local produce, so you should make sure you are getting what you pay for.

*Look in your local area for
homegrown foods full
of vitality.*

323. Pick or Buy Flowers
and Stop to Smell Them

The scent and perfume of flowers will invigorate you very quickly. Where I previously lived, a vine called wisteria is very prevalent. It can be a nuisance sometimes because it grows very quickly and can cover trees and other things seemingly overnight. But the flower this vine produces has an unbelievably appealing scent. It's one of my favorite fragrances. Wisteria has a big purple blossom that hangs like grapes. I used to stop on the side of the road, pluck off the blossoms, and bring them inside my home just so I could enjoy the scent.

Any floral fragrance you like—whether it's roses, carnations, gardenias, honeysuckle, or any other flower—will touch you spiritually. Whatever scent you enjoy, get those flowers and put them in your home or on your desk. Throughout the day, stop to smell the flowers and enjoy the way they look in the room. How does the appearance of the flower and its unique scent make you feel? Does it make you happy or make you feel all warm and fuzzy inside? You can also purchase a plant that blooms at various times of the year so you can enjoy the plant and its flowering scent several times a year.

*Enjoy some
flowers everyday.*

324. Essential Oils

Essential oils are created by using steam or water to distill liquid from plants. These are called oils, but they're not really oils or oily. They are concentrated scents from the plant they're derived from. The aroma and smell of the essential oils, usually sold in small bottles, acts as an energy catalyst. You can also buy essential oils as blends with base oils. There are as many essential oils as there are plants that produce scent. These are popularly used in aromatherapy, which uses plant oils to enhance your psychological and physical well-being. You can use them in your cleaning solutions, laundry detergent, and some of them even act as a repellent to keep bugs away (citronella). To raise your vibration using essential oils, add them to boiling water and then indirectly breathe the steam, or put them on a tissue to sniff. As you look for essential oils, you'll also find synthetic ones, but these don't produce as many benefits as natural essential oils. Make sure you're getting the real thing and not a man-made copy. Many people use essential oils when they're working on their psychic abilities, when they want to destress, or to aid in concentration. Massage therapists often use essential oils in their practices.

*Add essential oils to your
bathwater for a fragrant,
relaxing soak.*

325. Change Your Paint

Pick a room, any room, grab a paintbrush and a gallon of paint, and change the energy vibration of the interior. If you paint the walls of a room yellow or add yellow tones with accessories or painted trim, you will give the room a happy, vibrant feel. Yellow is a sunny, cheerful, warm color that reminds us of the sun's rays, which in turn gives us happy feelings. It's stimulating and can raise the vibration of the people who occupy the room. Yellow is often associated with intelligence and power. It's also known to enhance creative energy. You can use yellow to add a touch of warmth to darker rooms, or you can open up a small room and make it appear larger by painting the walls yellow. When used in the home, it's a favorite for the kitchen or dining room since it complements most foods. This is just one example of how color can transform the energy of a space.

Reflect on the colors that are already in your home and decide if a room could benefit from a change in color energy. If your home decor has a lot of colors that are vibrant, tone down one room to make it a calm and peaceful place you can escape to when you're feeling stressed out. Green or sky blue can accomplish this and make you feel more relaxed. Some colors act as stimulants and others are calming. Consider the room's purpose and how you want to feel when you're in that room before choosing new paint.

*Use a variety of color in
your home to give each
room purpose.*

326. Simplify Your Life

If you are so busy that you're falling into bed at night too exhausted to even dream, then you have to make time to do nothing. Yes, that's right: nothing. For someone who is constantly busy, doing nothing can be cause for a panic attack. The hardest part in the process of doing nothing is to quiet your mind so that you're not making lists in your head of the things you should be doing instead of doing nothing at all. It takes a while to acclimate to this type of change—especially if you're a very busy person—but once you do, you'll feel refreshed instead of frazzled and on edge.

Doing nothing takes only time, but you might not feel you have any extra time. To free up time, start finding ways to simplify your life. Let go of some of the obligations that are keeping you so busy that you don't even have time to breathe. When you do too much and are constantly on the go, you can't begin to realize what your true vibrational rate is because you're running circles around your soul essence. Many times you can improve complicated areas of your life by going back to the basics. If you have a family, delegate some of the workload to others and let them share in the responsibilities of running the household. Today, take fifteen minutes to do exactly nothing—how do you feel?

> * *The simpler you can make*
> *your life, the better.*

327. Remove Clutter

When the space around you is overflowing with accumulated clutter, it disrupts your energy flow. Major cleaning can be time-consuming. Instead, try to declutter in little steps. Choose one place to declutter today—a kitchen cabinet, a garage shelf, the laundry area, or your car's trunk or backseat. Look at everything there. Discard extra items or put them out where you'll see and use them. Clear the space and organize it. Resist the urge to store the clutter in another location. You may even find forgotten treasures! This is a good time to donate items or have a yard sale. Regardless of how you dispose of the things you no longer need, just removing them from your environment will make you feel more open and free.

Just as you'll clear out the space in your home, office, or other space, you can also increase your soul energy with a spiritual clearing to remove that which no longer serves you—namely, negativity and attachments. Use creative visualization to clear clutter from within your soul. As you clear this away, you'll feel lightness within you. These may be grudges, issues with friends or family, or anger with yourself or another person or situation. Whatever these negative feelings are, they're clogging up your spiritual being and keeping your energy low. Dispel them from your person and you'll free up space within yourself to allow for more vibrant energy. This allows you to feel more in tune within yourself and your spirituality. Do you see any positive emotions or thoughts that have been hidden in the clutter? Bring them out into the light!

Open space allows a
free flow of energy.

Part Ten

*

Peaceful
and Stress-
Free

328. Walk Barefoot
in the Grass

I love being barefoot—the feel of the ground beneath my feet, the sand between my toes, how the blades of grass caress my feet as I walk upon it. You have to watch for bees and occasionally you'll step on something sharp like a rock, but that goes along with the territory. I'm very comfortable being barefoot and feel that it grounds me to Earth. I don't mind getting my feet dirty because I like touching whatever I'm walking on and feeling it with my skin. For me, walking barefoot raises my frequency. It feels natural and comfortable. There is even a movement of people who jog barefoot! Other people disagree. Some will not even walk around their house without shoes on their feet. They feel grounded when their feet are confined and safe from injury or gross things they may encounter when barefoot. While it's no fun to step in some of these things, that's what soap and water are for. As long as the area you walk on is relatively safe, going barefoot shouldn't pose a threat.

If you're a barefoot enthusiast like me, take a walk on a surface that you normally don't walk on. If you're a shoe lover, pull those things off and try walking in sand or grass. Feel it beneath your feet and move past the gross factor in your mind. You may be surprised to find it is enjoyable; with that joy, your vibration will rise.

*Feel the ground
beneath your feet.*

329. Visit a Sacred Site

Visiting a sacred site can be a powerful catalyst because of the energy in the area. It's essential that you show respect when visiting a sacred site because it's sacred for a reason: the beliefs associated with it by people who live near the site or who used it as a place of worship. Sacred sites usually have very high energy; when you visit them, you can tap into that energy in order to raise your own personal vibration. During your visit, you may want to use creative visualization to send white light into the area surrounding you—not to change the energy of the site, but to clear away any energy that other people may have left behind. This way your energy has a clear, direct connection to the site without any interference from the lingering energy of previous visitors. You're enhancing your spirituality during visits to sacred sites, which always increases your personal vibration. Sacred sites and places that are considered holy locations can enlighten you on a spiritual level and allow you a deeper connection with your soul energy. Many times people come away from a sacred site feeling renewed, aware, and with a deeper peace than when they arrived. This is due to increased frequency within them.

> *There are many sacred sites around the world. Find one close to you to visit today.*

330. Walk Down a Dirt Road in the Country

If you're a city dweller, hop in the car and take a drive to the closest "country" atmosphere that you can find. Next, locate a dirt road and take a stroll. If you live in the country, get out of the house and take a leisurely walk down a road. There's just something about a country road that elevates your energy and puts you in tune with nature. You will feel at one with earth and the sky, and you'll notice the animals and insects around you. You'll feel the quiet—not just hear it, but feel it. If you can take a walk at dawn, you'll notice that you become one with the changing degrees of light as the sun rises. Think of this light as the light within you. As you increase your personal vibration, you're becoming lighter and brighter. You will feel stronger as you realize that you're growing spiritually. As you walk, think of your true nature, your soul, who you are, and where you're going in life. Don't be in a hurry as you walk, take your time. Use this as a time of reflection on anything that is bothering you. As you spend time alone walking, you'll find that you gain a new sense of clarity. And even if you don't think about anything as you walk, it's a relaxing exercise.

*In the peace and quiet of
nature, you will know the
truth within.*

331. Watch Puppies Play

As I write this, I'm watching two eight-week-old German Shepherd puppies play on my living room floor. They're trying to decide who is boss. Watching puppies play is a fun way to increase your energy. You can even stop what you're doing and play with them—yes, I've done it several times because they're just too cute to resist! Have you ever seen puppies hop and lunge at the same time? They look uncoordinated and soft in their movement but it's sweet. Puppies lick, bite, chase, and pull on each other, all in the name of fun. They take a toy from each other, then bring it back to share with the other one to play some more. They scuffle, growl, bite, and bark in adorable puppy ways. If you prefer cats, kittens can provide a lot of the same amusement.

Puppies can get in somewhat vicious fights that last only seconds but show the other puppies who is boss. When it's over, it's over, and they immediately go right back to being best friends. This is a lesson we can apply to our lives. When you argue with someone, have the argument and then let it go. Don't dwell on it and hold in your anger. Get it all out and release it. Doing this isn't always easy, but it is best in the long run.

*Enjoy and learn from the
antics of puppies.*

332. Swing or Lie
In a Hammock

Swinging in a hammock is very relaxing. It's good for your soul to feel the flowing, back-and-forth movement of the hammock while you lie in it. Just lie there and feel the breeze. Feel the heat of the sun or the coolness in the air if it's autumn. Connect to the world around you while you're lying down. You may even fall asleep. It's very easy to fall asleep in a hammock because we're in our natural element: outside. Even though we all live in houses now, we came from people who lived their entire lives outside and in caves, and that is still ingrained in us on a very deep, primitive level. Being outside is good for the soul, and being in a big swing that you can lie down in is even better because you connect to your inner self, relax, and raise your connection with the world around you. The hammock hugs you, wrapping around your body for a cozy, protective feeling. It is also great for anyone who has back problems because unlike lying in a bed, a hammock doesn't put any pressure on your spine or muscles. You can even bring your hammock indoors if you have the space for it. Then you can enjoy its benefits year-round.

> *Have a lazy day swinging
> in a hammock sipping iced
> tea or sleeping.*

333. Choose a Place You've Always Wanted to Visit and Go There

It might be Timbuktu, it might be the South Pole, or it might be two towns over to check out the new statue they put up. Anywhere in the world you've wanted to go, but you've never been able to visit, make plans to go see that place. Plan a day trip. You're accomplishing a task that you wanted to realize in your lifetime and you're going to a place that you want to visit that you'll enjoy seeing. We're only on Earth a short time and it's a good idea to visit as many places as you can while you're here. It may be something you wanted to see in your own town but you just haven't gotten around to yet. Don't put it off; you may never do it simply because you're procrastinating. Don't limit your desires because you feel that you have obligations, and don't put limits on what you're trying to achieve or the things that you want to do in life by always looking at what you need to get done. If your dream place is far away, use today to research what it would take to go there. If you're not sure where you'd like to visit, try this: take a pin, close your eyes, and stick the pin in the map. Voilà! That's the place you should go.

> * What you want to do
> should sometimes take
> priority over the things
> you need to do.

334. Go on a Canoe Ride

Taking a canoe ride is a wobbly fun time. Your arms will get tired from paddling, but it's also very good exercise. If you haven't been on a canoe ride lately, find a park that rents them and take one out for a few hours. As you're going down the river or across a lake in the canoe, feel the way your muscles tighten and stretch as you lift the paddle and then pull it back through the water and the coordination it takes to keep the canoe going straight instead of going around in circles.

When you're canoeing down the river or across the lake, you're immersed in nature. You get to look at all the things around you: animals, vines twisted in unique patterns, and beautiful flowing plants. You might wish you had a camera so you could take a picture of it but you probably left it at home because you were afraid it would fall into the water and get ruined (see how negativity did that to you?). Try a waterproof disposable one; if it does get damaged, you're not out a lot of money. Take pictures of things you see on your canoe ride so you can have memories to look back on at a later date. Whenever you look at those pictures, it will be with the happy memories of that day.

*Paddling down a
river or stream can be a
grand adventure.*

335. GO CAMPING

Camping means sleeping outside under the stars. It's relaxing to be around the campfire with friends or family, singing campfire songs or telling scary stories. You may even wash dishes in a nearby creek if you're there for a few days. There are all kinds of things you can do when you're camping that will bring you back to a Wild West kind of lifestyle, when folks had to live off the land. Granted, you're going to take along your own food, cooking utensils, a cooler, and other basic necessities. And your car will be right there so you can leave whenever you want if the weather turns bad or if you've just had your fill of camping. Still, it's the experience of being outside in nature and the fun memories you can make with fellow campers that increases your soul energy. You will create memories that will last a lifetime if you go camping. It is also relatively inexpensive compared to other vacation options. You can buy camping equipment secondhand to save on the initial investment. Camping gives you a chance to connect with nature and with the people around you.

> *You can always pitch a
> tent right in your backyard
> and have a mini camping
> trip at home.*

336. Take a Bike Ride

Riding a bicycle means you're getting exercise, moving your legs at a fast rate, feeling the wind on your face, and getting your heart pumping. You're invigorating your physical body while getting outside to connect with nature. As you ride the bike, you can allow your mind to free itself from any ramblings that are going on in your head, any worries or stresses that are eating away at you. You can take this time on the bike to consider how you can make your life more positive overall. You can ponder over problems that are bothering you in order to find a solution in your mind.

Another way you can increase your personal vibration while biking is to focus on your physical body: putting energy into the muscles, imagine the blood flowing through your body, observing how you're breathing, and feeling your heart beating. By feeling the connection between your mind, body, and spirit during the bike ride and considering things of a spiritual nature, you will be able to increase your connection to your core spiritual essence. At the end of the bike ride, you'll be tired but you'll also be mentally invigorated because you did something good for yourself by getting out of the house and bike riding.

*Pedal fast, pedal slow,
watch the speed of your
energy flow.*

337. Swim in a Pool, Lake, or Ocean

Swimming can be a great workout for both your body and spirit. If you haven't been swimming in a while, and you don't have any medical conditions that would prevent you from swimming, then put on a suit and head down to the local lake or even the ocean if you live close to one, with the main purpose of increasing your personal vibration through swimming. For this exercise, it's preferable to swim in a natural body of water, not a man-made pool. If you love water like I do, there's nothing better than getting in and gliding through the water, floating on top of it and being part of it. As you swim, feel the water move over you. Pretend you're a mermaid or a merman as you swim beneath the water. Wear goggles to see beneath the water if it's not too murky. When you're swimming you are connected to your energy because you're immersed inside water and feel that you're part of that liquid. As you swim, think about how you feel being part of a big body of water or how you feel when you're under the surface. Can you hear anything? It's a very solitary feeling to be underwater, and you can connect to your inner self there.

*Use visualization to
become one with the energy
of water while you swim.*

338. Walk on a Beach

Walking on the beach is very relaxing. As you look out across the ocean's waves, consider the vastness of the body of water in front of you. When you feel the ocean lapping around your ankles or knocking you down and completely covering you, you're part of something bigger than yourself. You're now looking at the big scheme of things. Go barefoot, don't wear shoes. As you walk, feel the softness of the sand between your toes. Feel the hard, wet sand beneath your feet, the water swirling around your legs, and the way the sand is sucked out from under your feet with the retreating waves, leaving you with a feeling that it's disintegrating right beneath you. Let that feeling move throughout your body and give you a sense of peace and happiness of being in the now of the ocean and the beach. Listen to the seagulls. Feel the salt in the air as the wind blows against your hair. You'll feel a connection to God and the Universe. This feeling is what is going to raise your own energy as you make this divine connection to your spirituality. You will also feel different energies from the ocean depending on whether it's calm and flat or rolling with huge waves. If you do not live near the ocean, use creative visualization, soundtracks, and/or pictures to tune into the energy of the ocean.

> * Visit the ocean during
> various types of weather to
> feel the difference in energy.

339. Watch the Water on a Pond

Have you ever taken an hour out of your day to just sit by a pond and watch what happens? What do you think you'll see? You may see bugs on top of the water, ducks eating those bugs, a mama duck with her babies, or a snake. You may feel a breeze or the sweltering heat of the sun beating down on you. All of these things raise your vibration because you're paying attention to the smallest details. You may want to stick your toes in the pond—or, if you live where gators can surprise you, maybe not. Does the pond have fish? Do you see one jump up after a bug? Be part of nature, feel the connection to the wildness of the place. Being part of the life at the local pond, even if it's just for an hour, will invigorate and energize you. Try looking at the reflections on the water. Do you notice the clouds in the reflection? This can be really cool because sometimes you'll see faces appear; other times you may receive a message in the reflection. Just taking a few moments to wait and examine what you're seeing and how that can be beneficial to you makes it worth the hour you spend on this exercise.

*Take your lunch to a
pond and spend the hour
reflecting on what you see.*

340. Avoid Excess

When you are excessive in anything that you do—especially things that dull your senses or lower your inhibitions—there is the possibility that negative energy can attach to you. It can be the downbeat energy of another person, an unconstructive action you're taking, or contact from dark entities. If you can eliminate the things you're doing in excess, you'll avoid this negativity and find balance in your energy. For example, there's nothing wrong with having an alcoholic drink. But when you drink in excess, either to the point that you black out, or you drink on a daily basis to get drunk, that's excessive, negative, and lowers your inhibitions, which makes it easier for attachments to be made to your energy. The same thing can be said for eating. If you're going overboard, it's a negative action. Limit the things you're doing in excess so you can open yourself to higher levels of positivity and move away from negativity. Eliminate the actions that can attract unwelcome kinds of energy by uncovering the reasons you feel you need to do this activity in excess. Is it because you enjoy the feelings you get when you're doing the behavior, or is it because you're sad, depressed, and lonely so you use the behavior as an escape? Examine your reasons for excess in order to eliminate it. Look inside, delve deep, and find the cause in order to stop the behavior.

*Excessive behaviors have
repercussions later.*

341. Visit a Playground

Playgrounds aren't just for kids. I think the most fun thing to do at a playground is get in the swing and go higher and higher, trying to flip over the top (even though that's pretty much impossible), going as high as I can go, pointing my feet toward the heavens. The feel of the sun on your face, the wind in your hair—it's exhilarating and gives you a feeling of ultimate freedom. When was the last time you went down a slide? It doesn't matter how old you are. Climb to the top of the biggest slide and down you go! How did it feel? Did your legs stick to the slide? Was the metal or plastic hot? Now do it again to increase your energy even more. If you don't get motion sickness, get on that spinny thing and twirl around and around, watching the sky, hanging off the sides, laughing out loud at your silliness. If you think you'll be embarrassed to enjoy spending time on a playground to increase your energy, wait until you're the only one there and then have a blast. Or take a friend with you so you'll have someone to play on the see-saw with. Then you both can raise your vibrations together and have a lot of fun too.

*Find your inner child
on the playground.*

342. Sit with a Tree

Every living and every inanimate thing has its own unique vibration. Everything in the Universe has a frequency because it's made up of molecules that vibrate at a given rate. It might vibrate slowly or very quickly. If you think about the vibration of trees, how can you connect to its energy? You might have a favorite tree that you feel drawn to, or you can just choose one that you consider interesting for this exercise. Sit beside this tree with your back flat against its trunk, close your eyes, and notice how its bark feels against you. Really sense the bark through your clothing. Use creative visualization to feel the energy flowing within the tree, and then connect your energy with that of the tree. Make mental notes of what you feel. Does the tree's energy feel slow? Is it moving quickly? Also consider the time of year. Is it spring and the sap of the tree is moving at a faster rate so it can produce leaves and buds? Or is it winter and the tree is dormant? Taking a few quiet moments to sit with a tree will allow you to commune with nature, tune into the energy of the tree, and heighten your own awareness of nature's energy flow. Trees are an integral part of our daily life and we need them for life itself.

Feel the life force
in nature.

343. Go to a Museum

When you visit a museum, the silence inside urges you to connect to the quiet part of yourself as you learn about different objects with its walls. The art and pieces inside the museum have history, and you'll notice that some of them seem to draw you to them while others do not. As you view them, think about how these pieces could connect to your personal history in any way. For instance, is there a mask from Africa that appeals to you, and you're African American? Is there a Celtic clock, and you're of Irish descent? Find connections to your own personal history and background as you walk though the museum.

Just the act of enjoying the pieces of work in the museum—whether that's a painting, army tanks, horse-drawn carriages, or a variety of different things—will increase your vibrational rate. You can learn about history as you take a leisurely stroll through the building and enjoy the presentations. You've given yourself the gift of joy by visiting the museum. While you're there, make an effort to learn about what's held inside. There are many cool and unique museums around the world that you may find enjoyable. You may even like to donate your time to a museum, helping out with programs for schools and other outreach projects where volunteers are welcome.

> *Visit a museum to learn
> about a new subject and
> connect to history.*

344. Take a Salt Bath

There's nothing more relaxing to me than soaking in hot water. The jacuzzi where we live is great—even during the heat of summer—for easing the pain of sore muscles, which I often have because I work with Friesian horses and German Shepherd dogs. Soaking in a hot bath filled with fragranced salt is even better. Salt added to your bathwater can make sore muscles less sore, release tension, increase circulation, and reduce tenderness. If you have recurrent pain anywhere, a long soak in a salt bath may be just what you need. You can get salts in a variety of fragrances. Relaxing in the salt water helps you to focus and aids in creative visualization. There's just something about water that acts as a conduit to the Other Side. I've gotten some of my best ideas while soaking in hot water. Talking with your guides is also easier when water is involved (and no, they don't care if you're naked; to them, you're simply energy, the core spiritual essence of your being temporarily inhabiting a physical body). You can even do energy exercises while you're soaking for a more powerful result due to the water's conductive ability.

*Set aside an hour to soak
away your aches, pains, and
troubles in a salt bath.*

345. WATCH A
SUNSET OR SUNRISE

The exquisite beauty of the day coming to life or peacefully moving into night is a wonderful time to focus on your own spirituality. Really noticing the beautiful colors created by the sun's energy flowing through the clouds or simply lighting up a clear sky is a perfect way to connect to your inner energy. Feel it growing and changing just as the sun's rays makes things on Earth grow and change. If you live in an area where it's difficult for you to watch a sunrise or sunset, hop online and log into a reputable live webcam so you can watch. With the technology we have today, you can watch the sun rise or set in different areas all around the world. Consider how the rising sun is casting a fresh, new light on the day; it's as if the world is being reborn from darkness into light, taking on a golden cast with hues of blue and pink until the day shines forth clear and bright. Think of how you fit into this scenario. Are you being reborn into enlightenment? Make changes within yourself so your life is full of joy and happiness. Connect with your soul energy, feel your spirituality, and know that life is good. Everything will work out as it should.

> *Let the vibrant energy of
> a sunrise or sunset fill you
> with positivity.

346. The Sound of
Water in a Creek

Growing up on a farm, I often found myself sitting by the creek looking for crawdads or swinging from a vine to the opposite bank. Sometimes when I'd get angry or mad, I'd take off to the creek and just sit there, listening to the bubbling sound of water gliding over the rocks. These sounds were calming and eased the negative feelings inside of me. If you live near a creek, sit beside it, listen to the water flowing and allow your thoughts to flow as well. You'll be surprised at the wide variety of thoughts that will come to you.

If you don't live near a creek or any kind of running water, you can accomplish the same thing with one of those babbling brook waterfalls that plug into an electrical outlet. If that doesn't appeal to you, buy a music CD with the sound of water flowing down a creek on it. You can also find downloadable music online that you can buy for your phone or portable computer. Then you'll have it with you to listen to whenever you feel stressed or upset. Find a waterfall or soundtrack that is appealing to you. Then listen to it with your eyes closed and imagine that you're in the country sitting beside a creek.

> *The tumble of water
> splashing over rocks is
> soothing and refreshing.*

347. Skip to Your Lou

When you were a kid, you could skip joyfully without feeling any kind of self-consciousness. You were just happy and letting that joy come out through your body's movements. Times like these are when your frequency is at its highest. Look at a child when they skip: they don't have a care in the world, they're just merrily hopping up and down. Can you remember the last time you felt so happy and joyous inside that you were overflowing with these feelings and your body just broke into skipping? What's holding you back now? Is it because you're an adult and only children are supposed to skip? Maybe you're too sophisticated to be bothered with something as childlike as skipping. Do you keep the skipping under control because you think someone may make fun of you if they see you doing it? You can't worry about what others think. Maybe seeing you skip along happily will affect the person who happens to see you in a positive way. Break out of your hardened mold of adulthood and let your inner child out to play. If you absolutely will not skip in front of other people, skip though your house when you're alone. Feel the freedom that skipping brings; allow the movements to affect you positively.

* Feel the joy in skipping
and get a bit of a workout.

348. Have Fun in the Leaves during the Fall

If you live in a tropical climate like I do now, this one may be a challenge to do unless you take a trip up north during autumn. The beautiful colors of the changing leaves during this time of year are something that everyone should experience at least once in their lifetime. Seeing the majesty of the brilliant display of colors can make you feel small in the grand scheme of things. When I lived in Virginia and North Carolina, we'd take a drive into the mountains each fall to view the changing of the leaves, and it was always so spectacular. Enjoying the colors of the dying leaves also allows you to get in touch with your spiritual self. Think of this as a time of renewal. It's the shedding of the old in preparation for the new. Not only will looking at the colors raise your energy, but if you can rake up a big pile of leaves and run and jump into the middle of it, then you're freeing your inner child and jump-starting your joy. The slight chill in the air, the feeling of the leaves beneath you, the crunching sounds they make as you roll around in them—all of this contributes to the experience. Let your senses revel in the experience to connect with nature, the world, and your own spirituality.

> * *Nature's colors enlighten*
> *us with their beauty.*

349. Horseback Riding

Riding a horse in a full-blown gallop is an experience unlike any other. It's one of the most liberating feelings in my life. As a child I was a horse fanatic. I saved all my money to buy a mare that we later bred. The foal was born April fourth, so of course I named her April. I trained her to walk behind me with her hooves over my shoulders; I rode bareback and without a bridle, steering by her mane. I'd bring her into the basement to watch television with me—boy did I get in trouble for that! April was my best friend. I had my first paranormal experience when her mother came back to say goodbye to us after she was shot by a hunter. After years of not having horses, I now breed Friesians and realize how much I missed having a horse in my life.

Give horseback riding a try. Some people are afraid of horses; if you are afraid, try to put the fear behind you, then make sure to find a facility that has safe mounts that are used for the trails. It will be an experience that will allow you to connect to the noble majesty of the horse and with nature, both of which will touch you on a soul level.

★ Sit astride a horse, even if it's being led by someone else.

350. Walk in the Woods
or Hike a Trail

Not only is walking a good exercise for the body, it's also good for the soul. When I walk, I always leave the ear buds at home. I take the time to listen to the world around me instead of blocking it out with music or talk radio. There is much to see and feel while walking outside. I've found that paying attention to details greatly increases my energy. This is a great time to quiet my mind so my higher self and guides can communicate with me. I often ask for guidance from God and the Universe as I walk. I soon find that thoughts come to me out of the blue because they are an answer to my request for help. Most times these thoughts are appropriate to the situation I just asked about, and sometimes they don't seem associated with anything in my life. When I follow through on them though, I always realize that I received the thought for a reason. As you're walking, don't just power-walk with a straight-ahead focus. Instead, pay attention to the world around you. Look at the little animals that are sitting on the plant life. If you're in too much of a hurry, you'll miss them. Notice the blooms on flowers and the way the trees grow. Write about the sights and sounds when you get home.

*Quiet your mind
by immersing yourself
in nature.*

351. ROCK A BABY TO SLEEP

There's nothing quite like holding a little baby and rocking back and forth in a repetitive motion. You can feel the baby relaxing in your arms, the way he or she breathes, the way their body snuggles up to you. Babies have a fresh, new smell (most of the time) and their skin is soft and satiny. If you're feeding the baby, the way it clings and holds onto a bottle while looking up at you is precious. Nothing has connected me to my core spiritual essence more than having children.

Not everyone has children because it isn't part of everyone's life map. For those of you who don't, you can still find a way to experience holding an infant. You may decide to lend a new parent a hand with some babysitting, which means you'll likely have to feed the infant and rock them to sleep. You may find that you want to sing to the baby, and that's perfectly natural. This gives you a connection to another human being that is totally reliant on you for his or her care. You may have nurturing feelings that you hadn't expected if you've never been in this situation before. If you have rocked a baby to sleep but it's been awhile, ask a friend or relative if you can rock their baby. It will bring you joy and happiness.

> *Being part of a child's life,
> if only for a short time,
> can bring joy.*

352. Go Fishing

Fishing is something that I grew up doing and it's always been a relaxing pastime for me. Be forewarned: you've got to be willing to put the bait on the hook, get the hook off the mouth of any fish you catch, and either keep it for dinner or throw it back in to catch again later. If you can't stomach touching the fish, just wear gloves and you won't feel the slime. Fishing is relaxing. It gives you quiet time to clear your mind while allowing new ideas to enter your consciousness. If you need the fish to eat, this can provide you with a meal; if you don't need the fish for food, you can put it back into the body of water you took it out of. The act of fishing—of repeatedly throwing out the line and reeling it in, mildly complaining because the fish ate your bait and you have to rebait the hook—is an enjoyable experience. Fishing in the ocean is different than fishing in a pond, especially if you fish off the beach. If you've never tried fishing but think that you'll hate it, give it a try anyway. You never know, you may love it. People like many different things in life and you should make an attempt to try everything once.

** You may be a pro
fisherman and not even
know it because you haven't
tried the sport.*

353. Make Joy in
Your Life a Top Priority

Having joy in your life is one of the keys to complete happiness. When you experience joy in your everyday life and share it with others, you're more apt to live a full, happy life. You're creating and spreading joy, which increases your personal vibration. The more joyful you are, the higher your energy will elevate. Every day, find little ways that you can add joy to your life. Write down the things you experience during the day that brought a smile to your face. You may even discover that you found joy in something that was unexpected.

How can you add more joy to your life? Start by going back to the joy list you created in an earlier exercise, which includes all sorts of small and large things that make you smile. Make an effort each day to experience something that you've written. If a songbird's music makes you happy, take a walk and listen for the birds singing. If it's puppy breath, visit a pet store and play with the puppies. Maybe you experience joy when you sing; instead of just singing in the shower, participate in a musical or join a choir. Writing down all the things that make you happy and filled with joy makes you more aware of how much joy you already have in your life and gives you ideas for ways you can find more joyful moments. You'll find that you never stop adding to your list!

* *When joy abounds,*
happiness surrounds you.

354. BELLY LAUGH

When was the last time you had a real good, shake 'em up, full belly laugh? When you laughed so hard that your sides hurt, you couldn't breathe, and you couldn't stop laughing? Maybe you even snorted! The thing that happened was the funniest thing you've seen, heard, or done in a very long time. What better way to raise your energy than to laugh all the way to your soul? Many people believe that laughter is the best medicine for whatever ails you, and I agree. It's better to laugh than cry, isn't it? When you're able to experience laughter and really feel it deep in your belly, deep in your bones—the kind of laughter that rocks all of the way through you until your eyes are watering and you can't catch your breath and everyone around you thinks you've completely lost your mind—then you have truly experienced a belly laugh. Stress and negativity can't stay in you when laughter is flowing through you. There's just too much positivity in laughter. A belly laugh can also be a short, fully felt, hearty burst. When you experience the depth of a belly laugh, take note of how you feel inside. Are you happier, have you released stress, and do you feel relaxed?

*Laughter brings
lightness to your soul.*

355. Relax, Rag Doll

When you're keyed up, stressed out, and worried, it's harder to focus on energy work. If you don't seem to be getting the results you seek, you might be trying too hard. Take a few moments to relax not just your body but your mind as well.

You might want to do this exercise prior to working on frequency. You're going to become a rag doll. Stand on top of your bed. (Yes, really; I don't want you falling on the hard floor.) Now hold your hands above your head and imagine that you're turning into a rag doll. Feel that rag-doll energy, loose and floppy, entering the tips of your fingers. As it flows through you, your body reacts accordingly. Your wrists fall forward, then your arms drop to your sides; they're heavy and you can't control them. The rag-doll energy is in your head now, so your neck lolls forward. Now your upper body is unstable, moving from side to side. Next your knees give out and you're a big pile of rag doll lying on top of your bed. You can't move. You just lie there in whatever position you fell in. Rag dolls don't have stress or worry. They can't think, so neither can you right now. You're just lying there, just *being*. If a thought creeps in, set it aside. If you move, immediately go limp again. Lie this way until you feel completely and totally relaxed. It will be easy to drift off, but try to stay awake.

Once you feel you are relaxed, imagine a little tingle of positive energy in your toes. It moves into your feet, then your legs, and all the way though you to the tips of your fingers. It's invigorating, giving you focus. When you feel like you're back to an energized you and are no longer a rag doll, get up. Now you will find that energy work is easier and you'll feel invigorated throughout the rest of your day.

> *Let rag-doll energy
> release worry and stress.*

356. Choose to Be Happy

In life, you can choose to be happy, or you can choose to be miserable. When you decide to be happy, you look at life from a different perspective. You see situations positively instead of negatively, you make more of an effort to get things done and meet your goals, to have good times and good memories instead of sitting around in misery feeling sorry for yourself. If you are feeling dejected and remorseful, now is the time to choose to have a happy life. You don't have to be miserable, you don't have to cause problems for yourself or do things that will make you unhappy. Instead, decide that your life will be fun, entertaining, and fulfilled. Choose to leave negativity and misery behind you. Being miserable isn't benefiting you and it's probably making those around you miserable too. Choose to step above despair into joy. The choice is yours. You can choose to be happy with a higher personal vibration, or you can choose to be miserable with a lower energy rate. The choice is yours alone to make. What do you choose? Will you be happy or sad? Choose to be happy and you'll find that the world opens up to you in ways you couldn't have even imagined when you were miserable.

> *Choose to be happy in life
> and move forward on your
> spiritual path.*

357. Be Mindfully
Aware and Accepting

Being mindfully aware means you are present in the here and now. You notice all the little nuances around you, and you're fully engaged in each and every moment. When you are living a mindfully aware life, you are consciously participating in it on a daily basis. If you feel you're running on autopilot, stuck in the same old thought patterns, are "zoned out" and not in the moment, then you need to make a conscious effort to change these static patterns into more active ones. You may discover you have more negative thoughts than you realized. By ignoring those negative thoughts, you can take a step toward accepting the pessimistic parts of yourself. Face them head on, look at the reasons behind your feelings, and make a conscious effort to get them out of your life for good. This allows you to be more accepting of yourself emotionally and spiritually.

You may worry that if you accept yourself as you are right now—today, in this very moment—you'll no longer strive to achieve new goals. The exact opposite is true. In order to move forward, you have to accept all your flaws first and choose to be better or you will not be motivated to achieve further growth. You have to know yourself to grow.

> *Accept yourself with all
> of your flaws to truly live a
> mindfully aware life.*

358. Mud Pies

When I was a kid, we used to make mud pies after it rained or pour water into the dirt to make a mud puddle. There's nothing like having your hands in mucky goo to make you appreciate *not* having your hands in mucky goo. But that goo is a great way to raise your energy through creating something with nature. When making mud pies, you drip the sand though your fingers to create cities and roads and all kinds of cool things instead of it just being a blob of mud in a circle. You don't have to get filthy to make a mud pie, either. You can make up some mud from dirt and water and play with it on a cookie sheet if that's the only way you are comfortable doing this exercise.

If mud pies are still too dirty for you, you may want to weave a basket out of leaves or create a decorative plaque out of seashells or build something out of rocks. Whatever it is that you want to do, be creative and use materials from nature. Because the things you use from nature are living things with their own unique energy, that energy transfers into your creation.

* In your handiwork,
your light shines through.

359. Animals and Frequency

Animals are always connected to their higher selves and spirituality, and they honor us by sharing their presence on the earthly plane. They're a source of fun, entertainment, and love for us. If they don't know how they'll get what they want, they're very ingenious and will figure out a way to achieve their goals. They live in the moment with no worry. If you watch animals, you'll notice that some of the things they do are really hilarious. I have a Chihuahua who picks out one piece of food, carries it across the room, eats it, then goes back to get another piece. She'll act like she's burying her food with her nose and will make the motion of pushing some invisible substance over the dish to hide her food. It never works, but she does it every day. Moments like this bring you joy because sometimes animals are just out-and-out hilarious. Other times simply appreciating the beauty of the animal gives you joy. Watching the majestic beauty of our Friesian horses galloping across the pasture always gives me a frequency boost. Take time to look at animals, even if you don't own one, to see if they do anything that is cute or funny or that you can find joy in.

*If you don't have a pet
in your life, consider
getting one.*

360. Realize a
Dream Today

Do you dare to dream? Do you have aspirations you've yet to achieve? They don't have to be big dreams, they could be little dreams, something that you've wanted to do but haven't done yet. Do you have a dream to become an author? Write a short story and submit it to a local magazine. Do you want to run in a 5K? Hit the pavement and start training, working up to the length of time you'll need to be able to run in order to compete. Maybe you dream of having one day free of stress. Start the day out on a positive note and deflect any obstacles that come across your path.

By choosing a small dream and following through on it, you give yourself the motivation to achieve larger dreams. Big dreams may take longer to achieve but you can start today by taking steps toward the end result. If you want a new car, put away some money into savings every week for your down payment. If you want to be a more outgoing person, then you have to meet new people that you share a common interest with. Say you enjoy acting—take a class. Every ambition you have is achievable when you set your mind to it and work toward your dream.

> *Dream a dream of
> happiness and make
> it happen.

361. Listen to Music

Listening to music can be calming and relaxing; or it can rev you up and give you purpose, drive, and the determination that you can achieve anything you set out to do. Allow the thrum of the guitar, the deep pounding of the bass, and the high notes of the piano to move through you, filling each fiber of your being with its rhythmic energy. Each note has its own unique pitch and when combined together with other notes to make a musical piece, the tones build upon each other, raising the overall resonance to a beautiful melody of sound. Music can move you to connect with your higher self and your guides. Listen to music often. When it's missing from your life, your soul is missing a key part of itself. Try a wide variety of music, even tunes or genres you may not normally listen to. You never know what combination of musical tones will increase your soul's vibration. Music can be used during meditation to help you focus or as a stress reliever that can help you release negativity and pent-up frustrations. Choose music with positive words instead of dark negativity. You may decide that you like to make music as well. If that's the case, create your own beats and put them together with your words to create a song.

*Music can touch the
chords of your soul.

362. Sing a Song

I am not a gifted singer. I can carry a tune, but that's about as far as it goes. But whether or not I can sing well doesn't matter when it comes to raising my energy patterns on a soul level. It's the act of singing, the joy you feel by releasing emotion in song, that increases frequency, even if you're tone deaf. Singing can change your slow energy to a high vibration within minutes. Sometimes I really don't feel like singing, especially if I'm sad or blue. In times like these, singing is the absolute last thing on my mind, but if I make myself hum a little tune, even if it's something I make up, I can feel my spirits rising. Singing will increase your alertness, boost confidence, and bring about joy and happiness in your life. There is also a physical side effect of singing: it tones your abs! Start with a little hum and let the music move you into a full-blown song. Sing at the top of your voice, raise the roof, blow out the rafters, but most of all enjoy the warmth and energizing feelings surrounding you. Remember that you are in tune with yourself and the world when your energy moves at a high rate.

> * *There's a song in your heart—let it burst forth into the world.*

363. Take a Walk with Someone You Care About

The people in our lives are treasures that we should hold dear to our hearts. Our existence on the earthly plane is short, especially when we consider Universal time, so why not embrace the love we're given to share with the people in our lives? Spend time with those you love. Show them how much you care. You may think that they already know how you feel about them, but what if they don't? Always tell those you love that you love them, so there will never be any doubt. Besides, even when we know that someone loves us, it's always nice to hear those three little words, especially if they're heartfelt.

Walking together, spending time holding hands, sharing pieces of our lives, asking opinions of the other person—these are all ways we can share our souls and our divine spirits with someone we care about. Whether you live in a city or in the country, find a place such as a park or a quiet country road where your walk will be surrounded by nature. In a natural setting you'll feel more comfortable and free to share your innermost thoughts with one another. A true spiritual connection with another human being is one where you love unconditionally and whole-heartedly. Neither time nor space will change those feelings.

** Appreciate the people in
your life by spending quality
time with them.*

364. TOUCH

Are you a touchy-feely person, or do you prefer to keep your hands to yourself? It's fine to be either way, but the more you experience the touch of others—whether it's a warm embrace or a slap on the back, feeling the textures of material things or experiencing the frequencies within the world around you—the more you'll increase your personal vibration. Through touch we can pick up psychic impressions, empathic feelings, and clairvoyant thoughts that allow us to connect to others. Touch is one of our five senses, so when you're experiencing touch, try to really understand the feelings that go along with the act of touching someone or something. Feel the keyboard beneath your fingertips as you type, feel the softness of an animal's fur, notice the silkiness of your loved one's skin. Feel with your whole body: the chair you're sitting in, the horse you're riding, or the inline skates you're wearing as they touch the ground. As you experience touch on a deeper level—as you really think about how things feel, how you feel to others, and how they feel to you—you will increase your energy and the feelings you invoke in others will increase their energy too. Touch everything in your life, truly feel its unique energy, and allow your own vibration to grow through your sense of touch.

> * *When you touch, feel;*
> *when you feel, touch.*

365. GAIN SOUL PERSPECTIVE

You already have everything you need from a soul perspective. You have the capacity to love, the ability to give and share, and the knowledge of all time within you. It may take time and practice to dig within yourself and uncover all those layers of this knowledge so you can move along your spiritual path, and that's fine. As you learn more about your core spiritual being, how you relate to the world and others, you'll find that you'll gain a greater sense of peace within your soul. It's what you do with this knowledge that affects your frequency. As long as you work with positive intentions, you'll be successful. That doesn't mean you don't need other things on the earthly plane to live a happy and fulfilled life; you do, and you'll get those things as you grow and develop and by simply being alive. Understanding your spirituality and the soul's connection to the physical body, the Other Side, and Universal Energy will enable you to grow within your own personal energy flow, allowing your spirit to reach higher levels of energized fulfillment while on the earthly plane. Your soul perspective makes living in this dimension easier, which you'll discover as you do energy work to increase your frequency by learning about and connecting to your core spiritual being.

> *You were born with all
> you need; it's what you do
> with it that matters.*

Bibliography

Blum, Ralph. *The Book of Runes*. New York: St. Martin's, 1982.

Chiazzari, Suzy. *The Complete Book of Color*. Boston: Element Books, 1999.

Gienger, Michael. *Crystal Power, Crystal Healing*. London: Blandford, 1998.

Gimbel, Theo. *Healing with Color and Light*. New York: Fireside, 1994.

Goodman, Linda. *Linda Goodman's Star Signs*. New York: St. Martin's, 1987.

Graham, Helen. *Discover Color Therapy*. Berkeley, CA: Ulysses Press, 1998.

Hall, Judy. *The Crystal Bible*. Cincinnati, OH: Godsfield Press, 2003.

——— *The Illustrated Guide to Crystals*. New York: Sterling, 2000.

Kenner, Corrine. *Crystals for Beginners*. Woodbury, MN: Llewellyn Publications, 2006.

Lambert, Mary. *Color Harmony for Better Living*. New York: Cico Books, 2001.

Permutt, Philip. *The Crystal Healer*. New York: Cico Books, 2007.

Sapolin, Donna. *Decorating with Color.* New York: Hearst Books, 1997.

Wauters, Ambika. *Homeopathic Color & Sound Remedies.* Berkeley, CA: Crossing Press, 2007.

Whelan, Bride M. *Color Harmony 2.* Rockport, MA: Rockport Publishers, 1997.

To Write to the Author

If you wish to contact the author or would like more information about this book, please write to the author in care of Llewellyn Worldwide Ltd. and we will forward your request. Both the author and publisher appreciate hearing from you and learning of your enjoyment of this book and how it has helped you. Llewellyn Worldwide Ltd. cannot guarantee that every letter written to the author can be answered, but all will be forwarded. Please write to:

Melissa Alvarez
℅ Llewellyn Worldwide
2143 Wooddale Drive
Woodbury, MN 55125-2989

Please enclose a self-addressed stamped envelope for reply,
or $1.00 to cover costs. If outside the U.S.A., enclose
an international postal reply coupon.

Many of Llewellyn's authors have websites with additional information and resources. For more information, please visit our website at:

www.llewellyn.com.